Palgrave Studies in Modern European Literature

Series Editors
Shane Weller
School of European Culture and Languages
University of Kent
Canterbury, UK

Thomas Baldwin
Centre for Modern European Literature
University of Kent
Canterbury, UK

Ben Hutchinson
Centre for Modern European Literature
University of Kent
Canterbury, UK

Linked to the Centre for Modern European Literature at the University of Kent, UK, this series offers a space for new research that challenges the limitations of national, linguistic and cultural borders within Europe and engages in the comparative study of literary traditions in the modern period.

More information about this series at
http://www.palgrave.com/gp/series/14610

Stewart Smith

Nietzsche and Modernism

Nihilism and Suffering in Lawrence, Kafka
and Beckett

Stewart Smith
Independent Scholar
Dorchester, UK

Palgrave Studies in Modern European Literature
ISBN 978-3-319-75534-2   ISBN 978-3-319-75535-9   (eBook)
https://doi.org/10.1007/978-3-319-75535-9

Library of Congress Control Number: 2018934635

Cover illustration: R J McDiarmid/Getty Images

Printed on acid-free paper

This Palgrave Macmillan imprint is published by the registered company Springer International Publishing AG part of Springer Nature
The registered company address is: Gewerbestrasse 11, 6330 Cham, Switzerland

For Jenny

ACKNOWLEDGEMENTS

I would firstly like to acknowledge how fortunate I have been to have had two wonderful supervisors over the course of my Ph.D. at the University of Southampton: Devorah Baum and Will May. Both were incredibly generous with their time, feedback, and encouragement throughout the Ph.D. thesis which largely comprises this study. Academically brilliant and inspiring, I cannot thank them enough.

I am also grateful to Ros King at the University of Southampton and to the Higher Education Academy for providing the opportunity to obtain funding for my Ph.D.

I would also like to thank the anonymous reader at Palgrave for helpful comments and suggestions during the publication process.

Most of all, I would like to thank my partner, Jenny, for her lightness and fun—particularly invaluable when working with the theme of meaningless suffering over several years—as well as for her patience, support and love.

CONTENTS

Abbreviations of Nietzsche's Works

AC   *The Anti-Christ*, in *Twilight of the Idols* and *The Anti-Christ*, trans.
R. J. Hollingdale (London: Penguin, repr., 2003).

BGE   *Beyond Good and Evil: Prelude to a Philosophy of the Future*, trans.
R. J. Hollingdale (Harmondsworth: Penguin, repr., 1990).

BT   *The Birth of Tragedy*, trans. Shaun Whiteside (London: Penguin, 1993).

D   *Daybreak: Thoughts on the Prejudices of Morality*, trans. R. J. Hollingdale
(Cambridge: Cambridge University Press, repr., 2007).

EH   *Ecce Homo: How One Becomes What One Is*, trans. R. J. Hollingdale
(London: Penguin, repr., 2004).

GS   *The Gay Science: With a Prelude in German Rhymes and an Appendix
of Songs*, trans. Josefine Nauckhoff and Adrian Del Caro (Cambridge:
Cambridge University Press, repr., 2003).

HAH   *Human, All Too Human*, trans. Marion Faber and Stephen Lehman
(London: Penguin, repr., 2004).

OGM   *On the Genealogy of Morality*, trans. Carol Diethe (Cambridge:
Cambridge University Press, 1994).

TI   *Twilight of the Idols*, in *Twilight of the Idols* and *The Anti-Christ*, trans.
R. J. Hollingdale (London: Penguin, repr., 2003).

TSZ   *Thus Spoke Zarathustra: A Book for Everyone and No One*, trans.
R. J. Hollingdale (Harmondsworth: Penguin, repr., 2003).

WP   *The Will to Power*, trans. R. J. Hollingdale and Walter Kaufmann
(New York: Vintage Books, 1968).

All texts authored by Friedrich Wilhelm Nietzsche.

CHAPTER 1

Introduction: Nietzsche, Nihilism and Modernism

NIETZSCHE AND MODERNISM

In 1913 the tormented Franz Kafka wrote to break off his engagement with Felice Bauer:

> It certainly was not my intention to make you suffer, yet I have done so; obviously it will never be my intention to make you suffer, yet I shall always do so. [...] Felice, beware of thinking of life as commonplace, if by commonplace you mean monotonous, simple, petty. Life is merely terrible; I feel it as few others do. Often—and in my inmost self perhaps all the time—I doubt whether I am a human being. (Kafka 2000: xiii)[1]

While acknowledging that life is constituted by inevitable suffering, Kafka reveals his own particularly sensitive nature. Furthermore, his confession to possessing such an acute sensibility, and the juxtaposition of this acknowledgement with a condemnatory evaluation of life, evokes a passage from the philosopher Friedrich Nietzsche's *The Gay Science* (1882–1887). This entry is revealing of Nietzsche's perception of modernity:

> *Knowledge of distress.*—Perhaps nothing separates human beings or ages from each other more than the different degrees of their knowledge of distress—distress of the soul as well as of the body. Regarding the latter we

© The Author(s) 2018
S. Smith, *Nietzsche and Modernism*,
Palgrave Studies in Modern European Literature,
https://doi.org/10.1007/978-3-319-75535-9_1

moderns may well, in spite of our frailties and fragilities, be bunglers and dreamers owing to lack of ample first-hand experience, compared with an age of fear, the longest of all ages, when individuals had to protect themselves against violence and to that end had themselves too become men of violence. [...] But that is how most people seem to me to be these days. The general inexperience with both sorts of pain and the relative rarity of the sight of suffering individuals have an important consequence: pain is hated much more now than formerly; one speaks much worse of it; indeed, one can hardly endure the presence of pain *as a thought* and makes it a matter of conscience and a reproach against the whole of existence. The emergence of pessimistic philosophers is in no way the sign of great, terrible states of distress; rather, these question marks about the value of life are made in times when the refinement and ease of existence make even the inevitable mosquito bites of the soul and the body seem much too bloody and malicious, and the poverty of real experiences of pain makes one tend to consider *painful general ideas* as already suffering of the highest rank. (48: 60–1)

This passage may be used to characterise Nietzsche as a cruel philosopher, insensitive to human suffering.[2] I shall argue, however, that Nietzsche remained consistently sensitive to the issue of human suffering, that his central doctrines revolve around this theme, and his analyses of various cultures rest upon his examination of their respective responses to suffering. Moreover, what is worth stressing here is that Nietzsche regards the especially modern, heightened sensitivity to distress to foster 'a reproach against the whole of existence': the experience of suffering is bound to one's evaluative interpretation of life; in our case, according to Nietzsche, 'suffering is always the first of the arguments marshalled *against* life' (*OGM* II 7: 47). Suffering is thus entwined with nihilism, the pessimistic view that life is not worth living.

Nietzsche's explosive impact upon literary modernism is widely acknowledged. However, there is a paucity of critical literature exploring these central aspects of his thought with regard to its relationship to modernism. It may be argued that all four of the writers I am exploring in this study, Friedrich Nietzsche, Franz Kafka, D. H. Lawrence, and Samuel Beckett, were particularly sensitive to suffering and perhaps therefore predisposed to experience feelings of futilitarian resignation.[3] But this biographical point aside, what I wish to do in this study is to examine their shared concern with suffering and nihilism as it is presented in their respective work in order to offer a new perspective of modernist cultural output. By taking Nietzsche's thought on suffering and nihilism as a heuristic lens through which to explore these modernist figures, I shall diverge from related studies that chart Nietzsche's relation to modernism.

A common entry point for critics discussing the heterogeneous streams of modernist literary practice and outlook is to emphasise its discontinuity with previous cultural forms: the complex phenomenon of literary modernism can be generally understood as an ardent response to the imperative enunciated by one of its leading promoters, the poet and critic Ezra Pound, to '[m]ake it new!'. This call to aesthetic innovation, with its implicit critique of traditional forms, parallels Nietzsche's philosophical project. Otherwise put, critics studying Nietzsche's seminal impact upon modernist literature primarily figure the thinker as an iconoclast, as a revolutionary prophet.

The putative view of Nietzsche's heretical programme is evident within studies discussing Nietzsche's relationship to early twentieth-century literary culture. Robert B. Pippin, for instance, claims that Nietzsche is a 'paradigmatic "modernist"' insofar as he embodies the 'irremediable break with the past' that defines modernist work (Pippin 1983: 151–2). Robert Gooding-Williams in his *Zarathustra's Dionysian Modernism* (2001) similarly argues that Nietzsche's relationship to literary modernism is premised on an unprecedented 'creative break with the past' (Gooding-Williams 2001: 3). Roger Griffin identifies Nietzsche as the paradigmatic figure in what he calls programmatic modernism. This term considers modernism as 'a mission to change society, to inaugurate a new epoch, to start anew. It is a modernism that lends itself to the rhetoric of manifestos and declarations' (Griffin 2007: 2).[4]

Nietzsche's early reception corroborates this dominant view of the thinker and his relation to literary modernism. Nietzsche's thought first came to prominence in European intellectual circles in 1888 when the esteemed Danish critic Georg Brandes lectured on the philosopher and, noting both his elitism and iconoclastic appeal, defined his work as expressing an 'aristocratic radicalism' (Bradbury and McFarlane 1976: 79). Nietzsche himself eagerly approved of this epithet. In terms of the early Anglophone response to the philosopher, for instance, accounts of his reception and dissemination reinforce this interpretation.[5] Unsurprisingly, Nietzsche's radical voice was primarily disseminated in publications emphasising the pursuit of individual expression: Nietzsche arrived at a time when aesthetes were involved in a struggle to overcome the expectations of an ethical or didactic commitment proscribed by Victorian moralism. Nietzsche thus featured heavily in journals such as *The Eagle and the Serpent*, *The Egoist*, and *The New Age* along with other iconoclastic writers such as Ralph Waldo Emerson and Thomas Carlyle (see Bridgwater 1972; Thatcher 1970). Contributors such as A. R. Orage, Bernard Shaw and Havelock Ellis celebrated Nietzsche's radical emancipatory rhetoric not only because Nietzsche emphasised a rejection of what were held to be the prevalent nineteenth-century virtues of altruism and self-abnegation, but also as he was seen to privilege an individualistic or aesthetic engagement in its place. Thus Malcolm Bradbury points out that Nietzsche was part of the wider cultural shift in which the newer emphasis upon individual expression existed in conflict with outlooks that implicitly demoted the value of the individual (see Bradbury and McFarlane 1976: 75–9). Writers revolting against the twin hegemonies of Victorian religiosity and the generalising, abstracting theories of scientific discourse, as exemplified by scientific positivism and Darwinism, thus found in Nietzsche's romantic heroism, with its grand rhetorical gestures and devastating critiques, a renewed poetic resilience and a celebration of individual creation.

For the most part, then, Nietzsche is seen to be adopted as an elitist, sceptical voice championing individual self-creation and calling for a radical reappraisal of dominant social codes and conventions associated with traditional religion and mass democracy. Patrick Bridgwater thus argues that '[f]or most of those who fell under his spell, Nietzsche's aristocratic idea, his anti-democratic stance, was at the centre of his appeal' (Bridgwater 1972: 243). Otherwise put, the modernists can be aligned with Nietzsche's notion of an 'active nihilism', or his project of carrying out a 'revaluation of all values' (*WP* Preface 4: 3): Nietzsche encourages an active deconstruction and renewal of the 'directing viewpoints through which human beings orientate themselves' (Muller-Lauter 2002: 74). Both John Burt Foster's *Heirs to Dionysus: A Nietzschean Current in Literary Modernism* (1981) and Keith M. May's *Nietzsche and Modern Literature* (1988) make this argument. Foster works from the premise that Nietzsche's thinking 'is nothing if not radically distrustful of continuity, since he envisions a total revaluation of values' (Foster 1981: 4). May, too, argues that 'Nietzsche's overwhelming concern was always with values' (May 1988: 8), before aligning modernist writers with Nietzsche's fictional madman's 'opinion about the "greatness" of the deed of killing God' (150). As I shall demonstrate, however,

Nietzsche's acute awareness of modern nihilism stands to complicate the exultant tone highlighted by literary critics.

Nevertheless, there are critical voices that contest this celebratory assessment of Nietzsche's pertinence to literary modernism. Such views invert the positive readings of Nietzsche's so-called 'active nihilism' suggested thus far. For some, Nietzsche's call for a radical break from all traditional values implicates the thinker with the programmatic modernism of Nazism. This point is made by Griffin who sees the Holocaust as the most extreme example of the logic of 'creative destruction' espoused by Nietzsche's active nihilism (Griffin 2007: 59–60).[6] John Carey's polemic, *The Intellectuals and the Masses* (1992), is more insistent on the point of Nietzsche's connection to Nazi atrocities. Carey argues that Nietzsche's elitism and revolutionary programme, as it is both destructive and individualistic, necessarily involves the rejection of the community. More contentious still, Carey claims that Nietzsche's espousal of an extermination of the weak and the degenerate appealed to the beleaguered early twentieth-century intellectual who felt threatened by modern mass culture (see Carey 1992).[7]

Despite the partiality of these views, Carey is not a lone voice within literary studies arguing that Nietzsche's thought is associated with cruelty, appropriation, and the exclusion or destruction of otherness.[8] Among the critics I have invoked thus far, Bridgwater also asserts that one of Nietzsche's key doctrines, the will to power, can be understood as 'an exploitative drive for self-aggrandisement' (Bridgwater 1972: 228). Furthermore, Nietzsche's response to pessimism, according to Bridgwater, was to 'idealize the predatory type' (241). Peter Childs and Margot Norris similarly echo this view, identifying Nietzsche with a reactive or imperious ethic which seems to be founded on the domination of others (see Childs 2000: 57; Norris 1985: 58).

It is worth pointing out that the term nihilism itself, and the examination of its various meanings, is, however, mostly absent from discussions observing Nietzsche's seminal impact upon literary modernism: the heroic dynamic of this thought, associating Nietzsche with an 'active nihilism' or an 'aristocratic radicalism', is privileged to either celebrate or condemn the philosopher; further connotations of Nietzsche's writing on nihilism remain relatively unexplored in the discourse. In this book I am motivated to provide a more considered account of Nietzsche's thought on nihilism. By investigating this aspect of the philosopher, I thus concur with Mark Warren who contends that:

Knowing a thinker's problematic is perhaps the most important thing we can know about this person's thinking as a whole. [...] knowing what [Nietzsche] meant by the problematic of "nihilism" is the most important thing we can know about the nature and implications of his thought. (1988: 13)

Moreover, I hold that knowing Nietzsche's 'problematic' of nihilism entails charting his preoccupation with suffering. Regarding Nietzsche's relation to literary modernism and the critical responses he provokes, I contend that examining Nietzsche's complex writing on nihilism through its relation to suffering evinces the strains operating at the heart of his affirmative project while illuminating areas of his thought that generate such diverse interpretations. Otherwise put, investigating Nietzsche's discourse on suffering and its integral relation to nihilism helps to nuance extant readings of the reactionary elements present in his work.

Nietzsche and Nihilism

Shane Weller's recent study, *Modernism and Nihilism* (2011), does much to address the paucity of critical attention given to the issue of nihilism within modernist studies. Charting the shifting definitions of the term nihilism from its advent in the eighteenth century to the present day, Weller offers a valuable appraisal of modernist literature in relation to the fluid, protean usage of the concept. Furthermore, Weller observes that it is Nietzsche who not only 'exerts an influence greater than that of any other philosopher of the period', but that it was he who 'deployed the concept of nihilism to capture the essence of modernity' (Weller 2011: 6). Charles Glicksberg, in *The Literature of Nihilism* (1975), makes a similar claim: '[p]ractically the entire history of twentieth-century thought, its transvaluation of the values of the past, its rejection of the gods, is foreshadowed in Nietzsche's work. He predicted the eventual triumph of nihilism' (20). Yet even though the concept of nihilism has been closely identified with Nietzsche, scholars have picked up on the subsequent interpretative difficulties arising from Nietzsche's own polyvalent usage of the term. For instance, observing that the lack of clarity stems from Nietzsche, Karen L. Carr contends that '[u]nfortunately, Nietzsche was ambiguous, vague, and not entirely consistent in his usage of the term; this legacy was transmitted, so that much twentieth-century discussion is also ambiguous, vague, or inconsistent' (Carr 1992: 15). Noting that some of the usages in Nietzsche's work are 'in tension with one another', Carr attests to Nietzsche's multifarious deployment of the term in which nihilism is variously described as 'a historical process, a psychological state, a philosophical position, a cultural condition, a sign of weakness, a sign of strength, as the danger of dangers, and a divine way of thinking' (26–7). Along similar lines, Nietzsche scholar Bernard Reginster asserts that '[n]ihilism is the central problem of Nietzsche's philosophy. Although this view is not new, its nature and implication have not been well understood. One reason is that Nietzsche's conception of nihilism itself remains elusive' (Reginster 2006: 21).

Another dominant tendency when accounting for nihilism in Nietzsche's thought is to privilege the entries that appear in an edited selection of his unpublished notebooks, posthumously published as *The Will to Power* (1901). For instance, Carr asserts that 'his discussion of nihilism is restricted almost entirely to his notebooks' (Carr 1992: 26). Weller also contends that this unpublished text gives 'centre-stage' to the issue (Weller 2011: 27).[9] Here Nietzsche introduces such notions as 'active', 'passive', and 'incomplete' forms of nihilism. While these entries certainly offer key insights into Nietzsche's presentation of nihilism, over-reliance on these unpublished passages tends to lead commentators to consider nihilism solely as an intellectual or theoretical problem.[10] Yet, as Nietzsche points out in one entry, nihilism is both a 'practical and theoretical' condition (*WP* 4: 10).

I shall diverge from the aforementioned studies by stressing that what becomes evident when examining Nietzsche's published work in conjunction with these notebook passages is that he understands nihilism as inextricably tied to embodiment, to affective-erotic being. I contend that Nietzsche's repeated emphasis upon the interdependency of the somatic, or the affective, and the cognitive, means that nihilism must be approached in relation to the embodied experience of agency, and the embodied experience of suffering. Daniel Conway's observation is relevant: Nietzsche 'alternately refers to nihilism as psychological state and a physiological condition, both of which are marked by exhaustion, pervasive pessimism, a dissipation of will, and an unprecedented erethism' (Conway 1992: 14). I hold this notion of nihilism, denoting the incapacity to experience oneself as an agent of deeds, to be the overriding and consistent usage of the term in Nietzsche's discourse. Suggestive of what Nietzsche refers to as 'passive' nihilism in his notebooks, it is this condition of cognitive disorientation and affective exhaustion that Nietzsche identifies to be pervading modernity. It is this depiction of nihilism, one that registers a state of paralysis, a condition that precipitates or gestures towards suicide, which permeates the modernist texts that I shall discuss in later chapters.

The significance of agency in Nietzsche's thought cannot be overstated. For instance, his physio-psychological thesis of the will to power, as it is articulated in his *On The Genealogy of Morality* (1887), postulates that our most basic, natural need is to experience a pathos of power which, in the primary instance, is attained through the performance of 'deeds' (III 7: 81). While this concept of the will to power is modulated by considering the development of man's consciousness, nihilism is repeatedly signalled by a loss of willing, by feelings attending the dissolution of efficacious being. This inextricable tie between agency and feelings of power or powerlessness underpins Nietzsche's various analyses of nihilism.

As Weller notes, Nietzsche most often refers to nihilism in the context of religion (see Weller 2011: 28). Yet contrary to the standard view in modernist studies of Nietzsche's hostility to religion, the philosopher is often ambivalent regarding religion's worth.[11] Moreover, he praises religion insofar as it combats states of paralysis or depression that continually threaten humanity: claiming '[m]an is often fed up, there are whole epidemics of this state of being fed up' (*OGM* III 10: 94), he lauds Christianity's success in opposing this ever-present danger: '[f]or, to speak generally: with all great religions, the main concern is the fight against a certain weariness and heaviness which has become epidemic' (II 17: 102).[12] Given that human beings are both 'sensuous, worldly beings who suffer, feel, and act' and 'conscious, cultural beings who constantly interpret and evaluate the world and themselves', the ascetic ideal provides 'an orientation toward existence' whereby individuals 'fit experience and interpretation together to form a "will" to act' (Warren 1988: 17). One way the ascetic ideal does this is by providing a goal or purpose: namely, of becoming one with God and attaining transcendent bliss.

In his discussion of the emergence of the Christian ascetic ideal in his *Genealogy*, Nietzsche focuses on an original form of nihilism. While I elaborate upon this hypothesis in Chapter 2, here I shall briefly note that Nietzsche considers this primary expression of nihilism to attend the provenance and formation of primitive domestic society: it is the powerless slaves in his anthropological narrative, denied the means to configure themselves as agents and render their suffering significant, who adopt the exegesis of life formulated by the ascetic priest. As Nietzsche's argument reaches a crescendo in this text, he articulates the import of the ascetic ideal for the powerless:

> Within [the ascetic ideal], suffering was given an interpretation; the enormous emptiness seemed filled; the door was shut on all suicidal nihilism. [...]—man was *saved*; he had a *meaning*, from now on he was no longer like a leaf in the breeze, the plaything of the absurd, of 'non-sense'; from now on he could *will* something, —no matter what, why and how he did it at first, the *will itself was saved.* (*OGM* III 28: 127–8)

Averting 'suicidal nihilism', the ascetic ideal performs the life-preserving function of enabling its adherents to experience themselves as self-affirming, willing agents. It attends to the basic need to render unbearable suffering significant while promising the transcendence of this condition. Yet, discerning the life-negating spirit informing this willing, Nietzsche considers the paradoxical character of the ascetic ideal: on the one hand, it combats the original threat of suicidal nihilism by allowing its adherents to reflexively experience themselves as agents, while on the other, the ascetic ideal posits a superior metaphysical realm that is constructed antithetically to temporal, contingent, earthly existence: 'a world that is not self-contradictory, not deceptive, does not change, a *true* world—a world in which one does not suffer' (*WP* 585 (A): 316). Its promise of a fictional permanence and an absolute absence of suffering entails allegiance to both an interpretative schema that denigrates earthly existence and to ascetic practices that diminish corporeality. For Nietzsche, the ascetic ideal thereby expresses a 'hatred of the human, and even more of the animalistic, even more of the material' (*OGM* III 28: 128). Thus, pursuing 'nothingness' or the absence of the suffering as its goal, the ascetic ideal frustrates or denies affective-erotic being. Denying the basic constituents of human existence, it is ultimately exhaustive and serves only to permit a 'slow suicide' (*GS* 131: 123).[13]

Nietzsche's 'active nihilism' partakes in Christianity's 'self-overcoming'.[14] That is, Nietzsche considers the Christian idealisation of truth to foster an intellectual conscience that culminates in atheism, the belief in the Christian God becoming untenable. He considers his philosophical mentor, Arthur Schopenhauer, and the natural sciences to embody this development. As he argues in *The Gay Science* (1882–1887), 'the concept of truthfulness that was taken ever more rigorously; the father confessor's refinement of the Christian conscience, translated and sublimated into a scientific conscience, into intellectual cleanliness at any price' (357: 219). Nietzsche thus observes the consequences of this transformation:

> Looking at nature as if it were proof of the goodness and governance of a god; interpreting history in honour of some divine reason, as a continual testimony of a moral world order and ultimately moral purposes; interpreting one's own experiences as pious people have long interpreted theirs, as if everything were providential, a hint, designed and ordained for the salvation of the soul—that is *over* now; that has *conscience* against it; every refined conscience considers it to be indecent, dishonest, a form of mendacity, effeminacy, weakness, cowardice. With this severity, if with anything, we are simply *good* Europeans and heirs of Europe's longest and most courageous self-overcoming. (219)

Nietzsche views his philosophy to be advancing the collapse of values that are no longer life-preserving or life-enhancing; such values may only be deemed life-preserving for those whom he considers to be weak, ill-constituted and declining in life force. His philosophical project thus accelerates the inevitable nihilistic consequences that accompany the destruction of our highest values hitherto. Yet Nietzsche remained equivocal regarding our capacity to creatively respond to the resultant catastrophic disorientation. For instance, Nietzsche's fictional madman registers an ambivalence regarding '[t]he greatest recent event—that "God is dead"; that the belief in the Christian God has become unbelievable' (343: 199):

> Aren't we straying through an infinite nothing? [...] God is dead! God remains dead! And we have killed him! How can we console ourselves, the murderers of all murderers! [...] Is the magnitude of this event not too great for us? (*GS* 125: 119–20)

As mediated through his madman, Nietzsche doubts whether we are endowed with the resources to manage the consequent 'long, dense succession of demolition, destruction, downfall, upheaval that now stands ahead' (343: 199). As adherents to the perspective of life proffered by modern, secular science, we are God's 'murderers', rendering the interpretation of life provided by Christianity redundant. Accounting for the modern European experience of nihilism, Warren observes that this arises because there is a practical dislocation between experience and interpretation:

> Nietzsche's structural definition of nihilism [is] something that results from disjunctions between experiential and interpretive conditions of acting. Theoretically, a disjunction might be caused by changes in experience. Or it might result from failures of an interpretive schema. Or it might be caused by some combination of the two. (1988: 18)

Given that interpretation and agency are bound together, Warren notes that one way in which the human animal succumbs to the threat of paralysis is through an internal crisis of interpretation such that the existent orientation becomes inappropriate to experience. Otherwise put, the natural sciences, which constitute the latest manifestation of the ascetic ideal's pursuit of the unconditional truth, induce the realisation that Christianity's metaphysical picture does not have a transcendent origin.[15] Rather, as Nietzsche discerns, this other-world has been 'fabricated solely from psychological needs': namely, to experience ourselves as effective agents and to appropriate unbearable suffering through the notion of a rational, just God (*WP* 12 (A): 13). Nietzsche thus claims, in light of this realisation: '[T]he time has come when we have to pay for having been Christians for two thousand years: we are losing the centre of gravity by virtue of which we lived; we are lost for a while' (*WP* 30: 20). Anticipating my analyses of the characters populating the modernist texts in the following chapters, I shall briefly sketch Nietzsche's reflections on the pathos of nihilism deriving from the loss of our 'centre of gravity'.

Exploring nihilism as a 'pathological transitional state' in *The Will to Power* (13: 14), Nietzsche observes that our collective disenchantment is characteristically extreme, as a reaction from a now untenable ideal that had been absolute and all-encompassing: '[e]xtreme positions are not succeeded by moderate ones but by extreme positions of the opposite kind', he claims (55: 35). In other words, it is our disillusionment with a hitherto totalising exegesis claiming to account for all of variegated existence that propels this tremendous shift: '[o]ne interpretation has collapsed; but because it was considered *the* interpretation it now seems as if there were no meaning at all in existence, as if everything were in vain' (35). Falling into 'the opposite valuations', this violent reconstrual of life has devastating psychological consequences. Accordingly, where the ascetic ideal served to enable man to constitute himself as an agent contributing to and partaking in 'the "fulfilment" of some highest ethical canon' (12 (A): 12), Nietzsche now contends that 'we are *weary* because we have lost the main stimulus' (8: 11). That is, denuded of the overarching ascetic telos, '[t]he aim is lacking': we succumb to affective exhaustion and paralysis (2: 9). Nietzsche's concern with agency is thus at the forefront of his diagnoses of both original and modern experiences of nihilism.

Nietzsche detects a resultant reluctance or incapacity to posit one's own personal goal or meaning: 'one still follows the old habit and seeks *another* authority that can *speak unconditionally* and *command* goals and tasks' (20: 16). One thus moves from forms of 'passive nihilism', of feelings of disenchantment and weariness from the absence of an overarching 'meaning', to exemplify what Nietzsche calls 'incomplete nihilism', the 'attempt to escape nihilism' by remaining bound and directed by the derivatives of the ascetic ideal: 'the authority of *reason*. Or the *social instinct* (the herd). Or *history* with an immanent spirit and a goal within, so one can entrust oneself to it [...] Finally, *happiness*—and, with a touch of Tartuffe, the *happiness of the greatest number*' (16–17).

Modern manifestations of the nihilistic pathos are implicitly hedonically orientated, Nietzsche detects, continuing to express the deep-seated 'mortal hatred of suffering' that inflects the ascetic ideal (*BGE* 202: 126). He considers Schopenhauer's pessimistic philosophy to be similarly determined by its opposition to distress: advocating the renunciation of passionate, striving being—the source of conflict and ultimate dissatisfaction for Schopenhauer—it aims at a Nirvana-like state of calmness and peace. For Nietzsche, the philosophy of his mentor may entail an honest awareness of a 'de-deified', meaningless universe, yet by advocating a cessation of willing he propounds an exhaustive, life-negating denial of embodiment somewhat akin to that espoused by the ascetic ideal. Defining this philosophy to crystallize a 'second Buddhism' (*WP* 64: 43), Nietzsche contends that this perspective constitutes the 'great danger', the 'sublime temptation and seduction', facing modern European culture: it offers a further, more refined path to 'nothingness' (*OGM* Preface 5: 7).

Nietzsche, then, considers himself to be 'the first perfect nihilist of Europe who, however, has already lived through the whole of nihilism to the end, leaving it behind, outside himself' (*WP* Preface 3: 3). He is a diagnostician of its various forms who has surmounted the threat posed by 'passive nihilism'. Importantly, he has transcended the destructive stage of 'active nihilism' to stress that one must 'posit for oneself, productively, a goal, a why, a faith' (23: 18). The creative formation of one's singular goal or meaning is generated in acknowledgement of the world's senselessness. Accepting the loss of a universal, impersonal narrative or meaning, Nietzsche thus argues:

> It is a measure of the degree of strength of will to what extent one can do without meaning in things, to what extent one can endure to live in a meaningless world *because one organizes a small portion of it oneself.* (585 (A): 318)

The weak, Nietzsche holds, adopt various nihilistic positions, succumbing to desperate resignation in the depths of passive nihilism, or they may be attracted to the new 'Euro-Buddhism'. The stronger, on the contrary, can work through passive nihilism to express its counter-movement, the creative generation of one's own unique 'goal', 'why', 'faith'.

With the discrediting of the prevalent interpretative schema, one overriding issue now facing Nietzsche and modernity is how to account for the suffering that had been hitherto rendered significant by traditional discourses. That is, having briefly alluded to Nietzsche's response to modern European nihilism in terms of the necessity of individual goal-positing, I have yet to account of Nietzsche's answer to what is perhaps the most significant consequence of the decline of the ascetic ideal: the loss of any capacity to render our suffering transcendentally significant. This realisation itself constitutes experiences of 'passive' or 'extreme' nihilism, as Nietzsche observes: '[n]ihilism appears at that point, not that displeasure in existence has become greater than before but because one has come to mistrust any "meaning" in suffering, indeed in existence' (55: 35). Where previously man had 'discovered a '"meaning" in all events' and 'evil appeared full of meaning' (4: 10), now one interprets 'all that happens' to be 'meaningless and in vain' (36: 23). In these terms Reginster identifies the problem confronting post-theological culture, noting that '[t]he rejection of the "Christian interpretation" has "terrifying" implications simply because this interpretation gave an answer to the problem of suffering—it gave suffering a meaning' (Reginster 2006: 161).

Furthermore, as Warren suggested above, the interpretative schema itself may be discredited by experience, thereby provoking the evaluation that 'existence in general' is 'inherently worthless' while engendering feelings of apathy and indifference (*OGM* II 21: 67). In the following chapters, I contend it is the experience of unbearable or excessive suffering that dismantles the value of the available interpretive framework. This experience may relate to a personal emotional trauma, or it may signal the undergoing of extreme or persistent, chronic physical pain. It may also reflect a collective trauma, such as the experience of war. Such extreme or interminable forms of suffering dominate the respective worlds depicted in the literary works that constitute the focus of this study, Lawrence's *Lady Chatterley's Lover* (1928), Kafka's *The Trial* (1925) and Beckett's *Endgame* (1957). Each work dramatises the frailty of the ill, the impotent, and the traumatised modern subject denuded of the traditional means to justify or redeem one's suffering, to render distress bearable. I shall therefore diverge from existent studies considering Nietzsche's relation to literary modernism by bringing the dynamic of his discourse on 'senseless suffering' to bear on the reading of modernist texts depicting wounded, powerless subjects.

Modernism, Senseless Suffering and Nihilism

In Chapter 2, I shall focus on the relationship between suffering and nihilism in Nietzsche's thought by examining the issue of senseless or excessive suffering. Nietzsche, I shall show, was preoccupied with bestowing one's suffering with significance and thus with averting a nihilistic loss of willing. While outlining his opposition to the Christian exegesis of distress, this chapter shall attend to the tensions that beset his work to address critical appraisals of his thought within modernist studies: I contend that investigating his discourse on suffering offers a provocative approach to apprehending the strains in his thought that give rise to widely divergent readings of the philosopher.

In the first part of this chapter I shall examine Nietzsche's first major published work, *The Birth of Tragedy* (1872), where Nietzsche presents a paradigm of life-affirmation in the form of ancient Greek tragedy. Arguing that the ancient Greeks were particularly sensitive to distress and feelings of 'suicidal nihilism', Nietzsche nevertheless claims that through their tragic art they can confront and 'redeem' life's horrors. Nietzsche thus holds the ancient deity associated with tragedy, Dionysus, to symbolise this capacity to affirm life despite, and indeed because of, its senselessness.

In the next segment of this chapter I shall briefly consider Nietzsche's valorisation of aesthetic activity in relation to experiences of pain and illness. Noting his departure from the metaphysical implications of *The Birth of Tragedy*, I shall frame this discussion with reference to Nietzsche's naturalistic account of human subjectivity, of the notion of the will to power. I shall then consider how Nietzsche adopts this notion of subjectivity to approach experiences of suffering and illness before complicating these positions by invoking theorists Emanuel Levinas and Elaine Scarry.

Turning then to largely focus on a mature work, *On The Genealogy of Morality* (1887), I shall investigate Nietzsche's analysis of the ascetic ideal. Noting that, for Nietzsche, Christianity appropriates senseless suffering in terms of punishment, or guilt, I will show that his work seeks to surmount what he regards as a reactive, life-denying construal of existence. Nevertheless, by examining the discordant positions surrounding Nietzsche's thoughts on nihilism and suffering, I shall point to the appearance and persistence of reactive sentiments in his own thought, particularly in relation to others' distress. I shall suggest that tackling the conflicting stances characterising this area of Nietzsche's thought will serve to complicate partial readings that focus solely on Nietzsche's sometimes shrill, unsavoury rhetoric.

The primary aim of this chapter is to tease out insights that shall guide my reading of the modernist literary works under consideration. I echo Michael Bell's contention that Nietzsche's relation to modernism is 'one of anticipation rather than influence' (Bell 2003: 66): Nietzsche, Bell observes, 'articulated discursively and in advance the complex of themes and the composite worldview that can be deduced from a large part of modernist writing' (57). My approach in this chapter, then, is to bring into focus governing features of this 'composite worldview' hitherto overlooked in the critical discourse. I do not claim to offer a comprehensive picture of Nietzsche's complex, and often confusing, philosophical genius. Indeed, Nietzsche insistently resisted offering any systematic, coherent philosophy. However, I will argue that the dominant strands that I discern operating in his work are present in the modernist works I engage with: these literary texts, depicting fictional landscapes characterised by illness, exhaustion and impotence, are centrally concerned with the response to suffering and the issue of attributing meaning to senseless suffering.

In Chapter 3, I shall consider D. H. Lawrence's novel, *Lady Chatterley's Lover*, to be exploring the trauma that afflicts post-World War One culture. I shall also examine the novel's presentation of its characters' struggles to surmount personal grievances that are largely entwined with the collective war trauma. This will include accounting for, at both individual and collective levels: the denial or repression of wounding experiences; a growing sense of depression and loss of willing; a consuming indignation and bitterness; a defensive withdrawal from the other.

Discerning Lawrence's presentation of the propensity to recoil from others as central to the novel's characterisation, I shall note strong affinities between Lawrence and Nietzsche: both saw modernity to be dominated by restrictive, prudential concerns dictated by the desire to avert encounters with suffering. Aligning Lawrence with Nietzsche on these terms, I shall also read Lawrence's representation of Clifford with Nietzsche's analyses of the ascetic ideal: Clifford is not only a victim of war, but he also connives at his own negation of embodied-erotic being. I shall demonstrate that the novel focuses on the nihilistic consequences of Clifford's ascetic rejection of embodiment that propel his wife, Constance, into depression and irrevocable estrangement from him.

I shall then consider Lawrence's vision of the erotic as a remedy to pervasive experiences of passive nihilism. This, I shall show, entails a reconfiguration of one's suffering: Lawrence's protagonists, Constance, or Connie, and her lover, Oliver Mellors, exemplify the overcoming of a defensiveness deriving from previous emotional-erotic wounds; the depiction of the couple's sexual fulfilment gestures towards the constitution of new meaning. Nevertheless, I shall challenge Lawrence's vision of erotic revitalisation by pointing to similar strains that beset Nietzsche's work: defensive and reactive postures continue to reassert themselves in Lawrence's characters, highlighting the fragility of his affirmative vision and suggesting suffering's excessive force.

In Chapter 4, I shall focus upon Kafka's novel *The Trial*. Here I will primarily interrogate the protagonist Josef K.'s recourse to guilt to apprehend his suffering. In the first part of this chapter I shall highlight that the court's arbitrary, mysterious proceedings primarily operate to strip K. of his exegetical capacity: K. is subject to indeterminate charges and his attempts to understand the nature of the accusation are repeatedly thwarted. Observing Kafka's portrayal of K.'s consequent feelings of powerlessness regarding this experience of inexplicable distress, I shall claim that Nietzsche's penetrating insights into the economy of guilt shed light on the protagonist's trajectory.

The role of interpretation shall be central throughout this discussion. Stressing the point that one's interpretative position is reflective of one's will to power, or pathos of agency, in Nietzsche's thought, I shall discuss the ways in which Kafka's novel evokes Nietzsche's doctrine of perspectivism. This doctrine, which challenges traditional notions of objectivity or disinterestedness by arguing that knowledge claims are always reflective of one's embodied and socially embedded position, is particularly relevant to unpacking the characters' repeatedly contradictory behaviour and enunciations.

In the final part of this chapter I shall argue that K.'s self-incrimination and his suicidal complicity in his execution stem from a failure to render his suffering significant. His experience of useless distress, I shall claim, is crystallised by ruminations that resonate with Nietzsche's thought of the 'eternal recurrence'. Crudely put, on imagining the repetition of his experience at the hands of the court, K. heightens his state of fatigued resignation. By then invoking Nietzsche's analysis of the guilty sensibility, I shall conclude this chapter by arguing that K.'s suicidal collusion entails an attempt to configure himself as a willing agent. Nevertheless, the radical indeterminacy characterising the work as a whole persists until the end so that it seems to fall upon the imagined spectator, or reader, to redeem some significance from K.'s abject execution.

The theatricality of suffering comes to the fore in Beckett's play, *Endgame*, the focus of the Chapter 5. As in Kafka's novel, I shall read the characters' appeal to a witness to signal the self's incapacity to assimilate experiences of unbearable suffering: the performative dimension of one's suffering, I shall argue, suggests that other means to appropriate one's distress have been exhausted or fallen short. Here I shall discuss the various strategies deployed by Beckett's characters to bear their suffering in a world that is permeated by physical pain, ageing and decay, and by feelings of frustrated powerlessness, or *ressentiment*.

I shall also register a tension in Beckett's play that is evident in Nietzsche's work, namely the desire to be true to suffering's senselessness, to its excessive force, and the contrary need to master suffering and to render it significant. Beckett's pseudo-couple Hamm and Clov present contrasting approaches: Clov echoes Kafka's protagonist by interpreting suffering in terms of punishment, thus pointing to the continued pertinacity of the ascetic ideal; Hamm gestures towards a rejection of theological discourse, yet struggles to confront a Dionysian vision of existence shorn of value. Hamm's repudiation of, and yet continued dependence upon, Christian theodicy is therefore central to this chapter.

Parallels abound between Beckett's play and the other texts I discuss in this study. For instance, Beckett's characters exhibit the restricted, self-preservative postures that appear in *Lady Chatterley's Lover* and *The Trial*. Here this self-defensive economy develops and intensifies because of the characters' experience as chronic sufferers. By drawing on Nietzsche's thoughts on the experience of prolonged pain, I shall consider Beckett's characters to be particularly sensitive to suffering, and to the other. Noting, too, that the characters in all three texts express compensatory aggressive gestures, I shall invoke Nietzsche to illuminate the proliferation of seemingly arbitrary sadistic imaginings and actions in *Endgame*. I shall conclude this chapter by considering the role of the play's audience, observing similarities with the reader's position at the conclusion of *The Trial*: in both works the characters share their exegetical impasse with their actual or projected audience as a means to endow their suffering with some significance.

I shall focus upon literature's affective dynamic in the conclusion of this study. Here invoking Virginia Woolf's essay, 'On Being Ill' (1926), I shall draw out some of this study's salient points, particularly regarding others' suffering and its tie to suicidal nihilism. Examination of Woolf's essay, I shall show, proves to be particularly fruitful in highlighting a series of tensions operating in Nietzsche and the modernist works I have considered. Most pertinently, Woolf's desire to valorise the experience of illness or suffering simultaneously demonstrates an implicit awareness of suffering's excessive, useless character and the pathos of nihilism this engenders. With this notion of the excessive in mind, I shall turn now to examine Nietzsche's engagement with suffering.

Notes

1. Quoted in Idris Parry's, 'Introduction' to *The Trial* in Franz Kafka, *The Trial* (London: Penguin, repr., 2000), p. xiii.
2. Nietzsche ends this passage: 'the recipe against this "distress" is: *distress*'. I shall consider some of these views in Chapter 2.
3. I will develop this point in Chapter 2 on Nietzsche. On Beckett, see James Knowlson, *Damned to Fame: The Life of Samuel Beckett* (London:

Bloomsbury, 1996), p. 27; On Lawrence, see David Ellis, *Death and the Author: How D. H. Lawrence Died, and Was Remembered* (Oxford: Oxford University Press, 2008), p. 57.

4. Roger Griffin, *Modernism and Fascism: The Sense of a Beginning Under Mussolini and Hitler* (Basingstoke: Palgrave Macmillan, 2007), p. 2. Griffin also observes an 'unresolved tension in Nietzsche's creative response to modernity' marked by a turning inward and 'the cultivation of special moments.' See Griffin 2007: 62.

5. For discussions of Nietzsche's critical reception outside the Anglophone tradition see, for example: Steven E. Aschheim, *The Nietzsche Legacy in Germany, 1890–1990* (London: University of California Press, 1994); Christopher E. Forth, *Zarathustra in Paris: The Nietzsche Vogue in France, 1891–1918* (DeKalb: North Illinois University Press, 2001).

6. In line with this association, Jacques Derrida notes that '[t]here is nothing absolutely contingent about the fact that the only political regimen to have *effectively* brandished his name as a major and official banner was Nazi'. Jacques Derrida, *The Ear of the Other* (London: University of Nebraska Press, 1988), p. 31.

7. Cary makes numerous assertions that I aim to nuance in this study. See John Carey, *The Intellectuals and the Masses: Pride and Prejudice Among the Literary Intelligentsia, 1880–1939* (London: Faber and Faber, 1992), pp. 4, 12, 72, 73, 75.

8. Kirsty Martin has recently corroborated Carey's view of Nietzsche, appealing to Carey to differentiate D. H. Lawrence from the philosopher. See Kirsty Martin, *Modernism and the Rhythms of Sympathy* (Oxford: Oxford University Press, 2013), pp. 140–1.

9. Weller argues: 'While the term "nihilism" occurs repeatedly in the works of 1887–88, [...] it is only in *The Will to Power* that the concept of nihilism takes centre-stage in Nietzsche's critique of modernity'. Shane Weller, *Modernism and Nihilism* (Basingstoke: Palgrave Macmillan, 2011), p. 27.

10. I adhere to Keith Ansell-Pearson's recommendation to firstly 'pay careful and close attention to what Nietzsche says in his published texts [...] and then allow the notebooks from the 1880s to be used only on the basis of connections one can plausibly make between them and the published texts'. Keith Ansell-Pearson and Duncan Large (eds.), *The Nietzsche Reader* (Oxford: Blackwell, 2009), p. 305.

11. See for example John Carey, *The Intellectuals and the Masses: Pride and Prejudice Among the Literary Intelligentsia, 1880–1939* (London: Faber and Faber, 1992), p. 72; Pericles Lewis, *Religious Experience and the Modernist Novel* (Cambridge: Cambridge University Press, 2010), p. 27; and Roger Luckhurst, 'Religion, Psychical Research, Spiritualism, and

the Occult', in *The Oxford Handbook of Modernisms* (Oxford: Oxford University Press, 2016), pp. 429–44 (429–30).

12. See also *GS* 131: 123.
13. See also *WP* 247: 143.
14. See *OGM* III 27: 126.
15. See also *OGM* III 27: 127; *WP* 5: 10.

REFERENCES

Beckett, Samuel, *Endgame,* in Samuel Beckett, *The Complete Dramatic Works* (London: Faber, 1990), 89–134.

Bell, Michael, 'Nietzscheanism: "The Superman and the all-too-human"', in *A Concise Companion to Modernism,* ed. David Bradshaw (Oxford: Blackwell, 2003), 56–74.

Bradbury, Malcolm, and James Walter McFarlane, *Modernism: 1890–1930* (Harmondsworth: Penguin, 1976).

Bridgwater, Patrick, *Nietzsche in Anglo-Saxony: A Study of Nietzsche's Influence on English and American Literature* (Bristol: Leicester University Press, 1972).

Carey, John, *The Intellectuals and the Masses: Pride and Prejudice Among the Literary Intelligentsia, 1880–1939* (London: Faber and Faber, 1992).

Carr, Karen Leslie, *The Banalization of Nihilism: Twentieth-Century Responses to Meaninglessness* (Albany: State University of New York Press, 1992).

Childs, Peter, *Modernism* (London: Routledge, 2000).

Conway, Daniel W., 'Heidegger, Nietzsche, and the Origins of Nihilism', *Journal of Nietzsche Studies* 3 (1992): 11–43.

Foster, John Burt, *Heirs to Dionysus: A Nietzschean Current in Literary Modernism* (Princeton, NJ: Princeton University Press, 1981).

Glicksberg, Charles I., *The Literature of Nihilism* (London: Bucknell University Press, 1975).

Gooding-Williams, Robert, *Zarathustra's Dionysian Modernism* (Stanford: Stanford University Press, 2001).

Griffin, Roger, *Modernism and Fascism: The Sense of a Beginning Under Mussolini and Hitler* (Basingstoke: Palgrave Macmillan, 2007).

Kafka, Franz, *The Trial.* trans. Idris Parry (London: Penguin, repr., 2000).

Lawrence, D. H., *Lady Chatterley's Lover* (London: Penguin, repr. 2006).

May, Keith M., *Nietzsche and Modern Literature: Themes in Yeats, Rilke, Mann and Lawrence* (Basingstoke: Macmillan, 1988).

Muller-Lauter, 'Experiences with Nietzsche' in *Nietzsche, Godfather of Fascism, On the Uses and Abuses of a Philosophy,* ed. by Jacob Golomb and Robert S. Wistrich (Princeton, NJ and Oxford: Princeton University Press, 2002), 66–89.

Nietzsche, Friedrich Wilhelm, *The Will to Power*. trans. Walter Kaufmann and R. J. Hollingdale (New York: Vintage Books, 1968).

———, *Beyond Good and Evil: Prelude to a Philosophy of the Future*. trans. R. J. Hollingdale (Harmondsworth: Penguin, repr. 1990).

———, *The Birth of Tragedy*. trans. Shaun Whiteside (London: Penguin, 1993).

———, *On the Genealogy of Morality*. trans. Carol Diethe (Cambridge: Cambridge University Press, 1994).

———, *The Gay Science: With a Prelude in German Rhymes and an Appendix of Songs*. trans. Josefine Nauckhoff and Adrian Del Caro (Cambridge: Cambridge University Press, repr. 2003).

Norris, Margot, *Beasts of the Modern Imagination: Darwin, Nietzsche, Kafka, Ernst, & Lawrence* (Baltimore: Johns Hopkins University Press, 1985).

Pippin, Robert B., 'Nietzsche and the Origin of the Idea of Modernism', *Inquiry* 26 (1983): 151–80.

Reginster, Bernard, *The Affirmation of Life: Nietzsche on Overcoming Nihilism* (London: Harvard University Press, 2006).

Thatcher, David S., *Nietzsche in England, 1890–1914: The Growth of a Reputation* (Toronto: University of Toronto Press, 1970).

Warren, Mark, *Nietzsche and Political Thought* (Cambridge, MA: MIT Press, 1988).

Weller, Shane, *Modernism and Nihilism* (Basingstoke: Palgrave Macmillan, 2011).

CHAPTER 2

Friedrich Nietzsche, Nihilism and Meaningless Suffering

Introduction: The Interpretation of Suffering

Friedrich Nietzsche tells us in the preface to *On the Genealogy of Morality* (1887) that 'as a thirteen-year-old boy, I was preoccupied with the problem of the origin of evil'. Nietzsche's biography may be invoked to explain his early focus on this traditional religious problem: the deaths of his father, Carl Ludwig, in 1849 when Nietzsche was 5, and his brother, Joseph, the following year profoundly affected him into adolescence and adulthood (see Ansell-Pearson and Large 2009: xxii). His biography may also account for his continued exploration of the cognate issues of suffering and nihilism throughout his oeuvre. Discussing the plethora of physical afflictions that Nietzsche struggled with including paralysing headaches, digestive problems, and a painful eye condition that meant that most of his books needed to be at least partly dictated, Charlie Huenemann observes that '[n]o philosopher suffered as much as Nietzsche' (Huenemann 2013: 67). Yet, while Huenemann notes that Nietzsche's 'state of health was a critical concern for him at every waking moment', suffering has been marginalised in Nietzsche scholarship (67). As Kathleen Marie Higgins notes, 'the intensity and scope of his concern for suffering is a feature of his work that has been unappreciated' (Higgins 2008: 72). Furthermore, I endorse Higgins' view that 'sensitivity to suffering is the presupposition of Nietzsche's work throughout his career': suffering goes to 'the heart of his thought' (59–60). As

© The Author(s) 2018
S. Smith, *Nietzsche and Modernism*,
Palgrave Studies in Modern European Literature,
https://doi.org/10.1007/978-3-319-75535-9_2

I shall demonstrate, suffering, which is broadly conceived by Nietzsche to include various forms of physical pain, illness and psychic distress, is inextricably bound up with the pathos of nihilism, the feeling that life is not worth living.

Nietzsche's first book, *The Birth of Tragedy* (1872), pivots around the issue of meaningless suffering and the nihilistic threat to subjectivity this poses. Propounding that the Pre-Socratic Greeks were deeply sensitive to life's horrors, Nietzsche claims that they were disposed to a paralysing nausea bound to a particularly pessimistic outlook articulated in the ancient myth of Silenus: according to the myth Silenus informs his captor, King Midas, that for humanity, "'[T]he best of all things is [...]: not to be born, not to *be*, to be *nothing*. But the second-best thing for you—is to die soon'" (*BT* 3: 22). For Nietzsche, the ancient Greeks' ability not only to avert this nihilistic condition but also to embrace the reality of human existence through their tragic art form was to provide answers as to how modernity, in its comparable tragic condition, was to overcome its crisis of meaning: given the so-called death of the Christian God, Nietzsche, I contend, was acutely cognisant of the threat of suicidal nihilism presented by inexplicable distress, by suffering no longer interpretatively appropriated by the redundant Christian redemptive narrative.

It is also in this text that Nietzsche introduces Dionysus, the Greek deity at the centre of ancient tragedy who, according to myth, is dismembered and repeatedly reborn. Before examining Dionysus' role in Nietzsche's account of ancient tragedy, it is worth noting that in his later writings Dionysus reappears as a paradigm of life-affirmation whom Nietzsche repeatedly identifies with. For instance, directing the reader to the significance of this alignment in the final lines of his final published text, the self-styled autobiography, *Ecce Homo* (1888), Nietzsche pronounces: '[h]ave I been understood?—*Dionysus against the Crucified*' (*EH* XIV 9: 104).[1] This crucial, self-defining opposition can be elucidated by turning to a notebook entry which employs a similar combative rhetoric:

> Dionysus versus the "Crucified": there you have the antithesis. It is *not* a difference in regard to their martyrdom—it is a difference in the meaning of it. [...] One will see that the problem is that of the meaning of suffering: whether a Christian meaning or a tragic meaning. In the former case, it is supposed to be the path to a holy existence; in the latter case, being is counted as *holy enough* to justify even a monstrous amount of suffering. The tragic man affirms even the harshest suffering: he is sufficiently

strong, rich, and capable of deifying to do so. The Christian denies even the happiest lot on earth: he is sufficiently weak, poor, disinherited to suffer from life in whatever form he meets it. The god on the cross is a curse on life, a signpost to seek redemption from life; Dionysus cut to pieces is a *promise* of life: it will be eternally reborn and return again from destruction. (*WP* 1052: 542–3)

This passage indicates the importance that the hermeneutic of suffering assumes in Nietzsche's thought: the desire to oppose the Christian construal of suffering 'as an objection to life, as a formula for its condemnation', governs his philosophical project. In this chapter, I shall outline Nietzsche's presentation of these conflicting perspectives to demonstrate that while the Dionysian or tragic interpretation symbolises the affirmation or 'justification' of suffering existence, the Christian exegesis and its cognate practices are nihilistic in Nietzsche's view. Much of the subsequent discussion aims to explore the complexities gravitating around the theme of 'the problem [...] of the meaning of suffering' in Nietzsche's work. It will begin by concentrating on the figure of Dionysus in *The Birth of Tragedy* and then focus largely on his *Genealogy* in the later segments of this chapter to chart his diagnoses of the nihilistic pathos inflecting Christian values.

There is another reason for beginning this chapter with a consideration of Nietzsche's presentation of Dionysus: re-examining the particularly exultant rhetoric Nietzsche employs regarding his identification with the god has wider implications for the reading of modernism. That is, many commentators emphasise recent poststructuralist interpretations of Nietzsche's apparent Dionysian playfulness, scepticism and experimentalism in their readings of his relation to modernism.[2] Benno Wagner, for instance, considers Kafka with Nietzsche's celebration of the absolute squanderer who lives life dangerously and triumphantly (see Wagner 2006); Charles Glicksberg, before going on to analyse Kafka's *The Trial* (1925) and Beckett's *Waiting for Godot* (1952), claims that:

> Nietzsche struggled to find a way out of nihilism by resolving to accept life as it is for all eternity, despite the reality of suffering and the misfortunes that fell to his lot. By the concentrated and disciplined power of his will he would rise above the human condition. He would transmute suffering into sheer joy, pain into jubilation. Whatever befell him he would greet with a burst of Dionysian laughter and thus establish his control of life in a problematical and supremely indifferent universe. (Glicksberg 1975: 26)

Glicksberg is astute in identifying the Dionysian with Nietzsche's response to nihilism. However, I wish to nuance these readings of Nietzsche's philosophy by exploring the sense of vulnerability, or fear of collapse, which underlies and attends his discourse on suffering.[3] That is, I shall observe Nietzsche's sensitivity towards the problem of excessive or useless suffering, of distress that cannot be transmuted into 'sheer joy' or 'jubilation'. This shall enable me to engage with the discordant postures that characterise his thought and thus to move beyond extant, partial accounts of Nietzsche's relation to modernism.[4] As I shall argue in the last section of this chapter, I hold this sense of frailty regarding the issue of meaningless suffering to account for the defensive-protective postures which undermine his expansive, affirmative idiom. I shall begin by exploring Nietzsche's exalted Dionysian sensibility by looking at *The Birth of Tragedy*, a text that profoundly impacted modernist writers.

'DISCIPLE OF DIONYSUS'

The Birth of Tragedy involves an investigation into the pre-Socratic Greeks' capacity to confront and embrace suffering's senselessness through the medium of ancient tragedy. Here Nietzsche makes the celebrated proclamation that it is 'only as *aesthetic phenomenon* that existence and the world are eternally *justified*': it is the aesthetic 'tragic pattern' that transfigures and palliates the nauseating insights disclosed by tragedy (*BT* 5: 32). To follow Nietzsche's account of the success of tragedy—the tragic Greeks perform 'an affirmation without reservation even of suffering' through this transformative experience—entails an exploration of the two life-principles, or artistic drives or instincts, he invokes to expound his thesis, namely the Greek deities Dionysus and Apollo (*EH* IV 2: 50). Appealing to these two symbolic figures, Nietzsche argues that it is the combination and balance of Dionysus, the god of intoxication and excess who symbolises a raw, directionless energy that suffuses all being, with the Apollonian principle of dream-like illusions and boundaries that creates tragic art. Apollo corresponds to the surface world of appearances or phenomena, of individuated being, and relates aesthetically to sculpture, visual art and epic poetry. The Dionysian artistic urges manifest primarily in music and dance. The interplay of these two principles produces a rare, fragile tension in pre-Socratic culture to produce tragedy's paradoxical dynamic.

By observing that *The Birth of Tragedy* simultaneously works to provide a powerful critique of modernity, Nietzsche's celebration of the Dionysian and his appeal to the modernists can be noted. One of the main arguments in the text surrounds the demise of tragic perception, of the collapse of the delicate balance of the two principles that give rise to tragic art: according to Nietzsche, the fetishisation of reason, primarily instigated through Socratic optimism, continues to manifest itself in cultural forms such as Christianity and scientific modernity, forms which suggestively hold the world amenable to human knowledge. Nietzsche considers this ensuing over-dependence upon rationality, which is an extreme manifestation of the Apollonian impulse to establish the boundaries of autarkic selfhood, to dominate what he labels 'Alexandrian' culture; its exponent, the 'theoretical man', may inhabit an outlook which offers a safe distance from the terrifying tragic knowledge of the world's purposelessness and absurdity, yet divorce from the instinctive energies associated with Dionysus transmits into cultural stultification and sterility. Not surprisingly, Nietzsche's diagnosis of modernity's crisis in these terms, and his concomitant espousal of the revitalising energy of the Dionysian, held great sway in early twentieth-century literary and intellectual culture.

To account for the Dionysian energetic of primordial tragedy, it is important to mention something of ancient tragedy's religious context: 'tragedy originated—and continued to be performed—in the cult of Dionysus', as Richard Seaford notes (Seaford 2005: 25). Nietzsche understood the religious context to directly inform the content and form of primitive tragedy. The city Dionysia, the spring festival held to celebrate the Asiatic Dionysus' arrival in Athens, was characterised by revelry, wine drinking, and orgiastic sexual licentiousness. This experienced rupture of normal social codes and boundaries, and hence of autarkic selfhood, resonates in the narrative of tragic drama: the tragic hero's destruction signals the inessential, transient nature of personhood and its return to the larger, primordial reality.

Much of Nietzsche's idiom in the text is highly romantic. For instance, he rhapsodises on this ecstatic state and the attainment of a 'mystical sense of unity' where the self is connected to larger communal and hence cosmic being (*BT* 2: 18). This is a result of the dissolution of egoistical, Apollonian boundaries of selfhood:

> Not only is the bond between man and man sealed by the Dionysiac magic: alienated, hostile or subjugated nature, too, celebrates her

reconciliation with her lost son, man. [...] Now the slave is a free man, now all the rigid and hostile boundaries that distress, despotism, or 'impudent fashion' have erected between man and man break down. [...] Singing and dancing, man expresses himself as a member of a higher community: he has forgotten how to walk and talk, and is about to fly dancing into the heavens. His gestures express enchantment. (17)

This romanticised notion of the Dionysian experience as a harmonious reconnect with mankind and the natural world, signalling a freedom from alienated, Apollonian being and hence from suffering, is picked up on by several critics. Giles Fraser, for instance, reads Dionysus 'as a saviour figure who comes to unify human beings with nature' (Fraser 2002: 57). Michael Allen Gillespie alludes to this notion to contend:

To be born is to be an individual, to be severed or alienated from the whole. This experience produces suffering, the only way to relieve this suffering is to cease to be an individual, that is to die and return to the original unity. (Gillespie 1995: 206)

A more sophisticated account of Dionysian joy is offered, however, by Michel Haar as he emphasises the profound ambivalence of this affirmative experience. Complicating the readings proposed by Fraser and Gillespie, Haar recognises that Dionysian ecstasy entails the shattering of the rational ego. Thus, whether in the state of communal ecstasy or, relatedly, through profound identification with the hero's suffering, it is the fracturing of the individual's self-coherence that fosters a Dionysian permeability between the self and the whole. This dissolution of self-coherent identity, while gesturing to a radical openness to otherness, simultaneously suggests a powerful affect of vulnerability. Haar observes that this sense of fragility is key to tragic experience: the collapse of the self's centre induces a feeling of 'inadequacy' that 'translates into uncertainty, frailty, scattering and yet indeterminate hope' (Haar 1998: 172). Tragic experience, Haar stresses, is a paradoxical affect of 'religious joy', an anguished 'joy inexplicable in Apollonian terms' (Haar 1996: 164).

Nietzsche's idealised endorsement of life with all its suffering and questionable or repugnant aspects derives from this affective, rather than conceptual, relation to the world's otherness. Declaring this joyous perspective as the ultimate expression of Dionysian faith and affirmation, Nietzsche, in a related notebook entry, posits this as the goal of his philosophy:

My new path to a "Yes".

...Such an experimental philosophy as I live anticipates experimentally even the possibilities of the most fundamental nihilism; but this does not mean that it must halt at a negation, a No, a will to negation. It wants rather to cross over to the opposite of this—to a Dionysian affirmation of the world as it is, without subtraction, exception, or selection—it wants the eternal circulation: - the same things, the same logic and illogic of entanglements. The highest state a philosopher can attain: to stand in a Dionysian relationship to existence—my formula for this is *amor fati*. (*WP* 1041: 536)

It is from this profoundly religious experience that he declares '*amor fati*', or 'love of one's fate'. Nevertheless, it is necessary to highlight the complexity of the nature of tragic experience, to register that Nietzsche's account of the Dionysian also points to a fear of collapse into futilitarian resignation. Doing so will also safeguard against understating the role of the Apollonian in Nietzsche's schema.

Writing separately on tragedy, Iris Murdoch notes that tragedy's 'dreadful vision of the reality and significance of death' works to 'break the ego, destroying the illusory whole of the unified self' (Murdoch 1993: 104). At the core of *The Birth of Tragedy* is Nietzsche's contention that tragedy 'wishes us to acknowledge that everything that comes into being must be prepared to face a sorrowful end' (*BT* 17: 80). Dionysus' dismemberment pertains, then, to the inevitable dissolution of self-identity in death, to the violation of the self by time. In Nietzsche's account of ancient tragedy, awareness of the self's disintegration and of existence as ephemeral, entailing the inevitable pain of de-individuation, precipitates a loss of agency and feelings of nausea. For Nietzsche observes that, '[t]rue understanding, insight into the terrible truth, outweighs every motive for action' (*BT* 7: 39). This depiction of nihilism as a state of paralysis, or the loss of willing induced by such disclosures, signals the necessity of 'untruth', or illusion, to transfigure the horror:

This is something that Dionysiac man shares with Hamlet: both have truly seen to the essence of things, they have *understood*, and action repels them; for their action can change nothing in the eternal essence of things, they consider it ludicrous or shameful that they should be expected to restore order to the chaotic world. Understanding kills action, action depends on the veil of illusion—this is what Hamlet teaches us. (39)

Nietzsche subverts the Platonic-Christian reverence for truth to contend that true knowledge of existence is unpalatable: insight into the groundless and transitory nature of existence merely serves to highlight one's fragile mortal existence. Noting the nature of this insight disclosed by tragedy complicates simplistic views of the Dionysian which suggest a harmonious return to primordial unity. Rather, Nietzsche's depiction of the pathos of collective identification is deeply ambivalent: Nietzsche celebrates the re-energising, irrational and transformative value of Dionysian ecstasy, on the one hand; on the other, the collapse of autarkic selfhood simultaneously discloses the terrifying knowledge of existence. He therefore registers the Greeks' need to impose illusory meaning: they must give form to the chaotic meaninglessness of the Dionysian or be subjected to suicidal nihilism:

> Both [Apollo and Dionysus] transfigure a region in whose chords of delight dissonance as well as the terrible image of the world charmingly fade away; they both play with the sting of displeasure, trusting to their extremely powerful magical arts; both use this play to justify the existence even of the 'worst world'. Here the Dionysiac, as against the Apolline, proves to be the eternal and original artistic force, calling the whole phenomenal world into existence: in the midst of it a new transfiguring illusion is required if the animated world of individuation is to be kept alive. If we could imagine dissonance becoming man—and what else is man?—then in order to stay alive that dissonance would need a wonderful illusion, covering its own being with a veil of beauty. That is the real artistic intention of Apollo, in whose name we bring tighter all those innumerable illusions of the beauty of appearance, which at each moment make life worth living and urge us to experience the next moment. (25: 116–7)

This passage illuminates the dynamic interplay of the Apollonian and Dionysian to suggest that ancient tragedy, according to Nietzsche, makes 'life worth living' in two main ways: as previously noted, the dissolution of individuated being, communally experienced, entails an ecstatic pathos of power of being part of the whole, of connecting with the underlying unity of life and nature's omnipotence and abundance; nevertheless, given that this Dionysian disintegration of the phenomenal world precipitates feelings of 'the most fundamental nihilism', the Apollonian makes sensible these nauseating insights, giving dramatic form to the ecstatic anguish of the disintegration of individual being. The Apollonian capacity for beautiful representation imposes order on a dissonance that may overwhelm the fragmented individual. Anticipating Nietzsche's later thought, an implicit masochistic economy or a joyous vulnerability premised on the fracturing and reconstitution of selfhood informs this affirmative valuation of suffering.

A further point of continuity from *The Birth of Tragedy* to Nietzsche's middle and later writings is his privileging of aesthetic activity to counter the ever-present threat of futilitarian resignation. As he transposes the notion of the aesthetic from its larger cultural significance to the individual in his later texts, both the Apollonian, form-giving sense and the Dionysian idea of the relatedness to the whole remain evident. Yet there is a notable departure from *The Birth of Tragedy*: art no longer plays such a totalising life-redeeming function as he abandons the notion of its 'metaphysical consolation', and therefore of a primordial, underlying unity (*BT* 7: 39). Rather, as he comes to focus upon ideas of self-artistry that are framed by naturalistic explanations of selfhood, he declares: '[a]s an aesthetic phenomenon existence is still *bearable* for us' (*GS* 107: 104). That is, Nietzsche privileges artistic activity that entails imposing form or unity upon one's own inner 'dissonance', thereby constituting one's own personal meaning within a chaotic, meaningless world. I will now turn to briefly note Nietzsche's naturalistic physio-psychological account of subjectivity before considering how suffering and nihilism relate to this emphasis on self-artistry.

POWER AND SELF-ARTISTRY

The notion of dissonance resonates in Nietzsche's naturalistic articulations of human subjectivity in his later writings. In his quest 'to translate man back into nature' (*BGE* 230: 162), Nietzsche conceives of the self to be constituted by a 'tremendous multiplicity' of conflicting drives and affects, of quanta of forces that are determined by internal power constellations (*WP* 518: 281). The self, therefore, is no pre-given unity, but rather exists as a site of internal struggle, as a plurality of competing passions vying for dominance. One's outward activity is an expression of the constitution of one's primal drives and impulses, a reflection of 'the order of rank the innermost drives [...] stand in relation to one another' (*BGE* 6: 38). There is thus a need to generate form, to hierarchically organise one's passions: one's experience as an effective, willing agent is determined by the imposition of an aim-directedness, or telos, by the dominant drive or cooperating drives; one's feeling of power, of efficacious agency, is also reflective of the strength of the hegemony this ruling drive obtains in its struggle with the other drives. I shall speak more of the necessity of goal-positing below. Investigating the phenomenology of 'willing', of heeding a 'commanding thought', Nietzsche thus valorises the 'affect of command' and the necessary 'obedience' of one's subordinate drives (19: 48); the overcoming of resistances, here presented by one's countering drives, is central to Nietzsche's physio-psychological thesis of the will to power. Importantly, while this internal relation of the drives is fluid, the failure to engender unified form results in a state of debilitating contradiction and paralysis. Nietzsche relatedly claims:

> The multitude and disgregation of the impulses and the lack of any systematic order among them result in a 'weak will'; their co-ordination under a single predominant impulse results in a 'strong will': in the first case it is the oscillation and the lack of gravity; in the latter, the precision and clarity of the direction. (*WP* 46: 28)[5]

Society, then, consists of a spectrum of beings whose varying capacities to experience themselves as efficacious agents, to feel powerful, is determined by their respective abilities to self-regulate or organise one's inner 'souls' into coherent form.[6] The physiological basis of nihilism is here registered: 'disgregation' of our impulses precipitates decline and exhaustion.

In various passages in *The Gay Science* (1882–1887) Nietzsche appeals to literary models to exemplify the creative, or aesthetic, process of self-constitution: one must 'learn from artists' (299: 170) to become beings that are 'unique, incomparable, who give themselves laws, who create themselves!' (335: 189). Imitating artists' techniques, this self-fashioning entails obtaining sufficient 'artistic distance'—'the art of "putting oneself on stage" before oneself'—to view oneself as 'something past and whole'. Otherwise put, one must conceive of oneself 'simplified and transfigured' as a unified totality (78: 78–9). One of Nietzsche's well-known passages sums up this activity of becoming the 'poets of our lives' (299: 170):

> To 'give style' to one's character—a great and rare art! It is practiced by those who survey all the strengths and weaknesses of their nature and fit them into an artistic plan until every one of them appears as art and reason

and even weaknesses delight the eye. [...] In the end, when the work is complete, it becomes clear how it was the force of a single taste that ruled and shaped everything great and small—whether the taste was good or bad means less than one may think; it's enough that it was one taste! (290: 163–4)

The import of perceiving oneself from an 'artistic distance', of construing one's thoughts, desires and actions as inter-connected, reflecting the 'force of a "singular taste"', has been noted by several commentators. Alexander Nehamas, for instance, expounds Nietzsche's view that we must deploy our organisational capacity to construe our own actions, thoughts and desires with reference to the overarching narrative of our own lives: Nehamas discerns Nietzsche's thought to signal the need to 'fashion a literary character out of [one]self and a literary work out of [one's]life' (Nehamas 1985: 137). Julian Young similarly points to Nietzsche's stress on constructing a personal narrative. Observing that Nietzsche sees the death of God to signify the loss of 'anything that performs the function in human life that was once performed by the God of Christianity', Young argues that Nietzsche considers other grand, universal narratives such as Hegelianism or Marxism to also be rendered obsolete (Young 2003: 83). Furthermore, it is by way of contrast to such totalising stories, engendering impersonal meanings, that Nietzsche advocates the construction of unique, personal narratives of selfhood.[7]

This paradigm of aesthetic activity has a significant bearing on apprehending Nietzsche's approach to suffering. Higgins, for example, observes that Nietzsche's attitude to suffering 'is aesthetic because it involves interpreting suffering as an element in a larger whole, much as the artistic element is interpreted as an element essential to the larger organism of the artwork' (Higgins 2008: 60–1). As Higgins notes, just as *The Birth of Tragedy* insisted upon the value of perceiving oneself in relation to the whole, so one's suffering can be actively assimilated, or integrated into one's overall interpretation of one's life. Obtaining such a perspective, pain, various grievances, misdeeds, and other meaningless losses can be rendered valuable, or 'redeemed' in a non-theistic sense, by perceiving them as 'essential to the structure and development of that life as a whole' (61).

Several passages throughout Nietzsche's work corroborate this notion of performing an active appropriation of one's distress by relating it to one's overall personal narrative. In one notable entry, Nietzsche takes aim at the negative construal of suffering he discerns informing both Christian and putative secular attitudes to distress to argue that suffering can be transformative, as an occasion for self-growth. By taking the perspective of 'the entire economy' of oneself, Nietzsche claims, one can discern the 'whole inner sequence and interconnection' of one's experiences (*GS* 338: 191). Importantly, this remains 'inaccessible and incommunicable' to 'our nearest and dearest' (191). Therefore, while the self may engage with its profoundest experiences to construe their relationality according to one's predominant self-representation or narrative, 'our so-called "benefactors"', those compassionate others striving to remove the apparent source of our distress, are necessarily limited to a superficial knowledge of the significance of one's suffering (191). Pointing to the deeper level of selfhood constituted by one's past sufferings, Nietzsche accordingly valorises the potential for convalescence and self-renewal offered by one's present distress: 'the breaking open of new springs and needs, the healing of old wounds, the shedding of entire periods of the past—all such things that can be involved in misfortune' (191).

While I shall return to further explore Nietzsche's suggestion here of the self's ontological isolation in subsequent chapters, it is worth briefly noting that his claim that 'there is a personal necessity of misfortune' indexes a recurrent theme in Nietzsche's later work[8]: his explicit articulations of suffering's affirmative value seek to counter the negative value attributed to suffering by '*the religion of snug cosiness*', namely Christianity and Western modernity more generally (192). As these formulations should be considered with his analyses of modern nihilism, which I will outline below, I shall return there to give due attention to these arguments.

Indeed, Nietzsche's inversion of the dominant hedonic evaluation of suffering is apparent in the physio-psychological thesis of the will to power, briefly alluded to above. That is, Nietzsche privileges the pathos of power that derives from attaining self-mastery, from fashioning oneself according to a dominant 'taste'. As noted, this entails attaining feelings of command and the overcoming of the resistances presented by one's conflicting drives. Suffering, then, is integral to the pathos of power, to the attainment of self-unity. As Nietzsche puts it in *The Will to Power* (1901):

> Displeasure, as an obstacle to its will to power, is therefore a normal fact, the normal ingredient of every organic event; man does not avoid it, he is rather in continual need of it; every victory, every feeling of pleasure, every event, presupposes a resistance overcome. (*WP* 702: 373)[9]

The intrinsic dynamic of striving for power complicates the distinction between pleasure and pain that governs hedonic evaluations of existence: pain and pleasure are intertwined feelings involved in the overcoming of resistances. Bernard Reginster focuses on this notion of overcoming resistances to neatly encapsulate Nietzsche's reappraisal of the value of suffering:

> The doctrine of the will to power radically alters our conception of the role and significance of suffering in human existence. If, in particular, we take power—the overcoming of resistance—to be a value, then we can see easily how it can be the principle behind a revaluation of suffering. Indeed, if we value the overcoming of resistance, then we must also value the resistance that is an ingredient of it. Since suffering is defined by resistance, we must also value suffering. (2006: 177)

While this notion of overcoming resistances may be readily applied to active or volitional forms of suffering, and relate to both internal and external obstacles to the realisation of one's willing, this concept can also be applied to passive, non-volitional forms of suffering in Nietzsche's thought. That is, Nietzsche frequently presents distress, physical and psychic, as a 'powerful adversary' against which the self nevertheless triumphs, as a resistance overcome. For instance, Nietzsche contends that in confronting physical pain '[o]ur pride towers up as never before: it discovers an incomparable stimulus in opposing such a tyrant as pain' (*D* 114: 70). Consequently, suffering represents an opportunity for attaining self-mastery: surmounting the challenge presented by pain 'represents a triumph over ourself', Nietzsche argues (70). This experience thus ultimately entails an appropriative gain for the sufferer, and the possibility of self-insight: '[t]he tremendous tension imparted to the intellect by its desire to oppose and counter pain makes him see everything he now beholds in a new light' (70).[10]

Useless Suffering

Several commentators contest Nietzsche's re-construal of suffering. David Boothroyd, for instance, asserts that 'Nietzsche's discourse misses [the] discovery', put forward by Emanuel Levinas, that 'suffering is "for nothing"' (Boothroyd 2009: 158). Accordingly, Boothroyd asserts that Nietzsche seems to bypass the uselessness of suffering, the very fact that 'pain is that which "results from an excess", a "too much"' (158). This constitutes '[t]he significant difference between Nietzsche and Levinas' for Boothroyd (157). To explore Boothroyd's contention, it is useful to invoke Levinas alongside another thinker, Elaine Scarry, whose respective work on the phenomenology of suffering depicts its excessive character. Reference to the salient points of these two writers will allow a greater appreciation of Nietzsche's thoughts on 'senseless suffering'.

Levinas' discussion of the phenomenology of pain in his essay, 'Useless Suffering', involves the recognition that suffering is a mode of experience that consumes the self and annihilates the pathos of self-integrity the subject strives for. And while physical pain only constitutes one experience of suffering, by drawing attention to this, as Nietzsche and Levinas do, I shall analogise other forms of suffering to this under-standing. Following Nietzsche by applying a broadly Kantian under-standing of the self, Levinas observes that, unlike other sensations which can be ordered and assimilated by the unifying subject, extreme pain disrupts the pursuit of pleasurable self-relation, of subjective coherence. Levinas thus labels suffering to be 'unassumable', claiming that 'mean-ingless suffering is a tautology' (Levinas 1998: 79). That is, pain exacts a violence upon the self which escapes rational ordering; pain is that which cannot be economised. Furthermore, pain, for Levinas, is a modality which not only signals an incapacity to render whole, but pain 'absorbs' consciousness and determines how all other experiences are perceived (79). For Levinas, suffering thus signals the dissolution of coherence and identity and, registering a heightened awareness of the self's limitability, provokes a confrontation with the void. As Levinas puts it:

> All evil relates back to suffering. It is the *impasse* of life and of being—their absurdity—in which pain does not just somehow innocently happen to 'colour' consciousness with affectivity. The evil of pain, the deleterious per se, is the outburst and deepest expression, so to speak, of absurdity. (79)

This passage echoes Nietzsche's Dionysian vision: by considering pain to signal the self's loss of self-integrity or self-possession, as Levinas presents it, it is possible to say that pain is an anticipatory echo of death; pain is a foreshadowing of the self's utter disintegration.

Elaine Scarry makes the link between physical pain, meaningless-ness, and death more explicitly and extensively in her seminal study, *The Body in Pain* (1985). Scarry observes that 'physical pain always mimes death' in that both 'are radical and absolute' (Scarry 1985: 31).

Echoing Levinas' assertion that pain 'absorbs' consciousness, Scarry claims that both pain and death happen 'because of the body. In each, the contents of consciousness are destroyed' (31). Pain and death are, she holds, 'the most intense forms of negation, the purest expressions of the anti-human, of annihilation, of total aversiveness' (31). In other words, Scarry contends that, '[a]s in dying and death, so in serious pain the claims of the body utterly nullify the claims of the world' (33). The manner in which pain absorbs consciousness is described in terms of the shrinking of the subject's circumambient world; this is a consequence of the necessary, inevitable inward-directed attention that pain commands. Pain not only entails the annihilation of the subject's relation to the external world, but, Scarry claims, it also involves a correspondent shattering of meaning, identity, language. Pain violently gestures towards human finitude, and insofar as it obliterates language, is itself a clear indication of its capacity to violate our attempts to impose coherence. Thus, as Scarry observes, '[p]hysical pain does not simply resist language but actively destroys it, bringing about an immediate reversion to a state anterior to language, to the sounds and cries a human being makes before language is learned' (4). Pain denotes an excess: it is a force which shatters the self's boundaries and brings a heightened cognisance of our vulnerability to the world's otherness and its forces, forces which will inevitably invade and rend the individual apart. It can therefore be said that the phenomena of pain, in dispensing one's attempts at achieving physio-psychological coherence and delivering the individual before the void, parallels the threat presented at the height of tragic experience.

Does Nietzsche, who articulates a capacity or desire to perform a 'Dionysian affirmation of the world as it is, without subtraction, exception, or selection', miss suffering's excessive nature, as Boothroyd claims? Several commentators have perceived this notion of the Dionysian as a declared goal central to his philosophy. Fraser, for instance, notes that 'Nietzsche's own version of "love" is affirmation, and he believes total affirmation of human life is only possible and meaningful on the basis of a full apprehension of life's horror' (Fraser 2002: 165). Furthermore, Fraser asserts that 'Nietzsche clearly prides himself on his ability to outface horror' (126). Gillespie similarly detects a mood of triumphalism, contending that 'the Dionysian man [...] is able to affirm the chaos and contradiction of existence absolutely' (Gillespie 1995: 221). Fraser, moreover, goes on to argue that Nietzsche's affirmation is self-deluded, that he in fact 'fails to appreciate the full horror of human suffering' which

Fraser finds exhibited in the Holocaust (Fraser 2002: 2–3): 'Nietzsche's soteriology is incapable of facing […] the evil as revealed in the Nazi-death camps' (122). Invoking the Holocaust as a concrete example of the overwhelming horror presented by others' suffering, Fraser contends that Nietzsche's work reflects 'the imaginings of a more comfortable and innocent age' and exemplifies the inadequacy of abstract philosophical discourse with regards to the issue of human suffering (139). Indeed, Fraser accuses Nietzsche of glamorising or aestheticising suffering:

> The very idea of the Apollonian […] does suggest a desire to refract the experience of suffering so as to produce an aestheticized version of pain. […] It is as if the Apollonian idea is there to filter out the very painfulness of pain, leaving us simply with the idea of pain. (136)

Fraser continues to argue that insofar as Nietzsche holds distress merely 'to edify the noble spirit', Nietzsche is 'a most dangerous thinker; one who writes of suffering in such a way that much of the reality of suffering is actually hidden' (136).

Fraser is not alone in his indicting of Nietzsche's discourse on suffering. Martha Nussbaum similarly charges Nietzsche with 'play-act[ing] at romantic risk-taking and solitude—but who never seems to endure a moment's human grief or thirst or hunger, wrapped up, as he is, in his own self-commanding thought' (Nussbaum 1994: 161). This posture, argues Nussbaum, characterises a fundamental contradiction in his work and aligns him with the restrictive, self-defensive positions he is supposedly challenging. Both Nussbaum and Fraser thus argue that Nietzsche 'fails by his own standards': Nietzsche's affirmative project avoids a direct confrontation with the horror of existence that his philosophy's success depends upon (Fraser 2002: 122).

Countering these attacks, it may be noted that Peter Dews, on the other hand, does not question Nietzsche's capacity to face life's horrors. After all, as Dews points out, 'Nietzsche learned to philosophize at the feet of Schopenhauer, whose evocations of the wickedness and misery of human existence it would be hard to surpass' (Dews 2008: 149). In other words, pre-twentieth-century human history also unfortunately abounds in concrete examples of human suffering, brutality and stupidity, which, like the Holocaust, afford similar nauseating, debilitating insights; Nietzsche profoundly meditated upon such experiences having served as a medical orderly in 1870 during the Franco-Prussian war.

Further rejoinders to Fraser and Nussbaum are implicit in the above discussion of *The Birth of Tragedy*. For instance, it may be recalled that Nietzsche's vision of affirmation is posited as a goal, or an ideal: he does not describe this pathos of affirmation as a fixed or achieved state.[11] Additionally, that Nietzsche is cognisant of the threat of collapse that attends this occasion of affirmation, and thus of the very necessity of the Apollonian, seems to suggest that he does not belittle the power of suffering.

Moreover, Nietzsche complicates the positions proffered by critics who value his work in terms of either its capacity or incapacity to engage in a full confrontation with life shorn of its redemptive illusions by repeatedly favouring a language of degree. Otherwise put, Nietzsche's work seeks to transcend the assumption of extreme or absolute positions: as noted in Chapter 1, he identifies nihilism with the adoption of extreme perspectives[12]; elsewhere he highlights that language itself crudely posits binaries that are suggestive of its metaphysical residues.[13] Attending to this complaint in conjunction with his own stress of gradation or degree underlines his view that an absolute affirmation of suffering is impossible; the capacity to affirm life qualitatively varies according to the degree of physio-psychological strength possessed by the individual or culture.[14]

It is helpful to invoke Nietzsche's privileged metaphor of digestion to apprehend his nuanced notion of subjectivity. This will provide some insight into how Nietzsche considers the self to manage encounters with distressing experiences, of confronting life's horrors. I shall also repeatedly appeal to this notion to unpack the modernist texts in the following chapters. Dissolving the binary distinction of body and mind and to suggest instead an interdependent relation of the corporeal and the cognitive, Nietzsche postulates that '"the spirit" is more like a stomach than anything else' (*BGE* 230: 161). This articulation of subjectivity, of the will to power, is suggestive of his sensitivity to the individual's limits regarding the overcoming of obstacles that one may encounter. Accordingly, the self is porous, existing in a fluid dynamic relation to its surrounding circumstantial world. The healthy, functioning subject seeks to integrate, or 'digest', heterogeneous sensations and experiences to augment and expand. This is primarily an appropriative manoeuvre by which the self attains the pathos of power: the self's assimilative capacity, its ability to falsify and simplify, is tested, and suffers, as it overcomes the resistances presented by the complex, the contradictory, or the foreign.

Not only is falsification a necessary appropriative or creative function, but also, according to Nietzsche, the expansive, 'domineering' mind is simultaneously served by a self-protective mechanism: an 'apparently antithetical drive' to that of expansion comes into play in acknowledgement of the self's appropriative limits; this drive actively rejects that which it cannot assimilate. Accordingly, a 'kind of defensive posture against much that can be known [...] an acceptance and approval of ignorance' also characterises the self's relation to the external world (160–2).

The operation of this expansive-defensive digestive function is evinced in passages discussing the necessity of illusion, of the falsification and simplification of 'reality'. For, according to Nietzsche, 'life is not an argument; the conditions of life might include error' (*GS* 121: 117). As he puts it in a related passage:

> It might be a basic characteristic of existence that those who would know it completely would perish, in which case the strength of a spirit should be measured according to how much of the 'truth' one could still barely endure—or to put it more clearly, to what degree one would *require* it to be thinned down, shrouded, sweetened, blunted, falsified. (*BGE* 39: 68)

As mentioned in Chapter 1, to function as a willing subject the human animal needs to perform some form of an interpretative, artistic, or form-imposing activity. Karen Leslie Carr observes that, for Nietzsche, man is 'an organism that invariably and necessarily interprets' (Carr 1992: 28). Complicating simple, absolutist views of Nietzsche's engagement with suffering, the question that Nietzsche thus presents to his reader is: given that one would 'perish' from 'completely' knowing the world, to what degree does your active interpretative artistry engage with existence, with its horrifying meaninglessness and nauseating suffering, and to what degree does it need to blunt, falsify or sweeten existence? In other words, he asks: can you 'remain true to the earth' (*TSZ* Prologue 3: 42), as his fictional prophet Zarathustra proclaims, or do you impose or adopt an interpretation that strives for disengagement from empirical existence?[15] For Nietzsche such a wholesale thinning and shrouding of existence is symptomatic of a state of powerlessness to fashion oneself as a coherent subject; it bespeaks the failure to interpretatively assimilate one's own suffering or to digest encounters with the world's horror.

Furthermore, attending to Nietzsche's many considerations of wounded, impotent subjectivities throughout his work provides cogent evidence of his acknowledgment of suffering's excessive character. That is, Nietzsche's work focuses on the relationship between distress and impotence to show an awareness of suffering's power to overwhelm the sufferer and render him or her passive and powerless; he connects this to a pathos of reactionary vengefulness: insofar as we are both acting and interpreting creatures, suffering that is refractory to one's attempts to impose meaning, existing as an obstacle that cannot be overcome and hence frustrating our ability to function as effectual willing beings, provokes a compensatory reactiveness, an 'accusing' or vengefulness that is central to Nietzsche's understanding of human subjectivity. These insights, I shall show, demonstrate an acute sensitivity to suffering's extreme nature.

This nexus of insights can be briefly illustrated by referring to Zarathustra's teachings 'On Redemption' in the prophetic fictional work, *Thus Spoke Zarathustra* (1883–85). Here Zarathustra pronounces that his 'art and aim' is 'to compose into one and bring together what is fragment and riddle and dreadful chance' (*TSZ* II 20: 160). What specifically denotes 'fragment' and 'dreadful chance' in this passage is the past, or rather the past's imperfection: that which cannot be reversed by action or willing accordingly remains recalcitrant to assimilation. Zarathustra's teaching here pivots on the desire to reinterpret every '"[i]t was"' into an '"[b]ut I willed it thus!"' (163): '"[i]t was": that is what the will's teeth-gnashing and most lonely affliction is called. Powerless against that which has been done, the will is an angry spectator of all things past' (161). The power to perform a synthesising or appropriative exegesis is hence key: failure to bestow significance upon past events that are irreversible through concrete action finds expression in the sufferer exacting 'revenge for its inability to go backwards' (160). This identification of impotence with vindictiveness is central to Zarathustra's message. That is, as one's active agency is rendered impotent by reflecting on the past, the powerless sufferer consequently 'takes revenge upon him who does not, like it, feel wrath and ill-temper' (162).

It is with reference to this passage that Martin Heidegger notes that 'Nietzsche's thinking meditates on deliverance from the spirit of revenge' (Heidegger 1985: 69); this is 'the bridge to my highest hope', Zarathustra declares (*TSZ* II 7: 123). Yet Zarathustra also reflects that man's thinking has been dominated by feelings of vengefulness: '[t]he *spirit of revenge*; my friends, that, up to now, has been mankind's chief concern; and where there was suffering, there was always supposed to be punishment' (II 20: 160). Zarathustra suggests that punishment is tied to the need to appropriate, or compensate for, the experience of useless suffering: the desire to inflict suffering through punishment, or understand one's suffering as punishment, results from an awareness of impotence which, in the passage just discussed, derives from an inability to contain a form of psychic suffering. I shall now investigate the compensatory structure of punishment in more detail by turning to the *Genealogy*. Given Nietzsche's exploration of vengeance and powerlessness here, this text has considerable bearing on my exegesis of modernism: the modernist texts examined in the subsequent chapters focus on wounded, impotent and reactive subjectivities; Nietzsche's devastating disclosures of the modern predicament and human psychology illuminate the problem of rendering suffering meaningful. Furthermore, it is necessary to examine the text that literary critics frequently adduce to illustrate Nietzsche's own reactive, predatory and cruel tendencies.

SUFFERING AND THE ASCETIC IDEAL

Usually prized for its systematic rigour, the *Genealogy* offers a speculative historical account of the emergence and success of the Christian ascetic ideal. Crudely put, Nietzsche argues that the ascetic ideal provided the slave populations in antiquity with an interpretation of the senseless suffering that dominated their lives: the priest's meaning permitted the subjugated slaves to confer value on their meaningless distress and so resist the threat of 'suicidal' paralysis or nihilism. In contrast to the tragic Greeks' affirmative construal of existence, Nietzsche claims that the priestly 'artistry', or interpretation, stems from, or appeals to, a condition of 'powerlessness'.[16]

To briefly outline this argument, it is worth alluding first to Robert Solomon's assertion that '[i]f Nietzsche made us aware of anything in ethics, it is the importance of *perspectives*, the need to see all concepts and values *in context*' (Solomon 1986: 72). According to Nietzsche's hypothesis, the Christian exegesis of existence and its attendant values do not derive from an omnipotent and transcendent deity but rather find their provenance in the physio-psychological context of the ancient world: the enslaved Hebrew populace, thwarted from experiencing themselves as active self-affirming beings, formulated a redemptive narrative to envisage themselves as willing agents and to conceptually appropriate their suffering, to make their suffering purposeful. However, as I will show in more detail below, the spirit of impotent revenge, or what Nietzsche calls *ressentiment*, permeates this salvific discourse: the values that are subsequently developed by the Christian martyrs are reactive, premised on a negation of the 'other', and suffused with a rancour that bespeaks of a powerlessness to exercise an 'actual revenge' against the perceived source of their suffering, namely the cruel masters.

At this juncture, it is worth noting that the *Genealogy* offers divergent readings regarding Nietzsche's presentation of the slave revolt. That is, conflicting narratives and idioms operate throughout the *Genealogy*. Regarding the reading that largely informs literary studies examining Nietzsche's relation to modernist writers, there is a proclivity to emphasise Nietzsche's valorisation of the primitive nobles' self-affirming values. These values stand in contradistinction to the deleterious ideals of Christian *ressentiment*. Otherwise put, these readings stress the dominant binary structure informing this work. Indeed, the structure of the text, in which both the first and the concluding third essay highlight Nietzsche's oppositional logic, lends itself to this reading. Here I shall briefly consider this interpretation.

According to Stephen Mulhall, Nietzsche's narrative enacts his own equivalent of the Biblical myth of the Fall (see Mulhall 2007). By depicting the primitive nobles to originally embody an innocent, healthy physicality, Nietzsche repeatedly signals his lament at the demise of this self-affirmative mode of being and strongly suggests a nostalgia for a mythical golden age. Significantly, in contradistinction to the slaves' values, Nietzsche claims that 'chivalric-aristocratic value-judgements' derive from 'strong, free, happy action'. Such values elevate 'war, adventure, hunting, jousting' and, corresponding to an 'effervescent good health', reflect a predominantly corporeal, instinctive mode of self-relation (*OGM* I 7: 18).

The slaves' revolution, inverting the aristocratic investment in principles such as pride, heroism, and physical prowess, operates by propounding antithetical, and from their perspective realisable, values such as humility, poverty and chastity. With the eventual triumph of slave values, the reader thus infers that the ascetic priest manages to inculcate the nobles to orientate themselves towards the ideal of a non-natural, transcendent good posited by slave morality. Such values, particularly for the masters, induce a damaging self-doubt towards the physical being that largely defines them. As Dews notes, the perverse values serve to force the nobles' 'spontaneously outward-directed drives to turn inwards' (Dews 2008: 141).

Focussing solely on the text's oppositional binaries such as those of slave and master and sickness and health gives rise to a partial apprehension of the *Genealogy*, however. For instance, Fraser argues:

> The way Nietzsche presents his genealogy one could be forgiven for presuming there are only two 'lifestyle choices'. One can become a Christian ascetic, morbid and life-denying, or one can be a hero—a Polish cavalry officer, a Homeric nobleman, a Julius Caesar-type, a Napoleon-type, take your pick. (2002: 96)

Fraser notably stops short of exploring an alternative possibility to this dichotomous organisation. His consequent contention is one largely echoed in literary studies: 'Nietzsche clearly wants to return us to an ethic of action and glory' (47).[17] Perhaps the most obvious objection to this argument is that Nietzsche repeatedly holds artistic figures such as Goethe, Shakespeare and Beethoven as his exemplars.[18] Moreover, more discerning readers will note that the *Genealogy* primarily offers a narrative of transformation that is consonant with his ideal of overcoming or sublimation.[19] Attending to the often overlooked second essay, '"Guilt", "bad conscience", and related matters', Nietzsche's larger narrative framework offers a speculative anthropological hypothesis of the provenance of the primitive social 'state' that pre-dates the origins of *ressentiment* and the reversal of the nobles' values: this story suggestively deconstructs the binary pairs that prevail in the text's first and third essays. Furthermore, turning to this anthropological story provides another point from which to observe Nietzsche's engagement with senseless, excessive suffering.

Primarily, the *Genealogy*'s second treatise presents a hypothetical account of the origin and evolution of our internal reflexive capacity, or conscience. Depicting the violent formation of the earliest 'state', it begins by claiming that powerful pre-historic tribes ruthlessly subjugated disparate, nomadic peoples. Nietzsche's a priori of man's instinctive cruelty directs this narrative: he contends that the incipience of larger, collective living signals the repression of our primary aggressive drives. Adopting an urgent, cataclysmic tone, Nietzsche posits that the sudden advent of societal existence is 'the most fundamental of all changes which [man] experienced': '[a]ll instincts of the wild, free, roving man were turned backwards, *against man himself*. Those instincts which are not discharged outwardly *turn inwards*— this is what I call the *internalization* of man' (*OGM* II 16: 61). This repression of the basic, aggressive drives is graphically depicted in images evoking an appalling self-terrorisation commensurate with the savagery hitherto unleashed upon the other. Consequently, the majority of those incarcerated in early societal form are defined by an unharnessed aggression that results in endless, undirected self-laceration. They are also characterised by the accumulation of frustrated impotent rage, or *ressentiment*, deriving from their incapacity to exact revenge against the cruel masters.

Furthermore, according to Nietzsche's hypothesis, the unprecedented suffering incurred by the inward-turning of our aggressive drives is intensified by the traumatic displacement of those primary instincts with an inchoate reflexive capacity. Nietzsche theorises that '[t]he whole inner world [...] was expanded and extended itself and gained depth, breadth and height in proportion to the degree that the external discharge of man's instincts was *obstructed*' (61). The supplanting of those hitherto governing instincts with the emergence of this new faculty, consciousness, 'that most impoverished and error-prone organ', entailed an overwhelming sense of alienation in which the body came to be held as that which is both self and other (61). One way to apprehend the consequent distress is to note that, unlike the animals that unconsciously manage their affective economy, man has 'strayed' from an instinctive regulation of his affective expenditure, instead becoming dependent upon a 'fallible organ', namely his consciousness.

Moreover, Daniel Conway observes that, as a result of this shift in mode of being, '[o]ur reliance on consciousness requires us to pursue goals, in order to sustain a threshold level of affective investment' (Conway 1992: 33). Otherwise put, to achieve a phenomenal experience of effectiveness, and hence power, we now require a 'goal capable of exciting a vital level of affective engagement' (32–3). Whilst this goal may be self-generated, the majority are unable to harness the self's conflicting impulses to posit a unifying, commanding goal. They are consequently subject to the dispersal of their vital energies. In other words, they experience feelings of lethargy or depression, precipitating the pathos of suicidal nihilism. David Owen makes a corroborating point:

> Insofar as one develops consciousness at the expense of instinct, so the feeling of power is increasingly mediated through meaning; the development of consciousness entails that the feeling of powerfulness requires that one experience one's self as meaningful. (Owen 1995: 57)

Given, then, that the reflective capacities of the oppressed are greater due to the degree of internalisation experienced, it can be surmised that they possess a more urgent need to provide meaning to their lives. Indeed, the oppressed suffer from a particularly heightened awareness of their frustrated, violated condition, of their lack of agency and their incapacity to discharge their instinctive energies. Yet from what position do the oppressed generate meaning? One approach to this question, propounded by critics such as Boothroyd and Conway, is to stress the masters' role in bestowing significance to the slaves.[20] However, an exploration of Nietzsche's defence of the masters reveals further contradictory postures that undermine what Henry Staten refers to as Nietzsche's consolation of the 'cruel hero' (Staten 1990: 101).

Nietzsche's defence of the primordial masters and their externally directed cruelty is suggestive of his continued preoccupation with useless suffering, of his need to confer the apparent senselessness of pre-history with significance. Claiming that in pre-history 'life then played the trick which it has always known how to play, of justifying itself, justifying its "evil"', Nietzsche, I believe, legitimises the 'the hardness, tyranny, stupidity and idiocy' of pre-history by pointing to the accomplishment of the masters' 'unconscious' state-building 'artistry' (*OGM* II 2: 39): lauding the masters' generation of societal form, Nietzsche argues that the hitherto 'unrestrained and shapeless' populace have now been given 'a fixed form' within which 'there is absolutely no room for anything which does not first acquire "meaning" with regard to the whole'. Echoing his celebrations of self-artistry discussed above, Nietzsche appeals to Romantic aesthetic notions that conceive of beauty in terms of the unification of complex, disparate elements: Nietzsche valorises this state-building artistry in which 'parts and functions are differentiated and co-related' within this social structure (II 17: 63); through the aesthetic constitution of form or coherence meaning is generated. Thus, primarily through the institution of punishment, the masters' form-giving cruelty, and hence the slaves' attendant suffering, is 'justified' and 'explained': the primordial masters create 'a structure of domination that *lives*', Nietzsche contends (63).

Suggesting a Nietzschean defence of the predatory nobles' 'terrible tyranny', Conway asserts '[i]n bringing order and purpose to a formerly formless populace, the beasts of prey impart meaning and identity to their captives' (Conway 2004: 166). Yet, one can take issue with this argument by invoking Aaron Ridley's observation that the slaves' self-relation is dominated by their masters' perspective: the slaves do not possess their own construal of existence to affirm themselves; the slaves are derivatively deemed as 'low, low-minded, common and plebeian' by the masters and are merely 'object[s] of violation' (Ridley 1998: 37–8). Their suffering, from their own perspective, is meaningless.

The attempt to legitimise the primitive masters' cruelty in terms of meaning constitution is also undermined by Nietzsche's own climactic argument in the *Genealogy*:

> Except for the ascetic ideal: man, the *animal* man, had no meaning up to now. His existence on earth had no purpose; […] *This* is what the ascetic ideal meant: something was *missing*, there was an immense *lacuna* around man,—he himself could think of no justification or explanation or affirmation, he *suffered* from what he meant. Other things made him suffer too, in the main he was a *sickly* animal: but suffering itself was *not* his problem, but the fact that there was no answer to the question he screamed, 'Suffering for *what*?' Man, the bravest animal and the most prone to suffer, does *not* deny suffering as such: he *wills* it, he even seeks it out, provided he is shown a *meaning* for it, a *purpose* for suffering. The meaninglessness of suffering, *not* the suffering, was the curse which so far has blanketed mankind,—and *the ascetic ideal offered man a meaning*! (*OGM* III 28: 127)

That is, the ascetic ideal's success rests upon its response to the existential void presented by meaningless suffering: the slaves, whose lives are consumed by a suffering that is unaccountable from their own perspective, require a construal of their distress that allows them to avert suicidal paralysis. With no other suitable hermeneutic of suffering available, the ascetic ideal performs this function by bestowing the slaves' suffering with a purpose, rendering it bearable. I will now turn to the 'purpose' that enables the slaves to conceive of themselves as self-affirming, goal-directed agents.

'Deliverance from the Spirit of Revenge'

The ascetic ideal gives meaning to the oppressed by exploiting their existent apprehension of punishment as legitimised cruelty. To trace this claim, I shall emphasise Nietzsche's view of man's instinctive disposition to inflict suffering while registering again that 'suffering is the basic condition of [the slaves'] existence', as Ridley notes (Ridley 1998: 38). It is also worth recalling here that the oppressed not only suffer as recipients of their masters' cruelty but they are also subject to a more intense experience of internalisation given that they have less possibility to discharge their aggressive instincts outwardly. Their lives are characterised by powerlessness and unbearable, unrelieved distress. Furthermore, the build-up of dangerous feelings of frustration and rancour threaten to explode early societal form: these aggressive drives and emotions spill over and are unleashed upon the other, 'friend, wife, child and anyone else near to them' (*OGM* III 15: 99). It is accordingly the economy of punishment, premised on the notion of equivalence, which acts to curb instinctive, reactive, and immoderate feelings of vengefulness which accrue in the sufferers and threaten social cohesion.[21]

To substantiate this point on the role of primeval punishment, I shall begin by noting that Nietzsche claims that the sufferers involuntarily seek to palliate their distress by inflicting pain upon the other:

> For every sufferer instinctively looks for a cause of his distress; more exactly, for a culprit, even more precisely for a *guilty* culprit who is receptive to distress—in short, for a living being upon whom he can release his emotions, actually or in effigy, on some pretext or other: because the release of emotions is the greatest attempt at relief, or should I say, at *anaesthetizing* on the part of the sufferer, his involuntary longed-for narcotic against pain of any kind. (99)

Extreme suffering is assuaged by first locating a source for this distress. The sufferer now has a conceptual comprehension of the 'cause' of his or her suffering in identifying a '*guilty* culprit'. Moreover, the necessary 'release of emotions' is achieved by appealing to a 'logic' of 'compensation' whereby recompense 'is made up of a warrant for and entitlement to cruelty': the injured party can legitimately inflict suffering upon the guilty party and experience 'the elevated feeling of despising and maltreating someone as an "inferior"' enjoyed by the masters (II 5: 45). Notably, Nietzsche is here signalling the primacy of affective being, and registering the entwinement of the affective and the cognitive, in his account of this most 'formative' stage of human development. Nietzsche thus contends that this primitive logic of compensation derives from 'the oldest and most primitive personal relationship there is, in the relationship between buyer and seller, creditor and debtor' (II 8: 49): the sufferer construes the other as a debtor while constituting her or himself as a creditor who has 'the pleasure of having the right to exercise power over the powerless without a thought' (II 5: 44). Importantly, because of this structure of compensation, communal existence is maintained: the sufferer's 'anger was held in check and modified by the idea that every injury has its *equivalent* which can be paid in compensation, if only through the *pain* of the person who injures' (II 4: 43).

Echoing Zarathustra's teachings 'On Redemption', Nietzsche again presents externally directed cruelty as a reactive, compensatory gesture. Otherwise put, by observing that the perpetration of cruelty largely appears in Nietzsche's thought as a form of recuperation, an appropriative movement whereby the injured and aggrieved seek to recover their losses through the infliction of suffering upon the other, we can resist, or at least complicate, those voices within modernist studies that seek to associate his thought with an aggressive, imperious ethic, as noted in Chapter 1.[22] While I shall further discuss Nietzsche's thoughts on the heightened pathos of power that cruelty affords when I turn particularly to Kafka and Beckett and their respective depictions of suffering, impotent subjects, Heidegger's insightful comment on vengeance can help to explicate cruelty's appropriative dynamic:

> [Revenge] opposes its object by degrading it so that, by contrasting the degraded object with its own superiority, it may restore its own validity, the only validity it considers decisive. For revenge is driven by the feeling of being vanquished and injured. (1985: 71)

Heidegger's analysis is consonant with Nietzsche's understanding of punishment as 'compensation'. In both revenge and punishment there is a restorative, appropriative flow of energy towards the perpetrator as the other suffers and is diminished. Resonating with Zarathustra's desire to supplant our dominant punitive logic and sentiments, Nietzsche elsewhere explicitly attests to the persistence of the pre-historic 'logic of compensation':

> At present, to be sure, he who has been injured, irrespective of how this injury is to be made good, will still desire his *revenge* and will turn for it to the courts—and for the time being the courts continue to maintain our detestable criminal codes, with their shopkeeper's scales and *the desire to counterbalance guilt with punishment*: but can we not get beyond this? What a relief it would be for the general feeling of life if, together with the belief in guilt, one also got rid of the old instinct for revenge [...] Let us

do away with the concept sin—and let us quickly send after it the concept *punishment*! (*D* 202: 121)

Attending to Nietzsche's articulations of his desire to transcend retributive, punitive modes of reasoning offers one way to chart his opposition to the ascetic ideal, or the 'priestly interpretation' of existence. For the priest perpetuates and amplifies the import of the notion of punishment: the ascetic hermeneutic of suffering operates essentially by identifying whom to blame, whom to punish. Moreover, the priest convinces the slave to find him or herself culpable, proclaiming: '[s]omebody must be to blame [for your suffering]: but you yourself are this somebody, you yourself are to blame for it, *you yourself alone are to blame for yourself*' (*OGM* III 15: 99). The notion of 'sin', formulated as a primal transgression in the narrative of the Fall, grounds this exegesis of legitimised self-punishment. While I shall discuss the sadomasochistic dimensions of guilt in more depth in the Kafka chapter, I wish here to highlight that this narrative allows the slave to avert feelings of suicidal nihilism which result from experiences of 'senseless suffering'.[23] Firstly, blaming oneself allows 'every conceivable kind of suffering' to be assimilated by this interpretation of self-culpability: as Ridley notes, '[n]o external object can ever be held fully and convincingly accountable for *all* of your suffering' (Ridley 1998: 54). Christian soteriology therefore economises all of the slaves' distress, doing so according to 'the rational workings of divine providence', as Kenneth Surin observes (Surin 1989: 53). By fully accounting for suffering through its redemptive narrative, the ascetic ideal offers a 'narrow', simple, or reductive reading of existence: theodicy averts any form of confrontation with that which cannot be assimilated, namely suffering's excessive force, or the tragic, irredeemable nature of existence.

Moreover, the notion of guilt encourages the sufferers to rigourously scrutinise their own actions and thoughts, intensifying their reflexive capacities, to locate the source of their suffering. Such a manoeuvre, in terms of the ascetic ideal, entails commitment to a regime of purification which seeks to extirpate corrupt libidinous impulses. Importantly, the slaves' adoption of prescribed ascetic practices, motivated by the goal of attaining transcendent bliss and the end of suffering through the very denial of suffering, corporeal being, permits them to experience themselves as willing agents. This is key to Nietzsche's apprehension of the tenacity of the ascetic interpretation of existence:

The interpretation—without a doubt—brought new suffering with it, deeper, more internal, more poisonous suffering, suffering that gnawed away more intensely at life: it brought all suffering within the perspective of *guilt*...But in spite of all that—man was *saved*; he had a *meaning*, from now on he was no longer like a leaf in the breeze, the plaything of the absurd, of 'non-sense'; from now on he could *will* something, —no matter what, why and how he did it at first, the *will itself was saved*. (*OGM* III 28: 127)

Nietzsche's account of the slaves' subscription to ascetic practices that diminish corporeal being in the pursuit of an idealised, de-eroticised, non-suffering existence, gives rise to one of the *Genealogy's* most striking aphorisms: 'a basic fact of human will, its *horror vacui; it needs an aim [goal]*—, and it prefers to will *nothingness* rather than *not* will' (III 1: 72). Despite creating a 'more poisonous' form of suffering, the slaves may constitute themselves as goal-bound agents by adhering to the ascetic ideal. Nietzsche's analysis of the ascetic ideal therefore underlines the human need to construe oneself as a willing agent: the slaves' unregulated and disorderly inner drives are organised and orientated towards the fulfilment of the ascetic, externally-posited telos. The desire for paradisiacal peace promised by this telos reflects the slave's 'fundamental desire [...] that the war which he *is* should come to an end' (*BGE* 200: 121). As Wolfgang Muller-Lauter observes, even though the ascetic ideal rejects earthly corporeal existence, considering 'this life' as a mere bridge to another transcendent existence, 'that bridge must be constructed and thus life must be maintained' (Muller-Lauter 1999: 44).[24] These values are thus necessary for the preservation of a certain mode of life. Furthermore, this seemingly perverse self-directed intensification of one's suffering, as one legitimately penalises oneself for having failed to honour one's ascetic obligations, is itself constitutive of one's feeling of agency: one identifies oneself as a cruel and powerful master actively punishing those refractory aspects of the self.[25] With fascinated horror, Nietzsche thus charts the ways in which the ascetic ideal performs its paradoxical life-preserving function, promoting practices of 'self-discipline, self-surveillance and self-overcoming' in the pursuit of its (pernicious) idealised ontology (*OGM* III 16: 100).

The transcendent narrative also provides the slaves with a further life-preserving tonic: the slaves possess the conceptual wherewithal to palliate their suffering through the imagined cruelty exacted upon the masters. Thus, while only 'the suffering, the deprived, the sick, the ugly' are to be saved according to the ascetic hermeneutic, the transgressing masters are promised eternal punishment, to be 'eternally wretched, cursed and damned!' (I 7: 19). Nietzsche cites Tertullian and Thomas Aquinas to corroborate his claim that the Christian conception of paradise consists not only in freedom from one's own suffering but also significantly entails the lustful pleasure of witnessing those condemned to everlasting torment in Hell.[26] Even if only in a fictional form, this spectacle gratifies the slaves' desire to occupy the position of the cruel masters able to exercise punishment. Christian salvific discourse thus reflects, for Nietzsche, the values of those 'who, being denied the proper response of action compensate for it only with imaginary revenge' (I 10: 21).

The narrative of the *Genealogy* partakes in the drive to overcome the 'narrow', ascetic interpretation of existence premised on notions of legitimised punishment.[27] Furthermore, Nietzsche's ideal of self and cultural enhancement is integral to his vision of the sublimation of punishment. That is, pointing to the gradual surmounting of the deep-rooted punitive mentality, the notion of self-wounding underpins Nietzsche's ideal of mercy as it is performed by both the strong man and by the powerful community:

> As the power and self-confidence of a community grows, its penal law becomes more lenient; if the former is weakened or endangered, harsher forms of the latter will re-emerge. The 'creditor' always becomes more humane as his wealth increases; finally, the *amount* of his wealth determines how much injury he can sustain without suffering from it. It is not impossible to imagine society *so conscious of its power* that it could allow itself the noblest luxury available to it,—that of letting its malefactors go *unpunished*. 'What do I care about my parasites', it could say, 'let them live and flourish: I am strong enough for all that!'... Justice, which began by saying everything can be paid off, everything must be paid off', ends by turning a blind eye and letting off those unable to pay,—it ends, like every good thing on earth, by *sublimating itself*. The self-sublimation of justice: we know what a nice name it gives itself—*mercy*; it remains, of course, the prerogative of the most powerful man, better still, his way of being beyond the law. (II 10: 51)

In contrast to crude, primitive cultures that perpetrate severe punishment upon their criminals, Nietzsche elevates the individual and the community with the strength to endure its 'parasites', to exercise mercy. Strength is thus denoted by the ability to forego the compensatory, appropriative gesture of retaliation. This exemplary form thus entails suffering from absorbing the wounds inflicted by others and demonstrates its power through an ability to retain one's integrity or coherence. Such a capacity, Nietzsche argues, 'in the face of personal injury, of scorn and suspicion, well, that is a piece of perfection, the highest form of mastery to be had on earth' (II 11: 53). I will return to allude to this ideal in future chapters, especially in my discussion on Lawrence. Furthermore, it must be stressed that Nietzsche's noble exemplar, who demonstrates a denied discharge of externally directed cruelty and a consequent intensification of his or her own suffering, stands in opposition to claims that associate Nietzsche's thought with brutality, propounded by Fraser among others.

Moreover, Nietzsche's depiction of 'those unusual cases of spiritual and physical powerfulness' whom he describes to be engaged in forms of self-fashioning in his narrative of primitive social formation not only radically departs from the vision of the spontaneous, physical nobles, but also gestures towards the overcoming of nihilism through the intensification and development of our reflexive capacities (III 14: 94):

> Fundamentally, it is the same active force as the one that is at work on a grand scale in those artists of violence and organizers, and builds states, which here, internally, on a smaller, pettier scale, turned backwards [...] it is that very instinct for freedom (put into my language: will to power): only that the material on which the formative and violent nature of the force is let loose is man himself, his old animal self—and not, as in that greater and more eye-catching phenomenon, the other man, the *other* men. The secret self-violation, this artist's cruelty, this desire to give form to oneself as a piece of difficult, resisting, suffering matter, to brand it with a will, a critique, a contempt, a 'no', this uncanny, terrible but joyous labour of a soul voluntarily split within itself, which makes itself suffer out of the pleasure of making suffer, this whole *active* 'bad conscience' has finally [...] brought a wealth of novel, disconcerting beauty and affirmation to life, and perhaps for the first time, beauty itself. (II 18: 64)

Where the primitive nobles discharge their cruel drives externally in the 'grand scale' project of societal formation, Nietzsche similarly valorises this self-reflexive 'terrible but joyous labour' in which the self discharges its aggressive instincts inwardly in the project of giving form to itself.[28] In both instances, meaninglessness is averted through the imposition of form. In both instances, the human animal gratifies its instinctive need to perpetrate cruelty. However, as Staten notes, in contrast to the affirmative vision of the primitive nobles, Nietzsche's picture of self-artistry seems to be characterised by the same perverse drive to inflict suffering upon oneself as that of the slave motivated by guilt: in both forms the 'sickness' of internalisation is amplified as both the guilty man and these unusual self-artists similarly intensify the 'split within itself', expanding the self's inner pathos of distance (Staten 1990: 91). What distinguishes these celebrated artists' self-violation, however, is that they strive to intensify this inner feeling of distance in order to integrate as many drives as possible, to engender a coherence consisting of a rich multiplicity of affects and perspectives. This project of self-fashioning thus stands antithetically to the self-directed cruelty of the ascetic ideal that, in striving for de-eroticized being, or 'nothingness', ignores or annihilates certain drives.[29] This adduced passage thus concludes by suggesting that this 'artist's cruelty' contains the potential for 'the affirmation of life': self-artistry, engendering a tentative 'beauty and affirmation' is thus central to Nietzsche's project of overcoming *ressentiment* and the nihilism, or 'the will to nothingness', expressed by the ascetic ideal (*OGM* II 18: 64).

Modern Nihilism and Suffering

Despite offering a sustained and profound assault on the ascetic ideal's interpretation of existence, Nietzsche's *Genealogy* simultaneously focusses on the threat arising from its demise. Indeed, his genealogical project itself, investigating the origin, success and decline of the ascetic ideal, must be understood within the overall task of diagnosing and overcoming modernity's nihilistic predicament. The following passage, in which Nietzsche transfigures the traditional religious notion of redemption, suggestively captures the nature of this diagnosis:

> This man of the future will redeem us not just from the ideal held up till now, but also from the things *which will have to arise from it*, from the great nausea, the will to nothingness, from nihilism, that stroke of midday and of great decision which makes the will free again, which gives earth its purpose and man his hope again, this Antichrist and anti-nihilist, this conqueror of God and of nothingness—*he must come one day...* (II 24: 71)

Nietzsche observes that this 'man of the future' must combat existent life-denying forms, 'the ideal held up till now', and the nihilism deriving from the collapse of this ideal. That Nietzsche's tone is implicitly desperate as he invokes his 'man of the future' to 'redeem' the earth suggests the scale of the catastrophe he envisages. For Nietzsche, his future exemplars or legislators must provide, or rather propose, a new goal or meaning to repel this modern manifestation of nihilism:

> Only if mankind possessed a universally recognised *goal* would it be possible to propose 'thus and thus is the *right* course of action': for the present there exists no such goal. [...]—To *recommend* a goal to mankind is something quite different: the goal is then thought of as something which *lies in our own discretion*[.] (*D* 108: 63)

In *The Will to Power* Nietzsche extensively considers the psychological implications of modern nihilism, of the loss of the highest values hitherto.[30] As sketched in Chapter 1, Nietzsche associates nihilism with the realisation that '[e]xistence has no goal or end' (*WP* 12(A): 13). This awareness is primarily arrived at through the growing power of the natural sciences. Observing that 'any goal at least constitutes some meaning' (12), elsewhere he neatly captures the implications of the loss of the Christian grand narrative or orientating telos: '"I know not which way to turn; I am everything that knows not which way to turn"—sighs modern man' (*AC* 1: 127). Given that the human animal is impelled to will, that it requires a goal to organise its conflicting drives and impulses, the redundancy of the transcendent goal posited by the ascetic ideal presents new dangers: we are subject to the 'disgregation' of our drives; a debilitating contradiction of our impulses reigns. This precipitates our collapse into nihilism. As Owen and Ridley observe:

> Nietzsche argues that the self-destruction of the ascetic ideal threatens to undermine our capacities for "self-discipline", "self-surveillance" and "self-overcoming", and our disposition to truthfulness precisely because we now lack an overarching goal in the service of which these capacities and this disposition are cultivated. But this undermining does not entail any diminution of our dissatisfaction with our this-worldly existence: the suffering endemic to life itself remains; all that is gone is the (ascetic) mode of valuing that rendered such suffering meaningful, and hence bearable. (Owen and Ridley 2000: 149)

I will initially consider two related matters noted here. Firstly, given the redundancy of Christian soteriology, we have now lost the main stimulus

that directed our willing and cultivated forms of 'self-discipline' that ena-
bled us to experience ourselves as self-affirming beings; secondly, the
suffering that itself constitutes an 'objection to existence' and which was
envisaged to come to a promised end is now no longer cognitively appropriated. Vulnerable to the perspective that our efforts and grievances are
ultimately 'meaningless and in vain' (*WP* 36: 26), we are therefore susceptible to feelings of rancour, of *ressentiment*. As Zarathustra's teaching
'On Redemption' illustrated, a vindictive hatred of existence, a demand
for revenge, attends the incapacity to conceptually integrate one's experiences and one's suffering. Robert B. Pippin thus observes that:

> [with] no ultimate justice in the after-life, [...] human beings will come
> to see a finite, temporally mutable, contingent life as a kind of burden, a
> curse, or purposeless play, and they will exact revenge for having been arbi-
> trarily thrown into this condition. (Pippin 2006: xxiv)

This frightening assessment of the modern human condition, of the propensity of a reactive, powerless hatred to emerge with and attend the
awareness of experiences of senseless suffering, is expressed in each of the
fictional works I shall discuss in subsequent chapters. As I have argued
above, Nietzsche's affirmative project is preoccupied with overcoming
reactive sentiments and with diagnosing forms of nihilism. Bearing this
twinned project in mind is key to understanding his valorisations of suffering and his celebrations of the arduous project of self-fashioning.[31]

Furthermore, while I have suggested that a certain masochistic economy characterises Nietzsche's paradigm of self-artistry, he bemoans what
he perceives to be at the root of the problem facing secular modernity:
the prevalent 'mortal hatred of suffering in general', bequeathed by
Christianity and amplified by the loss of its redemptive narrative, forecloses the necessary and arduous task of self-cultivation.[32] For Nietzsche,
not only is the ascetic ideal's stimulating, organising telos rendered redundant, but its residual, implicit hedonism prevails, intensifying one's hostility to distress: since man no longer has 'a *purpose* for suffering', he actively
avoids discomfort; with the loss of the ascetic ideal's appropriation of distress, modern man is consequently deterred from undergoing the necessary 'severity towards oneself' involved in practices of self-formation (*EH*
Foreword 3: 4). Nietzsche consequently laments that '[t]oday we see
nothing that wants to expand', things will 'continue to decline', becoming
'more comfortable, more mediocre, more indifferent' (*OGM* I 12: 27).

What is more, for Nietzsche, the mediocre majority populating modernity perceive themselves to embody the new goal, 'the *attained* pinnacle of man, the sole hope of the future, the consolation of the present and the great redemption from all the guilt of the past' (*BGE* 202: 126).[33] Again signalling Nietzsche's acute sensitivity to the senselessness of human history, of its lack of overarching purpose, Nietzsche suggests the need to redeem humanity with a life-inspiring meaning 'so as to make an end of that gruesome dominion and chance that has hitherto been called "history"—the nonsense of the "greatest number" is only its latest form' (*BGE* 203: 126). Observing that '[t]he *redeeming* class and human being are lacking—the justifiers' (*WP* 1 (6): 8), it is the democratic herd who alone 'have the prospect of continuing on and propagating themselves': it is the mediocre who bestow their meaning of comfort, security, prudence and 'happiness'. Zarathustra's prologue memorably articulates Nietzsche's derision of modern values with its presentation of the little or last men.[34]

Some of Nietzsche's most controversial pronouncements should be understood in this context. His assault on prudentially orientated modernity and his hyperbolic valorisation of suffering can be aligned with his project of combatting the nihilistic realisation of man's pointlessness, of rendering the senseless, unappropriated suffering that constitutes human history with new significance. Accordingly, he famously rebukes the modern aversion to distress embodied in the goals of peace, prosperity and progress:

> You want if possible—and there is no madder 'if possible'—*to abolish suffering*; and we?—it really does seem that *we* would rather increase it and make it worse than it has ever been! Wellbeing as you understand it—that is no goal, that seems to us an *end*! A state which soon renders man ludicrous and contemptible—which makes it *desirable* that he should perish! The discipline of suffering, of *great* suffering—do you know that it is *this* discipline alone which has created every elevation of mankind hitherto? (*BGE* 225: 155)

For Nietzsche, it is only through the severe discipline of sustained adherence to 'arbitrary laws' that anything of value has been achieved:

> The essential thing 'in heaven and upon earth' seems, to say it again, to be a protracted *obedience* in *one* direction: from out of that there always

> emerges and has always emerged in the long run something for the sake
> of which it is worthwhile to live on earth, for example virtue, art, music,
> dance, reason, spirituality. (188: 111)

Furthermore, it is this necessary and arduous 'protracted constraint' that
the secular, democratic world repudiates according to Nietzsche: the
modern instinct is to live 'very fast' and 'irresponsibly'; enabling institu-
tions and forms or notions of authority and domination are denounced
as impingements upon one's sense of autonomy (*TI* IX 39: 105).
Characterised in this way, the modern world precludes the potential
emergence of 'something for the sake of which it is worthwhile to live on
earth'.

There is a related, further dimension to Nietzsche's hostility to 'the
contemptible sort of well-being dreamed of by shopkeepers, Christians,
cows, women, Englishmen and other democrats' (*TI* IX 38: 104): the
modern aversion to suffering precipitates greater impoverishment insofar
as the 'tremendous tension' necessary for 'life-preserving uniformity' is
relaxed. That is, dissolution and decay arise in the conditions of peace
and security coveted by the majority. For Nietzsche argues, '[a] *species*
arises, a type becomes fixed and strong, through protracted struggle
against essentially constant *unfavourable* conditions'. Shifting between
the internal and the external, and the individual and society, Nietzsche
repeatedly contends that it is in adversity that individuals and commu-
nities are 'thrown on their own resources' and generate 'stratagems
for self-preservation, self-enhancement, self-redemption' (*BGE* 262:
199–201). Elsewhere he contends: '[h]ow is freedom measured, in individuals as in nations? By the resistance which has to be overcome, by
the effort it costs to stay *aloft*' (*TI* IX 38: 103–4).[35] In adversity, one is
compelled by one's self-preservative instinct to unify and harness one's
inner resources. Failure to do so provokes dissolution and *ressentiment*.
In relation to this argument, we may then recall his alignment of illness
as one such adversary, conceiving of distressing experiences as opponents
or obstacles that are surmounted: Nietzsche reconfigures the suffering
that may engender a powerless teeth-gnashing and hatred of existence as
integral to life-affirming feelings of power, as a means to heighten one's
own awareness of one's own resources and strength.

Nevertheless, it is not only the weak or the degenerating individual or
society in the throes of decay that are subject to nihilism, of affective exhaustion and the correspondent judgement that it is better not to be alive.

The rich, complex self that Nietzsche lauds and associates with Dionysus, experimentally increasing its affects and perspectives, is itself extremely vulnerable to the collapse into nihilism. As Nietzsche puts it: '[f]or the corruption, the ruination of higher human beings, of more strangely constituted souls, is the rule' (*BGE* 269: 207). Indeed, I contend that Nietzsche's aforementioned exterminatory proclamation, his pronouncement that man's mediocrity 'makes it *desirable* that he should perish', signals a sense of fragility bound to his own fear of nihilistic collapse. The clue to this vulnerability is suggested in the following passage, where Nietzsche again registers his disgust at the mediocre last man:

> What is to be feared and can work more calamitously than any other calamity is not great fear of but great *nausea* at man; similarly great *sympathy* with man. Assuming that these might one day mate, then immediately and unavoidably something most uncanny would be produced, the 'last will' of man, his will to nothingness, nihilism. (*OGM* III 14: 94)

I shall conclude this chapter by exploring this tone of alarm and anxiety in Nietzsche's discourse as he engages with the problematic of others' suffering, of pity, and its tie to nihilism. The 'morality of pity', central to Nietzsche's diagnosis of the nihilistic character of the ascetic ideal, persists into modernity, albeit in different form, and remains a 'sublime temptation and seduction [...]to nothingness'.[36] Drawing attention to the discordant positions in his thought gravitating around the twinned themes of pity and nihilism in the chapter's final section, the aim is to further nuance extant readings of Nietzsche within modernist studies that rather uncomplicatedly hold him to be scathing of pity and a proponent of cruelty.[37]

Suffering's Abyss

Nussbaum argues that Nietzsche embodies a hardness, a stoical self-defensiveness that demonstrates a lack of 'willingness to be porous' (Nussbaum 1994: 160). Such a posture may be suggested by his claim that the '*narrowing of perspective*' is a 'condition of life and growth' (*BGE* 188: 122): the will to ignorance, as considered in relation to Nietzsche's metaphor of digestion, for instance, is a precondition for life-preservation and life-enhancement.[38] However, in contrast to Nussbaum's accusation of narcissistic self-enclosure, Nietzsche repeatedly articulates the desire to perform an expansive, totalising embrace of existence, to indefinitely increase one's affects and perspectives. Such a strategy is inherently precarious. One immediate approach, or consequence, of this posture is the identification with others' suffering. I hold that engaging with this area of his thought, as it is suggestive of Nietzsche's particularly heightened sensibility towards suffering's excessive force, discloses compelling insights regarding the contradictory stances that permeate his work.[39]

The appropriative movement in Nietzsche's thought, the drive to embrace and assimilate more of existence, is registered by the goal of multiplying one's perspectives. For instance, he famously contends:

> There is *only* a perspective seeing, *only* a perspective 'knowing'; and the *more* affects we allow to speak about one thing, the *more* eyes, different eyes, we can use to observe one thing, the more complete will our 'concept' of this thing, our 'objectivity', be. (*OGM* III 12: 92) [40]

Indeed, Nietzsche exhorts philosophers to abandon their proclivity, which he otherwise valorises, to attain distance from 'the crowd' in order to fulfil their drive for knowledge:

> The study of the *average* human being, protracted, serious, and with much dissembling, self-overcoming, intimacy, bad company—[...] this constitutes a necessary part of the life story of every philosopher, perhaps the most unpleasant and malodorous part and the part most full of disappointments. (*BGE* 26: 57)

As Nietzsche admonishes those avoiding this 'company', he considers this expansion of one's empathetic capacity a necessary and yet dangerous task for the philosopher or psychologist to undertake: one must courageously squander one's existent sense of self to inhabit more and more perspectives; new states of inner complexity and contradiction continually challenge one's capacity to fashion one's richer multiplicity of perspectives into coherent form. Reconstituting one's sense of wholeness, resolving the new tensions and harnessing this rich plurality of affects and interpretations, signals the expansive movement in this economy. Notably, the woman or man bravely striving to embrace more of existence and fashioning a more variegated, complex self, is consequently more vulnerable: she or he squanders the stability of existent selfhood in this appropriative process. In Nietzsche's thought this sense of fragility is particularly heightened when one empathetically engages with 'the *average* human being'.

An implicit tragic register, an awareness of an ultimate limit or potential collapse, attends this privileged squandering-appropriative dynamic. Significantly, this strain is evinced when Nietzsche meditates on identifying with others' suffering: the need to defensively recoil from others' distress gestures towards the limits of Nietzsche's affirmative, expansive capacity. An entry from *Human, All Too Human* (1878) is pertinent. Beginning this passage by claiming that the 'exceptional' man's empathetic capacity is distinct from the 'ordinary' man, whose 'sympathy for life in general, and for the suffering of mankind, is very weakly developed', he contends:

> Most men tolerate life without grumbling too much and *believe* thus in the value of existence, but precisely because everyone wills himself alone and stands his ground alone, and does not step out of himself as do those exceptional men, everything extrapersonal escapes his notice entirely, or seems at most a faint shadow. Thus the value of life for the ordinary, everyday man is based only on his taking himself to be more important than the world. The great lack of fantasy from which he suffers keeps him from being able to empathise with other beings, and he therefore participates in their vicissitudes and suffering as little as possible. On the other hand, whoever would be truly able to participate in it would have to despair about the value of life; if he were able to grasp and feel mankind's overall consciousness in himself, he would collapse with a curse against existence—for mankind, as a whole, has *no* goals and consequently, considering the whole affair, man cannot find his comfort and support in it, but rather his despair. (*HAH* 33: 36)

The exceptional man participates in the 'vicissitudes and suffering' of others: in contrast to 'most men', the extraordinary man is capable of a profound Dionysian sensibility.[41] Yet, Nietzsche insists upon the limits that any individual can bear. Echoing the earlier discussions on the 'necessity' for 'error' over truth, of Apollo's role in tragic art, and of the outline of the defensive-appropriative digestive economy, Nietzsche claims that 'whoever would be truly able to participate in' the 'vicissitudes and suffering' of others 'would have to despair about the value of life; [...] he would collapse with a curse against existence' (36). In other words, it is through a profound identification with others' distress, the very means by which the exceptional man tests and expands his limits, that precipitates nihilistic despair and the pathos of impotent rage. For this identification highlights that man 'has *no* goals': man has no meaning.

I hold this passage key to apprehending the contrary positions, the oscillations and vacillations that characterise Nietzsche's thought. I have noted his insistence upon the need to engage in an experimental, transformative philosophy that tests the self's affirmative boundaries. Often the rhetoric is exultant as he idealises the squandering of self-contained individuality to perform an expansive, totalising endorsement of existence. Nevertheless, such rhetoric belies a fear of being overwhelmed by others' suffering, a fear of the consequent dissolution of autarkic selfhood. Nietzsche's own heightened receptivity to others' hardship, as one such 'exceptional man' able to inhabit other perspectives and attain more comprehensive states, made him particularly susceptible to this threat of suffocation. Nietzsche's work thus celebrates openness and experimentation on the one hand, and defensively propounds autarky and isolation on the other. It expresses a persistent sense of vulnerability in the face of the threat of nihilism as Nietzsche reaches the limits of his affirmative capacity: engaging with the nauseating, paralysing truth of man's meaninglessness presented most starkly by others' suffering, Nietzsche reaches his digestive capacity and adopts restrictive, self-protective strategies. His purported lightness and halcyon tone mixes with a fear of nihilistic collapse and attendant reactionary rage.

Accordingly, it is no coincidence that the nihilistic depths, or 'abysses', in Nietzsche's philosophy are repeatedly associated with others' distress. For instance, Zarathustra observes that '[p]ity [...] is the deepest abyss: as deeply as man looks into life, so deeply does he look also into suffering'. For Nietzsche, 'the deepest abyss and the highest summits' are inseparable (*BT* 13: 66)[42]: his philosophy of self-cultivation advocates plummeting into 'the abysses of the Dionysiac' to attain a tragic-religious pathos of joy engendered by this confrontation (14: 67).[43] The binary of height and depth dissolves as that which involves the greatest suffering produces the greatest pleasure, or power.

Yet Nietzsche's writings convey an incapacity to plummet to such depths regarding others' suffering. Nietzsche tellingly confesses: 'I, too, know with certainty that I need only to expose myself to the sight of real distress and I, too, *am* lost.' Importantly, being 'lost' signifies abandoning 'one's *own path*', or one's goal, to compassionate feelings (*GS* 338: 192). In *Beyond Good and Evil* (1886) he similarly contends: 'the more a psychologist—a born and inevitable psychologist and unriddler of souls—applies himself to the more exquisite cases and human beings, the greater becomes the danger that he might suffocate from pity' (*BGE* 269: 206–7) In the *Genealogy* Nietzsche assumes repeated reactionary or defensive positions when discussing others' suffering. He insists that the 'pathos of distance' between the healthy and the sick 'ought to be the chief concern on earth' (*OGM* III 14: 97).[44] Elsewhere, in *Ecce Homo*, he is more extreme, claiming that 'everything weak, sick, ill-constructed, suffering from itself [...] *ought to perish*' (*EH* XIV 8: 104). This statement is particularly startling given that it immediately precedes his declared identification with Dionysus, his symbol of universal affirmation. A related entry in *The Anti-Christ (1888)*, in which he propounds the same exterminatory argument, is revelatory: '[w]hat is more harmful than any vice?—Active sympathy for the ill-constituted and weak' (*AC* 2: 128). Again, it is 'active sympathy' and the engagement with the senselessness of others' suffering that attends Nietzsche's reactionary discourse: the 'exceptional man' participates in others' distress to transfigure the self and affirm existence according to his digestive capacity; yet it is precisely the fear of being overpowered by a meaninglessness that is most conspicuous when empathetically engaged with those 'average' or 'weak' human beings that provokes Nietzsche's own 'curse against existence'.

In summary, then, Nietzsche's work evinces a great tension that may be apprehended by examining his preoccupation with 'senseless suffering'. It is particularly regarding this discourse that one can observe the discordant impulses in his thought. On the one hand, his writing offers generous, inclusive gestures, pointing to the strong soul embracing existence and the powerful community enduring and absorbing its parasites. This affirmative vision involves the overcoming of vindictive sentiments and actions. On the other hand, the same discourse gives rise to reactionary, hostile positions, evincing a defensive fear of falling into meaninglessness, of the collapse of autarkic selfhood, of being unable to surmount the ever-present threat of suicidal nihilism.

By focussing on D. H. Lawrence's concern with senseless suffering and nihilism in *Lady Chatterley's Lover (1928)*, I shall now argue that Lawrence's affirmative vision is beset by similar strains. As I turn to examine the tensions arising in Lawrence's novel, noting that its vision of erotic regeneration similarly entails the need to transcend vengefulness, it may be instructive to suggest that Nietzsche's formulation of his ideal of '*amor fati*' anticipates Lawrence's engagement with these powerful sentiments. For, as Nietzsche articulates this ideal, he remains cognisant of the persistence of this drive to 'accuse' the other and of the difficulty of surmounting such reactive feelings:

> I want to learn more and more how to see what is necessary in things as what is beautiful in them—thus I will be one of those who makes things beautiful. *Amor fati*: let that be my love from now on! I do not want to wage war against ugliness. I do not want to accuse; I do not even want to accuse the accusers. Let *looking away* be my only negation! And, all in all and on the whole: some day I want only to be a Yes-sayer! (*GS* 276: 157)

NOTES

1. See also *TI* X 5: 121.
2. On poststructuralist readings of Nietzsche, see Robert C. Solomon, '"A More Severe Morality": Nietzsche's Affirmative Ethics', in *Nietzsche as Affirmative Thinker*, ed. by Yirmiyahu Yovel (Dordrecht: Martinus Nijhoff Publishers, 1986), pp. 69–89 (p. 70); Michael Allen Gillespie, *Nihilism before Nietzsche* (Chicago: University of Chicago Press, 1995), p. 176.
3. Reading Nietzsche's discourse on suffering as inherently fragile, I would echo Martin Heidegger's comments on Nietzsche's enigmatic fictional text, *Thus Spoke Zarathustra* (1883–1891): 'One who has not previously and does not perceive the horror in all the discourses—seemingly arrogant and often ecstatically conducted as they are—will never know who Zarathustra is'. Martin Heidegger, 'Who Is Nietzsche's Zarathustra?', in *The New Nietzsche: Contemporary Styles of Interpretation*, ed. by David B. Allison (Cambridge, MA: MIT Press, 1985), pp. 64–79 (p. 72).
4. See Chapter 1, p. 5.
5. See also *BGE* 21: 50–2.
6. As Alexander Nehamas observes: 'Coherence, of course, can also be produced by weakness, mediocrity, and one-dimensionality. But style, which is what Nietzsche requires and admires, involves controlled multiplicity and resolved conflict'. Alexander Nehamas, *Nietzsche: Life as Literature* (Cambridge, MA: Harvard University Press, 1985), p. 7.
7. See also *AC* 11: 133–4; *D* 108: 63.
8. See, for example, Chapter 4, pp. 189–90.
9. See *AC* 2: 127–8.

10. See also *BGE* 44: 73.
11. See p. 29 above.
12. See Chapter 1, p. 11.
13. See also *BGE* 24: 55.
14. Notably, Lucy Bending accuses Scarry of denying 'the variability of pain' in her 'argument from extremes'. Lucy Bending, *The Representation of Bodily Pain in Late Nineteenth-Century English Culture* (Oxford: Oxford University Press, 2000), p. 87.
15. See also *TI* X 2: 118; *AC* 39: 163; *AC* 62: 199.
16. See also *AC* 5: 129.
17. See Chapter 1, p. 5 for similar views.
18. For example, see *TI* IX 49: 114.
19. I am indebted to Richard Beardsworth for this point. Richard Beardsworth, 'Nietzsche, Nihilism and Spirit', in *Nihilism Now!: Monsters of Energy*, ed. by K. J. Ansell-Pearson and Diane Morgan (Basingstoke: MacMillan Press, 2000), pp. 37–69. Countering Frasers' view, see also *TI* IX 43: 108. Here Nietzsche states: 'A reversion, a turning back in any sense and to any degree is quite impossible'.
20. See David Boothroyd, 'Beyond Suffering I Have No Alibi', in *Nietzsche and Levinas: "After the Death of a Certain God"*, ed. by Jill Stauffer and Bettina Bergo (New York: Columbia University Press, 2009), 150–64 (pp. 154–5); I shall refer to Conway's argument below.
21. See *OGM* II 4: 43.
22. See Chapter 1, p. 5.
23. See Chapter 4, p. 152.
24. See *OGM* III 11: 90.
25. See the discussion in Chapter 4, pp. 152–3.
26. See *OGM* I 15: 32–3.
27. See *WP* 616: 330.
28. This argument complicates the position of those who hold Nietzsche's account of the initial 'breach with man's animal past' to signal the equivalent of the Christian myth of the Fall in Nietzsche's thought.
29. See *TI* V 1: 52.
30. See Chapter 1, pp. 11–12.
31. For instance, regarding self-fashioning Nietzsche warns: 'Whoever is dissatisfied with himself is continually prepared to avenge himself for this' (*GS* 290: 164).
32. For examples of this masochistic structure in Nietzsche's thought see *GS* Preface 3, *BGE* 229, *BGE* 230, *AC* 57: 188.
33. Also *OGM* I 11: 26–7.
34. *TSZ* Prologue 5: 46. 'The earth has become small, and upon it hops the Ultimate Man, who makes everything small. His race is as inexterminable

as the flea; the Ultimate man lives longest / […] They have left the places where living was hard: for one needs warmth. One still loves one's neighbour and rubs oneself against him: for one needs warmth. / […] They still work, for work is entertainment. But they take care the entertainment does not exhaust them. / Nobody grows rich or poor any more: both are too much of a burden. Who wants to rule? Who obey? Both are too much of a burden'.

35. See also *BGE* 44: 71–3.
36. Nietzsche discusses Arthur Schopenhauer's philosophy of will-lessness and its espousal of pity. Schopenhauer exemplifies a 'new Buddhism'. *OGM* Preface 5: 7.
37. According to Carey, Nietzsche considers '[b]enevolence, public spirit and consideration for others are despicable herd virtues. The truly noble man is egotistic. He despised pity, which is unhealthy and valued only by slaves'. See John Carey, *The Intellectuals and the Masses: Pride and Prejudice among the Literary Intelligentsia, 1880–1939* (London: Faber and Faber, 1992), p. 13.
38. See also *EH* II 10: 37. Here an extreme posture of self-enclosure is suggested: 'at an absurdly early age, at seven, I already knew that no human word would ever reach me: has anyone ever seen me saddened on that account?'
39. This section of my chapter is inspired by Henry Staten's reading of Nietzsche in his wonderful *Nietzsche's Voice* (1990).
40. See also *BGE* 230, *BGE* 257.
41. See *TI* IX 10: 84.
42. See also *EH* III 3: 42–3.
43. See also TSZ I 8: 69.
44. See also *OGM* I 12: 27.

References

Ansell-Pearson, Keith, and Duncan Large (eds.), *The Nietzsche Reader* (Oxford: Blackwell, 2009).

Boothroyd, David, 'Beyond Suffering I Have No Alibi', in *Nietzsche and Levinas: "After the Death of a Certain God"*, ed. by Jill Stauffer and Bettina Bergo (New York: Columbia University Press, 2009), 150–64.

Carr, Karen Leslie, *The Banalization of Nihilism: Twentieth-Century Responses to Meaninglessness* (Albany: State University of New York Press, 1992).

Conway, Daniel W., 'Heidegger, Nietzsche, and the Origins of Nihilism', *Journal of Nietzsche Studies*, 3 (1992): 11–43.

———, 'Beasts of Prey: How We Became What We Are: Tracking the "Beasts of Prey"', in *A Nietzschean Bestiary: Becoming Animal Beyond Docile and Brutal*, ed. by Christa Davis Acampora and Ralph R. Acampora (Lanham, MD: Rowman & Littlefield, 2004), 156–79.

Dews, Peter, *The Idea of Evil* (Oxford: Blackwell, 2008).

Fraser, Giles, *Redeeming Nietzsche: On the Piety of Unbelief* (London: Routledge, 2002).

Gillespie, Michael Allen, *Nihilism before Nietzsche* (Chicago: University of Chicago Press, 1995).

Glicksberg, Charles I., *The Literature of Nihilism* (London: Bucknell University Press, 1975).

Haar, Michel, *Nietzsche and Metaphysics*, trans. Michael Gendre (Albany: State University of New York Press, 1996).

———, 'Nietzsche and the Metamorphosis of the Divine', in *Post-Secular Philosophy*, ed. by Philip Blond (London: Routledge, 1998), 157–76.

Heidegger, Martin, 'Who Is Nietzsche's Zarathustra?', in *The New Nietzsche: Contemporary Styles of Interpretation*, ed. by David B. Allison (Cambridge, MA: MIT Press, 1985), 64–79.

Higgins, Kathleen Marie, 'Suffering in Nietzsche's Philosophy', in *Reading Nietzsche at the Margins*, ed. by Steven V. Hicks and Alan Rosenberg (West Lafayette, IN: Purdue University Press, 2008), 59–72.

Huenemann, Charlie, 'Nietzsche's Illness', in *The Oxford Handbook of Nietzsche*, ed. by Ken Gemes and John Richardson (Oxford: Oxford University Press, 2013), 63–80.

Lévinas, Emmanuel, *On Thinking of the Other: Entre Nous* (London: Athlone, 1998).

Mulhall, Stephen, *Philosophical Myths of the Fall* (Princeton, NJ: Princeton University Press, 2007).

Muller-Lauter, Wolfgang, *Nietzsche: His Philosophy of Contradictions and the Contradictions of His Philosophy*, trans. David J. Parent (New York: University of Illinois Press, 1999).

Murdoch, Iris, *Metaphysics as a Guide to Morals* (London: Penguin, 1993).

Nehamas, Alexander, *Nietzsche: Life as Literature* (Cambridge, MA: Harvard University Press, 1985).

Nietzsche, Friedrich Wilhelm, *The Will to Power*. trans. Walter Kaufmann and R. J. Hollingdale (New York: Vintage Books, 1968).

———, *Beyond Good and Evil: Prelude to a Philosophy of the Future*. trans. R. J. Hollingdale (Harmondsworth: Penguin, repr. 1990).

———, *Ecce Homo: How One Becomes What One Is*. trans. R. J. Hollingdale (London: Penguin, repr. 1992).

———, *The Birth of Tragedy*. trans. Shaun Whiteside (London: Penguin, 1993).

———, *On the Genealogy of Morality*. trans. Carol Diethe (Cambridge: Cambridge University Press, 1994).

———, *The Anti-Christ* in *Twilight of the Idols* and *The Anti-Christ*. trans. R. J. Hollingdale (London: Penguin, repr. 2003).

———, *The Gay Science: With a Prelude in German Rhymes and an Appendix of Songs*. trans. Josefine Nauckhoff and Adrian Del Caro (Cambridge: Cambridge University Press, repr. 2003).

———, *Thus Spoke Zarathustra*. trans. R. J. Hollingdale (London: Penguin, repr. 2003).

———, *Twilight of the Idols* in *Twilight of the Idols* and *The Anti-Christ*. trans. R. J. Hollingdale (London: Penguin, repr. 2003).

———, *Human, All Too Human*. trans. Marion Faber and Stephen Lehmann (London: Penguin, repr. 2004).

———, *Daybreak: Thoughts on the Prejudices of Morality*. trans. R. J. Hollingdale (Cambridge: Cambridge University Press, repr. 2007).

Nussbaum, Martha C., 'Pity and Mercy: Nietzsche's Stoicism', in *Nietzsche, Genealogy, Morality: Essays on Nietzsche's Genealogy of Morals*, ed. by Richard Schacht (Berkeley: University of California Press, 1994), 139–67.

Owen, David, *Nietzsche, Politics and Modernity: Critique of Liberal Reason* (London: Sage, 1995).

Owen, David, and Aaron Ridley, 'Dramatis Personae: Nietzsche, Culture, and Human Types' in *Why Nietzsche Still?* ed. by Alan D. Schrift (London: University of California Press, 2000), 136–53.

Pippin, Robert B., 'Introduction', in Friedrich Wilhelm Nietzsche, *Thus Spoke Zarathustra*, trans. Adrian del Caro (Cambridge: Cambridge University Press, 2006), viii–xxxv.

Reginster, Bernard, *The Affirmation of Life: Nietzsche on Overcoming Nihilism* (London: Harvard University Press, 2006).

Ridley, Aaron, *Nietzsche's Conscience: Six Character Studies from the Genealogy* (Ithaca: Cornell University Press, 1998).

Scarry, Elaine, *The Body in Pain: The Making and Unmaking of the World* (Oxford: Oxford University Press, 1985).

Seaford, Richard, 'Tragedy and Dionysus', in *A Companion to Tragedy*, ed. by Rebecca Bushnell (Malden, MA: Blackwell, 2005), 25–38.

Solomon, Robert C., '"A More Severe Morality": Nietzsche's Affirmative Ethics', in *Nietzsche as Affirmative Thinker*, ed. by Yirmiyahu Yovel (Dordrecht, The Netherlands: Martinus Nijhoff Publishers, 1986), 69–89.

Staten, Henry, *Nietzsche's Voice* (Ithaca, NY: Cornell University Press, 1990).

Surin, Kenneth, *The Turnings of Darkness and Light* (Cambridge: Cambridge University Press, 1989).

Wagner, Benno, 'Insuring Nietzsche: Kafka's Files', *New German Critique* 99 (2006): 83–119.

Young, Julian, *The Death of God and the Meaning of Life* (Abingdon: Routledge, 2003).

CHAPTER 3

D. H. Lawrence's *Lady Chatterley's Lover* and the Erotic Transcendence of Nihilism

INTRODUCTION: 'AN ENGLISH NIETZSCHE'

That Lawrence's work shares much with Nietzsche's thought is a firmly established view within Lawrence scholarship. Amongst those studies examining this kinship, Colin Milton's 1985 monograph, *Nietzsche and Lawrence*, offers the most extensive discussion. Milton's exploration of Lawrence's fiction is premised on the claim that 'Nietzschean ideas underlie and determine the large-scale patterns and structures of Lawrence's writing' (Milton 1987: 19). Others tracing the relationship also emphasise the similarities, with Kingsley Widmer going as far as to claim that Lawrence had 'become an English Nietzsche' (Widmer 1985: 121).[1] Many facets of Lawrence's output have been analysed in this discussion. Eleanor H. Green, for example, has compared the political views of both men, while Greg Gerrard has discussed their shared relevance to ecological concerns (see Green 1974; Garrard 2006). Others such as Anne Fernihough and John Burt Foster have commented on Lawrence's more ambivalent stance towards the philosopher, observing both Lawrence's assimilation of Nietzsche, and yet his desire to resist certain ideas (see Fernihough 1993; Foster 1981). Both commentators concede, however, that despite Lawrence's distancing attempts, fundamental convergences primarily characterise this relationship. What I wish to do in this chapter is to consider another, hitherto neglected, dynamic in this relationship. Thus, having identified the entwined

© The Author(s) 2018
S. Smith, *Nietzsche and Modernism*,
Palgrave Studies in Modern European Literature,
https://doi.org/10.1007/978-3-319-75535-9_3

issues of meaningless suffering and nihilism to be central and consistent concerns in Nietzsche's work in the previous chapter, I will now argue that Lawrence's work can be similarly apprehended in terms of its depiction of responses to suffering. I shall focus upon Lawrence's final novel, *Lady Chatterley's Lover* (1928), to analyse these points of continuity.

While the many reasons for examining *Lady Chatterley* within a discussion of Lawrence and Nietzsche shall become evident through the course of the chapter, it is worth noting here that critics normally read the novel as Lawrence's significant departure from the philosopher. For example, in his consideration of Lawrence's indebtedness to the thinker, Widmer dismisses the pertinence of Lawrence's last novel by claiming that it only 'relate[s] more distantly to the Nietzschean' (Widmer 1985: 131). Widmer's approach is indicative of the critical tendency to focus on the texts that constitute what is commonly labelled Lawrence's 'leadership period' within this discussion, namely the novels *Aaron's rod* (1922), *Kangaroo* (1923), and *The Plumed Serpent* (1926).[2] Otherwise put, *Lady Chatterley*, which was originally written with a working title of *Tenderness*, announces Lawrence's abandonment of his exploration of the political power motif; this shift in Lawrence supposedly marks his disengagement from Nietzsche's notions of the will to power and aristocratic leadership.

I shall argue, however, that *Lady Chatterley* provides fertile ground on which to cultivate a considered approach towards understanding Lawrence's engagement with Nietzsche's principal preoccupations. Indeed, the narrator's opening, summative declaration frames the novel's action in terms suggestively evoking Nietzsche's diagnosis of modern nihilism as the loss of our highest values[3]: 'we are among the ruins', proclaims Lawrence's narrator, 'there is now no smooth road into the future: but we go round, or scramble over the obstacles. We've got to live, no matter how many skies have fallen' (Lawrence 2006: 5). This pronouncement recalls Nietzsche's view that, as future-orientated creatures, we are impelled to generate a goal to strive towards to constitute ourselves as willing agents: Lawrence's narrator points to the ineluctable need to posit significance 'or new little hopes' to counter a prevalent and catastrophic loss of energy and meaning (5).[4] As the novel focuses upon personal and collective experiences of paralysis and exhaustion, I shall stress that its depictions of erotic regeneration and power relations seek to address this nihilistic condition, to engender new hope and meaning.

Critics such as Michael Bell and Daniel Schneider have noted the critical reception of *Lady Chatterley* by Lawrence scholars (see Bell 1992: 209; Schneider 1984: 237). While Bell and Schneider defend the novel on its own terms, they also concur with the critical consensus to treat this text as inferior to Lawrence's great works, *The Rainbow* (1915) and *Women in Love* (1920). Nevertheless, while Schneider cites damning views of several critics regarding, for example, the novel's overt didacticism and the nature of the its sexual content, his corrective to these interpretations is pertinent: these readings overlook the key, sustained tone of cataclysm that permeates the novel (Schneider 1984: 237). In other words, there is a need to stress that Lawrence's preoccupation with the post-war predicament of pervasive nihilism is most explicitly and extensively treated in this work. Thus, as Hilary Simpson notes, 'although Lawrence's last novel is frequently seen as a pastoral, a timeless exploration of sexual passion determined more by myth than by history, the historical context is crucial' (Simpson 1982: 140). The novel, I hold, paints a portrait of the English nation and its experience of overwhelming, senseless suffering. It insists upon a disjunction between experience and interpretation, of a corresponding evacuation of meanings and values that is directly linked to the experience of the trauma from the war. Furthermore, Lawrence presents individual and collective suffering to be inseparably intertwined: personal grievances are twinned with and somewhat mirror the larger, collective experience of wounding. My subsequent discussion will firstly examine Lawrence's dramatisation of the modern nihilistic predicament to reveal its proximity to responses to suffering. I shall then go on to explore Lawrence's vision for the overcoming of the life-nausea that afflicts the novel's protagonists and modernity at large.

SUFFERING AND NIHILISM

Perhaps the novel's most emphatic dramatisation of suffering's excessive force and its tie to nihilism is evident with Lawrence's characterisation of Sir Clifford Chatterley. Returning from the war 'more or less in bits', Clifford is wounded and paralysed from the waist down (Lawrence 2006: 5). This physical paralysis also symbolises an internal, emotional paralysis Lawrence considers to be prevalent in the post-war culture. Leaving aside the point that narrative offers a central means to reconstitute a sense of selfhood for greater examination in Chapter 5 on Samuel Beckett's *Endgame* (1957), it is noteworthy that Clifford 'was back at Wragby, and writing his stories and feeling sure of life in spite of all, he seemed to forget, and to recover all his equanimity' (49). However, his wife Constance notes that his convalescence 'is only an appearance' (49). Rather, the wound 'had been so deep as to be numb' and 'the paralysis, the bruise of the too-great shock' re-emerges, 'gradually spreading in his affective self' (49). This insight, that the physiological-affective wound 'only slowly deepens its terrible ache, till it fills all the psyche', is conveyed with gravitas as 'one of the great laws of the human soul' (49). Notably, Lawrence's apprehension of the all-consuming character of emotional distress parallels those observations regarding physical pain propounded by Emanuel Levinas and Elaine Scarry discussed in the previous chapter.[5] The wound thus renders Clifford emotionally paralysed: 'he had been so much hurt, something inside of him perished, some of his feelings were gone. There was a blank of insentience' (6). This devastation of Clifford's affective self is central to the novel's trajectory: his incapacity to sympathise with others intensifies the gulf between Clifford and his wife, Constance, or Connie; this estrangement impels Connie to seek emotional fulfilment elsewhere, firstly in the disastrous affair with the playwright, Michaelis, and later with the gamekeeper, Oliver Mellors.

Clifford's trauma can be illuminated by drawing a parallel with Nietzsche's notions of Apollo and Dionysus, first outlined in *The Birth of Tragedy* (1872).[6] Recalling that the Apollonian artistic urge engenders the illusion of the self's individuated existence, the experience of extreme pain can be related to the Dionysian, an excessive force that overwhelms or ruptures these boundaries of selfhood, shattering one's sense of self-possession. As John Sallis notes, the 'Dionysian state is an abysmal loss of self', it is an excess that 'is at the same time the dissolution of subjectivity, the utter disruption of determinate selfhood, being torn to pieces' (Sallis 1988: 5). Accordingly, the experience of acute suffering signals an annihilation of self-definition that evokes the Dionysian, tragic awareness that everything that 'comes into being must be prepared to face a sorrowful end' (*BT* 17: 80). Pain, in its various forms, anticipates the self's total disintegration. In terms of the novel, Lawrence stresses that Clifford 'was haunted by anxiety and a sense of dangerous, impending void' (Lawrence 2006: 139). His trauma has induced an encounter with life's senselessness, with what Nietzsche refers to as the '*horror vacui*', the fear of nothingness (*OGM* III 1: 72). In Nietzsche's account of tragic art, this Dionysian disclosure of one's absolute expenditure and of life's inherent senselessness entails the attendant threat of a suicidal, depressive loss of willing.[7] Lawrence marks his depiction of Clifford's anxiety, of his haunting fear of annihilation, by noting that there is an accompanying depressive, nihilistic fatigue, concomitant with and intensifying his lack of self-coherence: '[a] terrible hollow seemed to menace him somewhere, somehow, a void, and into this void his energy would collapse. Energyless, he felt at times he was dead, really dead' (Lawrence 2006: 140).

Significantly, in Nietzsche's account of ancient tragedy, Apollonian illusion counters the nauseating horror of the Dionysian insights. As noted in Chapter 2, Nietzsche later formulated the notion of the will to power in somewhat parallel terms, repeatedly suggesting that this doctrine relates to the capacity to impose form upon one's own plurality of instincts or drives, or the Dionysian forces of the self. Clifford's loss of energy, or will, suggests, however, an incapacity to perform a correspondent recuperative gesture to resist the disintegrative force of the Dionysian. The following passage suggests that Clifford has failed to fashion the sense of coherence required to reflexively experience himself as an effective agent:

> When Clifford was roused, he could still talk brilliantly and, as it were, command the future [...] But the day after, all the brilliant words seemed like dead leaves, crumpling up and turning to powder, meaning really nothing, blown away on any gust of wind. The words were not the leafy words of an effective life, young with energy and belonging to the tree. They were the hosts of fallen leaves of a life that is ineffectual. (49–50)

This passage implies that the excessive force of the trauma to which Clifford is subject impacts his capacity to constitute an ordered, meaningful life mediated through language. Lawrence's depiction of Clifford's nihilistic state in terms of a disjunction between language and action recalls Mark Warren's analysis of Nietzsche's notion of nihilism which, Warren holds, entails a discrepancy between interpretation and experience:

> The fundamental structural contradiction in nihilism, then, is between humans as sensuous, worldly beings who suffer, feel, and act, and humans as conscious, cultural beings who constantly interpret and evaluate the world and themselves. Individuals lose their orientation and become nihilistic when they cannot fit experience and interpretation together to form a 'will' to act: that is, when they fail to organize their powers of agency. (1988: 16)

In line with this analysis, Clifford evinces a disconnect 'between experiential and interpretive conditions of acting' due to his experience of extreme suffering (18). There is a consequent evacuation of the significance of existent discourse as the self is unable to interpretatively appropriate its suffering, to give form, order and meaning to its experience. The existent interpretative framework, or ideals, constituted to secure and reflect the subject's sense of agency, therefore appears at odds with empirical existence.

The novel repeatedly insists upon an emptying of meanings and values and ties this to the experience of overwhelming or senseless suffering on both personal and collective levels. Connie's brief and ultimately devastating affair with Michaelis may be invoked to illustrate this regarding personal experiences of extreme distress. For example, what is telling from Connie's perspective concerning Michaelis' cruel rejection of her following intercourse was that it was 'particularly unexpected' as '[s]he felt so innocent' (Lawrence 2006: 54). It constitutes an act of 'incomprehensible brutality' and is described as 'one of the crucial blows of Connie's life' (54). In other words, Connie is unable to rationally appropriate 'this unexpected piece of brutality' because it dislocates the extant sense of significance inflecting the signifier 'sex', 'the last of the great words' (54). Echoing Warren's analysis of nihilism as arising from 'disjunctions between experiential and interpretive conditions of acting', Connie's consequent ruminations upon the inadequacy of existent meanings and ideals gesture towards an attendant inner dissolution (Warren 1988: 18):

> All the great words, it seemed to Connie, were cancelled for her generation: love, joy, happiness, home, mother, father, husband, all these great dynamic words were half-dead now, and dying from day to day. [...] As for sex, the last of the great words, it was just a cocktail term for an excitement that bucked you up for a while, then left you more raggy than ever. Frayed! It was as if the very material you were made of was cheap stuff, and was fraying out to nothing. (Lawrence 2006: 62)

Connie's reflections on Michaelis' 'brutality' evoke Nietzsche's description of 'passive nihilism', or a disillusionment with existent ideals. As Nietzsche contends in his notebooks: '[n]ow everything is false through and through, mere "words", chaotic, weak, or extravagant' (*WP* 30: 20). Otherwise put: '[w]hat does nihilism mean? *That the highest values devaluate themselves*' (2: 9). Recalling Nietzsche's descriptions of 'passive nihilism' discussed in Chapter 1, Connie seems to undergo an extreme shift in perspective.[8] That is, having adhered to those collective ideals that had hitherto directed human willing, she now reflects: '[n]othingness! To accept the great nothingness of life seemed to be the one end of living' (Lawrence 2006: 55). Furthermore, Connie's disillusionment with those 'great words' engenders a depressive loss of energy: attending 'her inner resentment' deriving from this unredeemed suffering, she is subject to an 'overwhelming inertia' (94). Her condition thus echoes Nietzsche's claim that nihilism entails an affective exhaustion accompanying a cognitive disorientation: 'we are *weary* because we have lost the main stimulus', meaning, or goal (*WP* 8: 11).

It is also noteworthy that Clifford's nihilistic pathos precedes his war injury. The personal and the collective intertwine as we are told that, before going to fight in Flanders, he shares in the growing bitterness towards the political establishment and the war effort: '[h]e was only caught in the general, popular recoil of the young against convention and against any sort of real authority'; everything is consequently 'ridiculous' for Clifford and his generation (Lawrence 2006: 10). Noting Clifford's departure from the prevailing values suggests, then, that his subsequent wounding serves to intensify an already present disposition and extant sense of disjunction. Furthermore, while Clifford may be read to be partaking in a form of what Nietzsche labels 'active nihilism', of advancing the dissolution of established values and social hierarchies, it is necessary to observe the passive dynamic of this economy of feeling as Lawrence presents it.[9] Firstly, as this recoil from existent ideals seems to be a pervasive feeling or consciousness that one is subject to, Lawrence does not depict it as essentially volitional. Furthermore, Lawrence highlights that there are no values supplanting those that are collapsing. Ruminating on the paucity of meaning in the extant social hierarchies and values, Clifford turns to self-reflect on his own inadequacy:

> Clifford felt his father was a hopeless anachronism. But wherein was he himself any further ahead, except in a wincing sense of the ridiculousness of everything, and the paramount ridiculousness of his own position? (12)

Beset by an existential crisis stemming from the cultural malaise, Clifford's vulnerability is highlighted as he resolves that he needed a wife to be an 'anchor' in 'the vast seething world' (11–2). For Clifford,

Connie's very anchorage consists in her capacity to engender meaning: striving to ameliorate others' suffering during the war, Connie, by way of contrast to Clifford, 'believed in something', was 'earnest about *something*' (11). Clifford's dependence on Connie on such terms signals an incapacity or reluctance to construct his own meaning. In Nietzsche's words, Clifford's external orientation towards an other is a 'sign of a lack of strength to posit for oneself, productively, a goal, a why, a faith' (*WP* 23: 18). Significantly, Connie is attractive to Clifford as he requires the 'assurance' that comes from her greater sense of self-mastery: '[s]he was so much more mistress of herself in the outer world of chaos, than he was master of himself' (Lawrence 2006: 10).

This experience of passive nihilism, characterised by the absence of a meaning or goal and a concomitant depressive loss of energy, permeates the culture at large. At the novel's denouement, for instance, Mellors conveys to Connie that the men in the north of England are 'very apathetic. [...] There's no sort of conviction about anything—except that it's all a muddle and a hole. [...] The men are limp, they feel a doom somewhere, and they go about as if there was nothing to be done' (299). Mellors' bleak assessment underlines the prevalent resignation to the industrial horror and the post-war catastrophe. Indeed, through Michaelis, Lawrence seems to be suggesting that this nihilistic pathos suffusing the culture precedes and determines the individual: Michaelis' 'fathomless disillusion' has been 'built up of layers of disillusion, going down in him generation after generation, like geological strata' (23). Lawrence's novel repeatedly suggests immediate historical-contextual and personal sources of life-weariness as well as larger cultural impulses that frame and determine the phenomena of modern nihilism.

What is more, Lawrence's depiction of the purposeless, general populace echoes Nietzsche's character type of the 'Ultimate' or 'Last Man', the figure that the philosopher repeatedly demonises. Perhaps this type is most memorably described in *Thus Spoke Zarathustra* (1883–85) where the thinker uses this symbol to capture the state of comfortable mediocrity he discerns to be characterising modernity.[10] Lawrence similarly portrays the working classes, and, indeed, the social elite, to be motivated by the pursuit of pleasure and an aversion to suffering. For instance, informing Connie that nothing can '"make"' the workers '"serious"', that physical activities and sports such as football are considered '"too much like hard work"' (108), Mrs Bolton surmises that '"all the lads want is just money to enjoy themselves, and the girls the same, with fine clothes: and they don't care about another thing"' (104). The connection of the pursuit of pleasure to a lack of meaning is shared in later passages. For example, as Connie travels to Venice and encounters thrill-seeking travellers and holidaymakers she complains of 'too much enjoyment' and ponders: '[w]hat did people mean, with this simply *determined* enjoying of themselves?' (Lawrence 2006: 255). Connie's observation, suggesting the pointlessness of the pleasure-seeking surrounding her, echoes Nietzsche's identification of hedonism with nihilism. That is, one dimension of Nietzsche's critique of modernity is that, in broad terms, he considers pessimism, the judgement of a '"preponderance of suffering over pleasure" or the opposite (hedonism)' as 'already signposts to nihilism': '[f]or in both of these cases no ultimate meaning is posited except the appearance of pleasure or displeasure' (*WP* 35: 23). The pursuit of happiness merely signals an absence of a goal, or an incapacity to constitute one.

Connie's lament also suggests a more poignant motivation underpinning the ubiquitous pursuit of pleasure. Discerning that pleasure 'was a complete narcotic', she observes, '[a]nd that was what they all wanted, a drug: the slow water, a drug; the sun, a drug; jazz, a drug; cigarettes, cocktails, ices, vermouth—To be drugged! Enjoyment! Enjoyment! (Lawrence 2006: 259). Connie's use of the term 'narcotic' implies that the pleasure-seeking primarily serves to palliate pain. This corroborates her earlier observation of the 'bruised' populace, the colliers who are consumed by an emotional-psychic wound deriving specifically from the war: 'the vast black clot of bruised blood, deep inside their souls and bodies', she thinks, will take generations to 'dissolve' (50). She also perceives that the traumatised populace 'would need a new hope', or a new cognitive orientation, to redeem their suffering and restore a sense of agency: for the colliers' prospective strike was 'not a manifestation of energy' but only the indignation of senseless suffering 'slowly rising and creating the great ache of unrest, the stupor of discontent' (50).

Connie's perceptions of the colliers, suggesting that the pursuit of pleasure serves to anaesthetise extreme pain, evoke Nietzsche's claim that Christianity contains 'so much to refresh, soothe and narcotize' deep suffering and depression (*OGM* III 17: 101). In his *On the Genealogy of Morality* (1887), Nietzsche elaborates upon this analgesic role by asserting that the ascetic ideal provides a number of palliative techniques that aim to distract the sufferer, or to effectively repress 'dull, crippling, long-drawn-out pain' (III 19: 107) in practices that seek to achieve a state 'akin' to '*hibernation*' (III 17: 102–3). In effect, by preventing the sufferer 'coming to consciousness', the ascetic ideal perpetrates a wholescale denial of embodiment. For, in acting as a 'narcotic against pain of any kind', these techniques seek to remove the sufferer from desire, from striving, from affective-erotic being (III 15: 99). As Nietzsche observes: '[I]f possible, absolutely no more wanting, no wishing; everything which arouses the emotions and "blood" must be avoided' (III 17: 102–3). There is a corresponding evaluative position accompanying these practices:

> the hypnotic feeling of nothingness, the tranquillity of deepest sleep, in short, *absence of suffering*—this may counted as the highest good, the value of values, by the suffering and by those who are deeply depressed, it *has* to be valued positively by them and found to be *the* positive itself. (II 17: 104)

According to Nietzsche, the ascetic ideal, then, entails a systematic repression of pain, and thus of embodiment. Insofar as it operates to prevent contact with the Dionysian excesses of earthly, bodily existence and suffering, it appears to be a particularly heightened form of the Apollonian exemplified by the Alexandrian or 'theoretical' man in Nietzsche's *The Birth of Tragedy* (see *BT* 18: 85–9).[11] *Lady Chatterley's Lover* explores the consequences of repressing such 'tormenting, secret pain which is becoming unbearable', and the effective denial of Dionysian embodiment that such an approach to suffering involves (*OGM* III 15: 99). The novel offers a complex picture. For while it gestures towards the need to confront rather than repress such suffering, for this offers the potential for affirmation and flourishing, it also suggests that such encounters with overwhelming suffering may induce a nihilistic *ressentiment*. Before investigating these ubiquitous feelings of powerlessness and vindictiveness, I firstly wish to examine the nihilistic consequences of this repression of pain by largely focussing on Clifford's rejection of embodiment.

THE SELF-PRESERVATIVE ECONOMY

Clifford seeks to deny full consciousness of his trauma. As mentioned above, on returning from the war he had resumed habitual life and 'seemed to forget' his paralysis. Yet this characteristic strategy of repression engenders a state of dissonance. This is evident, for instance, regarding Clifford's conscious suppression of the knowledge of Connie's affair with the gamekeeper. On disclosure of the relationship the narrator conveys that, '[i]nwardly he had known for a long time she was leaving him. But he had absolutely refused any outward admission of it' (Lawrence 2006: 288). Clifford's perspectival interpretation is marked by an extreme disconnect from empirical actuality: for 'he knew' about the affair, 'and all the time tried to kid himself it wasn't so' (289). He thus 'felt the devil twisting his tail, and pretended it was the angels smiling on him' (289). Such a highly illusory perspective, severed from, and shielding oneself from, life's unpalatable elements is, however, inherently fragile and subject to radical disturbance: for the revelation of Connie's affair 'came as the most terrible blow and shock' to Clifford (288), inducing a 'crisis of falsity and dislocation, hysteria, which is a form of insanity' (289).

Furthermore, Clifford's repression of this negative knowledge of Connie's affair evokes Nietzsche's entry on the self's appropriative or its 'digestive' capacity, alluded to in the previous chapter.[12] According to Nietzsche the expansive, appropriating self incorporates knowledge of the other and the world according to its *'plastic strength'* by synthesising the contradictory and domesticating the unfamiliar (Muller-Lauter 1999: 39). Key here is the need to constitute oneself with a sense of coherence in one's relation to the world. Prior to the devastating disclosure of the affair, Clifford has apparent mastery of Connie within his stable, coherent, and familiar perspective and world: '[h]e was used to her. She was as it were embedded in his will' (Lawrence 2006: 294). To retain this mastery and interpretative security, however, Clifford evinces the limits of his 'digestive' ability. For resembling Nietzsche's description of the self's antithetical, restrictive drive, Clifford exemplifies the 'acceptance and approval of ignorance' with regards the foreign, the contradictory, or the disturbing: that is, the knowledge of the affair (*BGE* 230: 161). Indeed, Clifford's chief complaint towards his wife is that this news has shattered his familiar, routine world, destroying 'the fabric of his daily existence' (Lawrence 2006: 294). Clifford's active rejection of consciousness of the affair thus marks what Nietzsche would call Clifford's 'defensive posture', signalling the limits of his ability to emotionally and cognitively assimilate this refractory experience (*BGE* 230: 161).

Indeed, the term 'defensive posture' could be applied to summarise Clifford's character more generally. This defensiveness primarily takes the form of a pathological, narcissistic self-enclosure that is characterised by a withdrawal from painful relations with others. On the one hand, Clifford's self-enclosure is a protective, self-preservative recoil following the previous violation of his selfhood: having had the coherence and continuity of his being ruptured by his war injury, his withdrawal marks the closure of the self's boundaries in relation to the perfidious outside world. Clifford's self-prudential strategy is tropistically represented by his treatment of Wragby Wood: he wanted to 'protect' the wood, to have the 'place inviolate, shut off from the world', as it had been denuded to contribute to the war effort (Lawrence 2006: 42). However, on the other hand, his desire for impervious self-containment predates the war and this can be tied primarily to his sense of emotional vulnerability, of what Morag Shiach calls Clifford's 'precarious sense of self' (Shiach 2001: 92).

Lawrence's stress on Clifford's recoil and defensiveness evokes his first critical work, his *Study of Thomas Hardy* (1914). This essay, which originally had the Nietzschean title, *Le Gai Savaire*, sees Lawrence broadly follow Nietzsche's contestation of the Darwinian argument that the cardinal drive of organic life is that of self-preservation. According to Nietzsche, the healthy organism accumulates force only to discharge this in activity. The drive to self-expenditure, rather than that of self-preservation, is illustrative of the organism's abundance of power. Nietzsche thus argues that '[t]he wish to preserve oneself is a sign of distress', reflective of a particularly weak disposition (*GS* 349: 207). Lawrence deploys a similar dichotomy and adduces the image of the phoenix to exemplify the squandering economy: the phoenix 'attains to fatness and wealth and all things desirable, only to burst into flame and expire in ash' (Lawrence 1985: 10). Taking the symbol of the phoenix's rebirth to convey a plenitude that induces self-transcendence, Lawrence challenges what he assumes to be the dominant interpretative orientation of modernity: '[w]e always hold that life is the great struggle for self-preservation; that this struggle for the means of life is the essence and whole of life. As if it would be anything so futile, so ingestive' (13). What is more, not only does this restrictive perspective foreclose self-realisation, but Lawrence predicts that the prudential impulse will be intensified by the suffering experienced in the war:

> And we must be prepared to fight, after the war, a renewed rage of activity for greater self-preservation, a renewed outcry for a stronger bushel to shelter our light. We must also undertake the incubus of crippled souls that will come home. (17)

Clifford can be seen to embody this 'renewed rage' for 'greater self-preservation'. And just as Nietzsche sees physiological, affective decay tied to the ascetic ideal and its self-preservative drive, Lawrence follows suit in his portrayal of Clifford. Indeed, Lawrence's characterisation of Clifford as exemplifying this heightened prudential posture echoes Nietzsche's claim that 'the ascetic ideal springs from the protective and healing instincts of a degenerating life which uses every means to maintain itself and struggles for its existence' (*OGM* III 13: 93). For, together with Nietzsche's 'theoretical man', Clifford resembles the two character types that Nietzsche identifies with the reactive values of the ascetic ideal in the *Genealogy*, namely the ascetic priest and the slave. This is firstly apparent regarding the aristocrat's assumption of a metaphysical or ascetic perspective, the dual world view that posits an idealised existence in contrast to inferior, earthly being. Clifford explicitly espouses such views: embodied being, he informs Connie is 'an encumbrance' (Lawrence 2006: 234); in further contradistinction to Nietzsche's privileging of bodily consciousness, Clifford argues that God is 'slowly eliminating the guts and alimentary system from the human being, to evolve a higher, more spiritual being' (235). In other words, Clifford evinces what Nietzsche refers to as a 'hatred of the human, and even more of the animalistic, even more of the material' (*OGM* III 28: 127).

The aristocrat Lady Bennerley corroborates Clifford's opinions. She is more explicit in attributing human suffering to embodied being and likewise considers scientific progress to signal a departure from afflicted corporeality:

> "So long as you can forget your body you are happy," said Lady Bennerley. "And the moment you begin to be aware of your body, you are wretched. So, if civilization is any good, it has to help us to forget our bodies, and then time passes happily without our knowing it". (Lawrence 2006: 74–5)

This endorsement of hedonic principles, in which pleasure or happiness is viewed as the highest good, holds scientific methodology as the instrument towards attaining the transcendent. The intellectual elites thus assume the optimistic outlook of Alexandrian culture, as Nietzsche presents it in *The Birth of Tragedy*, believing in 'the rectification of the world through knowledge and in a life guided by science' (*BT* 17: 85). As Nietzsche later aligns science with the ascetic ideal, considering science as its latest manifestation of the ascetic idealisation of truth, so Lawrence presents Clifford 'reading one of the latest scientific-religious books' as he 'was egocentrically concerned with the future of his own ego' (Lawrence 2006: 233).[13] Suggesting the proximity of science to religious-salvific discourse, Clifford turns to such literature to avert the terrifying encounters with the void at the core of being and hence contemplation of the self's absolute expenditure.

Lawrence depicts the aristocrat in terms strikingly close to Nietzsche's figure of the ascetic priest. Emphasising the perversity of Clifford's denial of erotic-affective being, Lawrence's narrator asserts that Clifford is 'triumphing over life in spite of life' (140). This judgement evokes Nietzsche's insight that the 'ascetic life is a self-contradiction', seeking 'to be master' over 'life itself and its deepest, strongest, most profound conditions' (*OGM* III 11: 91). That is, on the one hand, 'the ascetic ideal is a trick for the *preservation* of life' (II 13: 93): it allows its adherents to order and harness antagonistic passions in their striving towards a fictional 'true world'. On the other hand, however, the excision of those refractory instincts impeding realisation of one's pure, transcendent being induces a 'slow suicide' (*GS* 131: 123). This observation points to Nietzsche's claim that man would prefer 'to will *nothingness* rather than *not* will' (*OGM* III 1: 72). Clifford, suffering from an incapacity to engender feelings of self-mastery and thus failing to constitute himself as a goal-bound agent, thereby conforms to Nietzsche's view that the ascetic ideal is a radical means of self-preservation adopted by degenerating life forms failing to control the self's conflicting drives. Through this connection with Nietzsche's priest, I hold Lawrence to be suggesting that Clifford also connives at his own emotional insentience in his ascetic pursuit of transcendence.

Clifford's defensive self-enclosure evokes another dimension of Nietzsche's analysis of the ascetic ideal: slave morality's restrictive ontology 'says "no" on principle to everything that is "outside", "other", "non-self"' (*OGM* I 10: 21). For, as Connie discerns, Clifford's isolation, his need to be 'shut in' and 'cut off' from the industrial midlands, is related to his fear of, and attendant negation of, the other: '[h]e was in some way afraid' of the miners, 'his own men; but he saw them as objects rather than men, parts of the pit rather than parts of life, and crude raw phenomena rather than human beings along with him' (Lawrence 2006: 15–6). Clifford's reification of the workers derives from his prudential, self-protective posture. According to Scott Sanders,

Clifford is 'locked within the fortress of his ego', maintaining the 'illusion of the isolated ego, self-sufficient and all-powerful' (Sanders 1985: 3). While concurring with this assessment, it is important to emphasise that his isolation derives from his sense of woundedness, as the narrator observes: 'he could not bear to have them look at him now he was lame' (Lawrence 2006: 15–6). That is, this sense of fragility informs and attends his defensive-appropriate posture. As Sanders notes, Clifford thus 'regards the rest of the cosmos as the infringement of his bloated self' (Sanders 1985: 5): this 'illusion of separation', or contrived distance between self and the other, is directly related to his fear of 'infringement' (4). He correspondingly fosters distant and hierarchical, instrumental relationships. As Sanders puts it, 'the attitude of domination presupposes a master and something *else* to be mastered' (4).

Jeff Wallace similarly notes in his discussion of Lawrence's critique of instrumental reason that the domination of the other forecloses the possibility of fluid, porous relations between the self and the other. Suggesting a defensiveness at the heart of this economy, Wallace argues that, '[t]he promise of domination' must keep 'a safe distance between subject and object' (Wallace 2005: 237). The self 'must remain non-dialectical', preventing an 'intimate relationship with the other' (237). Consequently, 'nothing really touched' Clifford (Lawrence 2006: 16). And it is in these terms of rigid, closed dichotomies of self and other that Lawrence examines the denial of emotional and physical intimacy in Clifford's relationship with Connie: for 'they were so utterly out of touch'; 'he never touched her. He never even took her hand and held it kindly' (112).

Give and Take

Connie's relationship with Clifford is characterised by ascetic self-denial. The couple are contained within fixed, Apollonian boundaries of separate identity that preclude intimacy. However, while Connie is largely a victim of Clifford's paralysis and emotional deadness, she is also complicit in her own self-abnegation. For instance, prior to meeting Clifford, the youthful Connie shares a similar ascetic demotion of the physical: her 'whole dignity and meaning in life consisted in the achievement of an absolute, a perfect, a pure and royal freedom. What else did a girl's life mean?' (7). Desiring to extricate herself from embodied and socially-embedded being, her early goal is to 'shake off the old and sordid connections and subjections' (7). The erotic is one such 'sordid connection', for sex is considered merely 'a sort of primitive reversion and a bit of an anti-climax' (7). Not only does this citation suggest that hitherto the common goal or meaning directing Connie's generation is that of transcending the corporeal, it also indicates that outside this conventional perspective Connie lacks her own personal meaning.

The novel stresses that the drive for a spiritually pure, transcendent, or cerebral existence is unsustainable: while Connie is originally attracted to Clifford's intellectual superiority, over time 'the mental excitement had worn itself out and collapsed' (97). Therefore, '[a]s the years drew on, it was the fear of nothingness in her life that affected her. Clifford's mental life, and hers—gradually it began to feel like nothingness' (50). Principally due to the absence of emotional-erotic intimacy, she becomes aware of a 'growing restlessness' and a vague feeling that 'she was going to pieces in some way' (20).

One of the chief purposes of the novel is to present the practical nihilistic consequences of the ascetic denial of erotic, embodied being. With regards to Lawrence's portrayal of Connie in this respect, her physiological demise conveys the impact of the couple's characteristic neglect of the corporeal. For instance, Connie observes that, '[h]er body was going meaningless,' that it was '[o]ld through neglect and denial' (Lawrence 2006: 70–1). Attending this awareness of her decline 'she began to be afraid' of her own finitude. And, echoing Clifford's fear of the *'horror vacui'*, Connie's further contemplation of her own dissolution terrorises her, inducing a paralysing loss of agency: perceiving the world to be permeated by 'hopeless inertia', she becomes 'immensely depressed, and hopeless' (70); she consequently feels that '[t]he days seemed to grind by with curious painfulness, yet nothing happened' (76). Lawrence, like Nietzsche, depicts the pathos of nihilism as a twinned cognitive and affective phenomenon.

The doctor's diagnosis of Connie's deterioration is significant: referring to her loss of '"vitality"', he warns her that she is '"spending"' her life '"without renewing it"' (78). The doctor's analysis of her degenerative condition, induced by her selfless care of Clifford, anticipates her own later perception of the modern condition: 'weary, worn-out for lack of a little tenderness, given and taken' (254). What is more, for Connie this absence of a vital exchange of sympathy in the relationship brings about a bitter, 'cold indignation against Clifford and his writing and his talk' (71).

Briefly turning to Lawrence's near contemporaneous essay, 'We Need One Another' (1929), where he similarly articulates subjectivity as porous and fluid, illuminates his description of Connie's bitterness in the novel. Here Lawrence argues that '[i]t is in the living touch between us and other people, other lives, other phenomena that we move and have our being' (Lawrence 1961: 190). He describes this 'living contact' of 'give and take' as 'a quivering and flowing towards someone, something that will receive [an] outflow and send back an inflow, so that a circuit is completed' (191). There are a couple of things worth noting here. Firstly, it is implicit that there is ultimately a reflexive nature of this dynamic encounter with the other: there is a further gain or return to the self, or an intensification of selfhood, even as there is some form of self-expenditure as the self 'gives' to the other. Furthermore, Lawrence stresses that should this 'circuit' be frustrated, then the individual becomes discordant and vindictive, seeking to hurt 'everyone within range' (191).

Lawrence's emphasis on revenge and its association with frustration or impotence recalls Nietzsche's notion of *ressentiment* as it is explored in the *Genealogy*.[14] Moreover, the erotic nature of Connie's frustration evokes Zarathustra's 'The Night Song', where the prophet discloses his own rancour at his lonely isolation. Here, finding that '[a] gulf stands between giving and receiving', Zarathustra conveys the bitterness arising from an unrequited love, of a gift-giving that is not reciprocated:

> A craving for love is in me [...] But I live in my own light; I drink back into myself the flames that break out of me. I do not know the joy of the receiver [...] A hunger grows from out of my beauty: I should like to rob those to whom I give – thus do I hunger after wickedness [...] Such vengeance does my abundance concoct: such spite wells from my solitude. (*TSZ* II 9: 129)

Connie's vindictive indignation mirrors what Henry Staten calls Zarathustra's 'economy of erotic *ressentiment*' represented in this song (Staten 1990: 156). For a deep 'sense of injustice, of being defrauded, had begun to burn in Connie' against Clifford and the selfless outpouring of the substance of herself (Lawrence 2006: 72). And there is an explicit moment of realization where Connie seeks to justify her otherwise irredeemable sense of loss:

> A sense of rebellion smouldered in Connie. What was the good of it all! What was the good of her sacrifice, her devoting her life to Clifford? What was she serving, after all? (72)

Connie's sense of 'deep physical injustice' (71), and the need to find an explanation for her suffering, recalls a key claim Nietzsche makes in the *Genealogy*: '[w]hat actually arouses indignation over suffering is not the suffering itself, but the senselessness of suffering' (*OGM* II 7: 48). And, just as Nietzsche analyses these overpowering feelings of 'indignation' at unassimilated distress in his account of the slaves' *ressentiment*, Lawrence focalises this experience of useless suffering through Connie to observe that, '[t]he physical sense of injustice is a dangerous feeling, once it is awakened. It must have outlet, or it eats away the one in whom it is aroused' (Lawrence 2006: 72). This 'outlet', as Nietzsche discerns, which allows 'a release of the emotions' to provide the 'greatest attempt at relief', is the identification of a guilty party:

> For every sufferer instinctively looks for a cause of his distress; more exactly, for a culprit, even more precisely for a guilty culprit who is receptive to distress,—in short, for a living being upon whom he can release his emotions, actually or in effigy, on some pretext or other. (*OGM* III 15: 99)

Tellingly, Lawrence stresses the instinctive, emotional power of this 'physical sense of injustice' consuming Connie. This manifests in her reproach of Clifford. Connie's attempts to rationalise these sentiments, to exculpate Clifford by reflecting that '[h]is was the greater misfortune' in which he was 'part of the general catastrophe', are overridden by the persistent need to attribute culpability: '[a]nd yet, was he not in a way to blame? This lack of warmth, this lack of simple, warm, physical contact, was he not to blame for that?' (Lawrence 2006: 72). Lawrence's representation of the potency of these vindictive feelings suggests the largely imaginary form such sentiments take, and again echoes Nietzsche's analysis of *ressentiment* in the *Genealogy*:

> And she realized for the first time, what a queer subtle thing hate is. For the first time, she had consciously and definitely hated Clifford, with vivid hate: as if he ought to be obliterated from the face of the earth. And it was strange, how free and full of life it made her feel, to hate him and to admit it fully to herself. (192)

By highlighting the sense of liberty and power that such thoughts induce, this elicitation of Connie's relish at the imagined extermination of Clifford surpasses the evocations of Mellors' annihilatory rage. Examining the protagonists' respective struggles to surmount their grievances and these attendant reactive sentiments in more depth below, I shall turn to focus on Lawrence's complex portrayal of sympathy in the novel: compassionate feelings may entail self-loss, and hence engender reactive postures, on the one hand; on the other, a deep sympathetic identification with the other contains the potential to establish a life-enhancing, reciprocal contact and exchange. Doing so, sympathy gestures towards the overcoming of vindictive sentiments in Lawrence's vision.

'Pity Is *Practical* Nihilism'

Commentators have noted Lawrence's antipathy towards notions of compassion and pity. For example, Jae-Kyung Koh claims that, '[t]he central criticism which Lawrence levelled at Western Civilisation was that, due to its Christian foundations, it had given too high a value to ideas of altruism and sympathy' (Koh 2007: 16). Adam Phillips and Barbara Taylor echo this reading of Lawrence's negative appraisal of sympathy: '[a]ll compassion is self-pity, D. H. Lawrence remarked, and this usefully formulates the widespread modern suspicion of kindness' (Phillips and Taylor 2010: 7). According to these critics, Lawrence's view exemplifies what they see to be a general proclivity to withhold sympathetic feelings towards others. However, having noted that the novel was originally conceived with the title of *Tenderness*, it is pertinent to invoke Mark Spilka's insightful reading of Lawrence's oeuvre given that Spilka detects a paradigmatic shift regarding Lawrence's treatment of sympathy, of feeling with others, in his later work (see Spilka 1967). Attributing this to biographical reasons—Lawrence overcame his own personal defensiveness deriving, for instance, from an intensely close relationship with his 'devouring' mother—Spilka claims that this transformation sees Lawrence come to embrace the qualities associated with expansive personal emotions, of tenderness, warmth and sympathy. Nevertheless, close attention to the role of compassion in this text reveals a complex portrayal of sympathetic feelings. To explore the tensions at work here, I shall begin by pointing to the strong parallels with Nietzsche's largely negative analyses of the dynamics of pity. Doing so, I will show that, as with Nietzsche, Lawrence's highly complex portrayal of sympathetic sentiments resonates again with the theme of meaningless suffering.

Nietzsche's objection to the valorisation of sympathy or pity which he sees at the core of Christian morality can be crudely summed up by referring to passage 134 from *Daybreak*: pity 'increases the amount of suffering in the world' (85). In manifold ways pity, Nietzsche argues, merely intensifies suffering for both the sufferer, the recipient of pity, and the pitier, the one who identifies with the sufferer. Pity, for Nietzsche, is a '*harmful* affect' that entails 'losing oneself' (85).

Lawrence's novel amply demonstrates the validity of Nietzsche's analyses of, and negative view of, the role of pity. For instance, Connie's relationship to Clifford can be adduced with regard to the '*harmful* affect' that others' suffering can have upon the pitier. Given, then, that her name Constance evokes a sense of loyalty, that her compassionate nature is evident in her youthful participation in social ameliorative projects as well as her role in the provision of aid to wounded soldiers, she can be seen to be particularly receptive to Clifford's suffering.[15] The narrator thus points out that Clifford 'was a hurt thing. And as such, Connie stuck to him passionately' (Lawrence 2006: 15). Furthermore, Clifford's injuries invoke a conventional sense of duty, as Bell puts it: '[t]here is a sense of compassion, imbued with ethical value, which requires her to respond to Clifford in a positive way' (Bell 1992: 215). However, having already discussed the life-denying consequences of the absence of warmth between the couple, Connie's depression is arguably compounded by sympathetically identifying with Clifford's distress. Echoing Nietzsche's contention that pity is 'contagious' and has 'a depressive effect', the pain that consumes Clifford's being, rendering him insentient, induces Connie's own depression: as the deep, overwhelming wound 'spread in him, Connie felt it spread in her. An inward dread, an emptiness, an indifference to everything gradually spread in her soul' (Lawrence 2006: 49). This sense of 'emptiness' Connie is subject to corroborates Nietzsche's claim that 'pity is *practical* nihilism. [...] pity persuades to *nothingness*!' (*AC* 7: 130).

The potentially nihilistic consequence of identifying with others' pain is again registered with Lawrence's portrayal of Connie's relation to Michaelis. Here Lawrence conveys that the pitier may be manipulated by the recipient of pity. Repeatedly Michaelis is described in terms which emphasise his sense of grievance, his nihilistic 'disillusion', bitterness, and vulnerability (Lawrence 2006: 23). Moreover, he actively seeks to impress his suffering upon Connie, 'sending out an appeal that affected' Connie as 'an infant crying in the night' (25). He consequently 'roused in the woman a wild sort of compassion and yearning' (29) and 'she was utterly incapable of resisting' his 'awful appeal' (26). Connie's response signals an absolute self-abandon, self-sacrifice to the other: 'she must give him anything, anything' (26), observes the narrator. With Connie's yielding to Michaelis' 'appeal' to her sympathetic sensibility, she ignores her better judgement, and her instinctive repulsion of the play-wright. These instincts are proven correct when Michaelis blames her for their sexual incompatibility, bringing about her own nihilistic disillusion.

A further dynamic of pity presented in the novel, which accords with Nietzsche's analysis of the phenomenon, regards its harmful impact upon the recipient of pity. Lawrence's presentation of Clifford's relation to his carer, Mrs Bolton, highlights the danger of being subject to the other's pity. This is particularly evident when Mrs Bolton consoles Clifford when he receives notice of Connie's affair with Mellors. Here, resolving that Clifford 'must weep' in order to overcome his hysterical reaction, Mrs Bolton determines to simulate identification with Clifford by recollecting her own loss. Notably, this act of 'suddenly summoning up all her old grief and sense of woe, and weeping the tears of her own bitter chagrin' suggests both the persistence of unredeemable wounds and an incapacity to really identify with the other's distress (290). Nevertheless, and while reinforcing the narcissistic subjectivities Lawrence is exploring, the car-er's exhausting conjuring of past wounds works to 'release his self-pity': 'in a contagion of grief', Clifford was soon 'weeping for himself' (290). Moreover, Clifford's outflow of grief is described as 'sheer relaxation on his part, letting go all his manhood, and sinking back to a childish position that was really perverse' (291). There is a corresponding shift in power relations between the couple: as he yields 'absolutely', Mrs Bolton becomes 'the Magna Mater, full of power and potency, having the great blond child-man under her will and her stroke entirely' (291). Clifford's surrender, in shared suffering, marks an extreme loss of autarkic selfhood which the narrator disparages as '[t]he wallowing in private emotion, the utter abasement of his manly self' (291). Furthermore, Mrs Bolton's domination recalls Nietzsche's view on pity as a mode of 'conquest' in which others' suffering presents an 'opportunity to take possession' of the one in distress (*GS* 14: 40).

This continuity between love and pity in Nietzsche's thinking, and his somewhat defensive resistance to these twinned forms of emotional vulnerability, is noted by Staten: '[l]ike pity, love is a permeability of the boundary of individuation or a pouring-out of the substance of the self' (Staten 1990: 155). From this perspective, pity and love thus both signal a heightened fragility with the potential loss of autonomous self-hood to the other. The Clifford-Mrs Bolton relationship is repeatedly depicted in these terms of appropriative 'love', suggesting this point of continuity with Nietzsche's negative appraisal of pity. For, particularly in the role of Clifford's carer, Mrs Bolton's love for her patient and subsequent domination of Clifford strongly resonates with Nietzsche's analysis of the 'egoism of love': 'submission, making oneself indispensable and useful to those in power; love, as a secret path to the heart of the more powerful—so as to dominate him' (*WP* 7: 406). Lawrence, then, follows Nietzsche in undermining notions of pure selflessness associated with love and pity according to romantic ideals and conventional morality: while Mrs Bolton '*thought* she was utterly subservient and living for others' (Lawrence 2006: 97), in actuality according to the narrator, '[g]radually, with infinite softness, almost with love, she was getting him by the throat, and he was yielding to her' (98). Mrs Bolton's apparent selfless subordination, marked by her early deference and compliance, is contrasted with an increasingly perfidious possession of the other. Lawrence, then, subtly dramatises the fluid dynamic of power relations: not only does he capture the shifting relationality of this energetic, he also depicts the Nietzschean realisation that passive yielding and active domination are inextricably bound in a power continuum.

In light of this threat to autarkic selfhood presented by love and pity as it is depicted in this pathological relationship, one can apprehend the posture assumed by the novel's social elites: like the Chatterleys, the Wragby intellects are 'all inwardly hard and separate' (72), maintaining clear, Apollonian 'boundaries of the individual' (*BT* 4: 26). Furthermore, what Lawrence stresses in his depiction of the cerebral coterie is their excessive recourse to a calculative rationality that precludes any form of sympathetic identification with the other. Like Clifford, they, too, exemplify the posture of the Alexandrian or theoretical man who dare not glimpse the Dionysian. For example, the writer Hammond considers that the other's suffering is a '"concern only [for] the person concerned, and, like going to the privy, [has] no interest for anyone else"' (Lawrence 2006: 32). He thus espouses disengagement from '"the matters of ordinary life"' (31), which are '"all utterly senseless and pointless"' (32). While my previous analysis of Connie's identification with

Clifford's trauma would seem to corroborate such a view given that I pointed to the limits of such deep sympathy and the resultant pathos of nihilism that Connie experiences, it would be mistaken to see the novel gesture towards such an antithetical defensive posture. For, as I pointed out above, the novel makes it clear that such a prudential position, characterised by rational mastery and fearful detachment, ultimately leads to barren sterility. Indeed, Lawrence's portrayal of the intellectual elites brings to mind the philosopher Martha Nussbaum's analysis of Stoicism. According to Nussbaum, the Stoic argument for self-command appeals to 'images of softness and hardness to contrast vulnerability to external conditions with the dignified absence of such vulnerability' (Nussbaum 1994: 146). What is more, she claims that, '[t]he Stoic looks like a fearful person, a person who is determined to seal himself off from the risk' involved in 'attachments that can go wrong and cause deep pain' (159–60). That is, at the core of the defensive position is a desire to avert any encounter of senseless suffering, of relationships that may entail self-loss. It is thus through the novel's exemplary relationship between Connie and Mellors that Lawrence presents a counter to the prevalent self-preservative impulse that dominates the world of the novel. Yet, even with Lawrence's desire to present an affirmation of one's vulnerability and the 'deep pain' that the intimate relationship entails, there remains the pull of an Apollonian mode of separate, individuated existence.

LOVE AND DEATH

As the novel's protagonists embark on their affair, they, too, are presented to be in states of recoil and withdrawal from the painful contact with the other. Again, the shoring up of the self's boundaries is tied to their respective experiences of past suffering. Mellors, for instance, is described in terms strikingly close to Clifford's defensiveness:

> Especially he did not want to come into contact with a woman again. He feared it: and he had a big wound from old contacts. He felt, if he could not be alone, and if he could not be left alone, he would die. His recoil away from the outer world was complete. His last refuge was this wood. To hide himself there!' (Lawrence 2006: 88)

Prefiguring the great disturbance to self-contained identity that the erotic encounter holds, the initial contact between the couple is primarily depicted in terms of a violent intrusion of the other upon the self (see 69). Moreover, Lawrence stresses the involuntary, embodied nature of the sympathetic feelings that instigate the affair. The description of Mellors' response to Connie's depression evokes both his loss of rational self-possession and the proximity of, or entwinement of, these tender feelings with the erotic: Mellors perceives 'something so mute and forlorn in her, compassion flamed in his bowels for her' (115); he is rendered 'powerless' and, '[w]ithout knowing', his 'helplessly desirous hand' performs a '[b]lind instinctive caress'; the 'flame' at the 'back of his loins' intensifies as he reaches out to her in sympathy (115–6). The erotic encounter is thus depicted as an extension of, or intensification of, compassionate feeling. This is clearly evident, for instance, in a later passage: '[a]nd he went into her softly, feeling the stream of tenderness flowing in release from his bowels to hers, the bowels of compassion kindled between them' (279).

In portraying the loss of rational self-possession in the erotic-sympathetic relation, Lawrence echoes Nietzsche in identifying the ecstatic Dionysian experience with the erotic. For instance, in *The Birth of Tragedy* Nietzsche claims that 'the nature of the *Dionysiac*' refers to 'the blissful ecstasy which, prompted by the same fragmentation of the *principium individuationis,* rises up from man's innermost core' (*BT* 1: 16). The Dionysian, which is 'most immediately understandable to us in the analogy of *intoxication*' according to the thinker, thus also represents the internal libidinous urges that overwhelm and annihilate personal self-identity. This is suggested throughout the text: cue Nietzsche's reference to the orgiastic licentiousness at the Greek Dionysia; and the image of the Dionysian Greek in the form of the satyr, is, for instance, presented as a 'symbol of nature's sexual omnipotence' (8: 40).

Having registered Lawrence's negative portrayal of sympathy above regarding the attendant threat of nihilism, how then does one apprehend this apparent valorisation of these feelings in the Mellors-Connie relation? One approach to reading the novel's complex rendering of compassionate relations is to heed the narrator's self-conscious interjection with regards to the role of the novel. This intrusive narrative voice articulates what Bell calls 'one of Lawrence's classic statements about the novel' (Bell 1992: 213):

For even satire is a form of sympathy. It is the way our sympathy flows and recoils that really determines our lives. And here lies the vast importance of the novel, properly handled. It can inform and lead into new places the flow of our sympathetic consciousness, and it can lead our sympathy away in recoil from things gone dead. (Lawrence 2006: 101)

According to this authoritative narrative voice, the 'properly handled' novel operates to exemplify or inculcate 'a spirit of fine, discriminative sympathy' (101). As Bell puts it, '[t]he detection of false feeling, the wrong kind of "sympathy", is central to the book' (Bell 1992: 211). Lawrence's implied reader is thus 'to recognise that sympathy can have a minus sign' (213). Focalising through Connie, Lawrence highlights the negative, exhaustive impact of compassionate feelings insofar as they are performed to comply with a hitherto privileged ethical principle: while practicing compassion implicitly bestows purpose to her life during the war prior to her marriage with Clifford, it is her selfless care of the paralysed Clifford, expressing a persistent sympathy towards 'things gone dead', that induces her growing feelings of emotional exhaustion and bitterness. In challenging the viability of our hitherto highest values and its moral imperatives, examining their life-enhancing or life-denying impact, Lawrence's novel is partaking in the deconstruction of their abstracted, absolutised and ossified formulation. Bell's point, that Lawrence communicates the necessity of possessing a discriminatory capacity, that sympathy requires finesse, is equally instructive for reading Connie's sympathetic response to Michaelis given that she ignores her better instincts in yielding to his affective call. Yet, as shown above, Lawrence's complex rendering of the erotic-sympathetic relation suggests that one's capacity to determine one's flow of sympathy, and to detect false feeling, is foreclosed once one enters a deep identification with the other: Lawrence's evocation of the couple's tender, compassionate feelings emphasises the largely involuntary and overwhelming nature of this Dionysian affective flow.

Lawrence's vision of the Dionysian erotic encounter registers the strains entailed in the necessary and painful surrender of autarkic selfhood. Coinciding with Nietzsche's presentation of Dionysian intoxication as a transformative loss of self-possession that is marked by profound anguish, Lawrence dramatises the tension between the impulse to relinquish oneself and the opposing desire to maintain autonomous control in the midst of the erotic encounter. That is, the erotic relation can be read to correspond to Nietzsche's insights regarding tragedy's paradoxical energetic: in both Nietzsche's account of ancient tragedy and in

Lawrence's depiction of the Connie-Mellors affair the loss of individuated form may be celebrated as it permits contact with the other and with larger, vital cosmic forces that transcend the individual. However, this self-fragmentation is accompanied by an affective vulnerability, provoking cognisance of self-loss, of one's ultimate ephemerality. Relatedly, Lawrence portrays the characters' impulse to reconstitute the Apollonian boundaries of individuation following any surrender of self-control. Examining the lovers' respective responses to their mutual erotic awakening thus reveals a profound ambivalence. For Lawrence presents the concomitant resistance to the sympathetic flow or interexchange as their respective egos battle this overwhelming force of erotic-sympathy: Mellors 'fought against' his tender and erotic feelings (Lawrence 2006: 115); concerning Connie, Shiach notes that such passion 'leads to a loss of self which she both celebrates and fears' (Shiach 2001: 93). Particularly through Connie, Lawrence captures the self's sense of precarious exposure as it submits to the other in the sexual encounter. This fearful loss of autonomous selfhood that grips Connie is attended by an intimation of one's finitude: as Connie 'went all open to him', '[s]he yielded with a quiver that was like death' (Lawrence 2006: 173).

The association of love and death is familiar within the Western canon (see Dollimore 1998). Nietzsche's contribution to this discourse, in the pronouncements of Zarathustra, anticipates Lawrence's depiction of Connie's 'death' in love. Articulating this relation between love and death within the context of a parable that evokes *Thus Spoke Zarathustra's* central theme of self-overcoming, the prophet declares: '[l]oving and perishing: these have gone together, from eternity. Will to love: that means to be willing to die, too!' (*TSZ* II 15: 145). Zarathustra's ideal of squandering, or 'perishing', through love seems to suggest that love offers one mode to create 'beyond oneself', of attaining self-transcendence. The death of Connie's existent self is attended by the birth of a new, fragile self:

> Another self was alive in her, burning molten and soft in her womb and bowels, and with this self she adored him. [...] In her womb and bowels she was flowing and alive now, and vulnerable, and helpless in adoration of him as the most naïve woman. (Lawrence 2006: 135)

Lawrence depicts her transfiguration through an idiom of liquescence to stress the self's porous delicacy in this most intensive, dynamic interexchange with the other. Furthermore, Lawrence suggests that this fluid, protean self experiences a heightened sensibility towards the larger circumambient world: for Connie, on her way home following intercourse, 'the trees in the park seemed bulging and surging at anchor on a tide, and the heave of the slope to the house was alive' (178). The affirmative erotic experience is the basis of a centrifugal, expansive sensibility, an animistic receptivity to the world's otherness. This portrayal of the erotically energised self reverberates with Nietzsche's description of the Dionysian re-enchantment of nature, offering a temporary release from alienated, individual being.[16]

It is important to stress that Lawrence emphasises the delicacy of this heightened, affirmative state. Recalling the earlier discussion of Nietzsche's Dionysian man, where I noted simultaneous feelings of anguish accompanying those of enraptured ecstasy, Lawrence highlights Connie's profound ambivalence at the peak of affirmation.[17] Her torment leads to a reactive closure of the self's breached boundaries, a resumption of conscious mastery. While suggesting a necessary Apollonian reconstitution of individuated being, her oscillations register the strain that the self undergoes in this heightened state: 'tormented by her own double consciousness and reaction', this divided state constitutes her 'real grief' (172). What is more, focalised through Connie, Lawrence portrays this need to self-augment as entailing a compensatory appropriation of, or violation of, the other. Dionysian imagery of *sparagmos*, or the sacrificial destruction of the victim, is heavily suggested here as Connie reacts to her terrifying loss of self-control: 'if she adored him too much, then she would lose herself, become effaced, [...] a slave' to the other (135); consequently, a reactive 'hard passion flamed in her for a time, and the man dwindled to a contemptible object'; she feels 'the force of the Bacchae in her limbs and her body,' and the man is 'the mere phallus-bearer, to be torn to pieces when his service was performed' (136). Inverting the image of the expansive Dionysian vision, the defensive-appropriative dynamic of these thoughts is stressed. For Connie the man is reified as a 'pure god-servant to the woman'; fearing the non-objectified, non-subjugated other disturbing this vision of self-aggrandisement, she reflects, '[t]he man, the individual, let him not dare intrude' (136).

Conveying Connie's possessive desire as largely reactionary, as a compensatory augmentation of her fragile sense of selfhood, Lawrence's novel adds another dimension to Nietzsche's notion that 'sexual love' reveals itself 'as a craving for new *property*' (*GS* 14: 40). For while the philosopher claims that sexual love 'may in fact be the most candid expression of egoism' in that it is characterised by a drive to absolutely possess the beloved other, Lawrence's exposition of Connie's anguish further suggests that this possessiveness also arises as a reactive fear to the self's dissolution in moments of heightened intimacy, particularly 'in the flux of new awakening' (Lawrence 2006: 136). Additionally, Connie's articulation of this temptation to reify and instrumentalise the exposed other for one's own self-intensification recalls the description of her youthful affairs:

> A woman could take a man, without really giving herself away. Certainly she could take him without giving herself into his power. Rather she could use this sex thing to have power over him. For she only had to hold herself back, in the sexual intercourse, and let him finish and expend himself without herself coming to the crisis; and then she could prolong the connection and achieve her orgasm and her crisis while he was merely a tool. (7–8)

Again sex is considered in these appropriative-instrumental terms. However, what marks Connie's transformation, or self-overcoming, is her resistance to these strong and familiar defensive-appropriative urges. Realising that '[i]t was early yet, to begin to fear the man', she admits that she is 'weary' of these 'barren, birthless' instrumental relations (136). Otherwise put, as this mode of being entails self-conscious mastery, foreclosing the deep sympathetic circuit of give and take with the other, there is no necessary ego dissolution and correspondent Dionysian rebirth. Nevertheless, this compensatory re-assertion of selfhood is indicative of a necessary limiting of one's self-expenditure; it is suggestive of a fragility deriving from previous emotional-erotic wounds. Thus while the excessively prudential Clifford and his coterie are associated with emotional sterility, on the one hand, Connie's heightened anguish in response to her erotic-affective vulnerability registers the dangers attending an extreme breach of one's boundaries, on the other. This point can be further discerned when examining Lawrence's presentation of Mellors within the depiction of the erotic encounter. Together with Connie's resolution to relinquish 'her hard bright female power' at the height of erotic intensity, the description of Mellors in these scenes gestures to the novel's gender ideology (136).

THE POLITICS OF EROS

A number of critics writing on Lawrence's presentation of erotic-sympathetic relations suggest that both the man and the woman undergo an equal, somewhat democratic experience of self-relinquishment in the novel's valorised erotic encounter. For instance, Simone de Beauvoir asserts that, '[w]oman must, like man, abdicate all pride and all will' (de Beauvoir 1953: 252). More recently, Martina Ludwigs argues that the novel subverts the 'inherently hierarchical sexual relationship' with both partners 'giving up control and willing self-abasement' (Ludwigs 2011: 4–5). Kirsty Martin also observes that sympathy in Lawrence's work 'involves submission' and the loss of 'one's personal control' (Martin 2013: 132, 138). These readings fail to discern, however, that Lawrence depicts a subtly distinct position with regards to the male: while Mellors realises that he, too, must yield to his deeper sympathetic impulses, that coming 'into tender touch' with Connie was 'the thing he had to do', it is noteworthy that he resolves to do so 'without losing his pride or his dignity or his integrity as a man' (Lawrence 2006: 279). There appears to be a tension in Lawrence's presentation of the squandering ideal: while he seems to celebrate an intensive, involuntary sympathetic-erotic experience, which involves the Dionysian dissolution of one's rational self-possession on the one hand, he simultaneously gestures towards Mellors' need to maintain some sort of integral core of selfhood on the other. While this observation may align my argument with feminist critiques that highlight the woman's subordinate role, I shall nuance this reading by remaining attentive to the novel's dominant thematic of the problem of nihilism. This preoccupation, I contend, governs Lawrence's depictions of gender relations in the novel.

One way to account for Mellors' contradictory posture is to read it as signalling a defensive need: like Connie, he similarly struggles to courageously yield and 'perish'. Indeed, Mellors' protective desire to retain his 'integrity' is understandable when one observes that his recurrent feelings of embittered indignation largely derive from past erotic hurt. For instance, somewhat echoing the idiom of Dionysian *sparagmos* alluded to above, he complains to Connie that his estranged wife, Bertha Coutts, '"always ripped [him] up"' (Lawrence 2006: 280). From Mellors' point of view, he has been the sacrificial victim of the devouring, appropriating female, experiencing a pointless dispersal of his selfhood. His resolve to retain a degree of conscious mastery may thus imply a need to safeguard against the abandon that dangerously exposes the self to the other.

This apparent defensive strategy evokes Nietzsche's comment in his unorthodox autobiography, *Ecce Homo* (1888), in which the thinker expresses his resistance to the devouring female: '[t]hey all love me [...] Happily I am not prepared to be torn to pieces: the complete woman tears to pieces when she loves' (III 5: 45). However, where Nietzsche's entry ambiguously contains positive connotations of the 'perfect woman', Mellors' account of his wife aligns her with the cold, compensatory cruelty that Connie ultimately manages to suppress and overcome. For Mellors relays that his wife oscillated in the sexual relation, that she 'loved [him] in moments. But she always took it back, and started bullying' (Lawrence 2006: 279). Bertha seems to be recovering her sense of self through the devastation of the other.

Nevertheless, despite gesturing towards a reading of Mellors' restrictive economy as a reactive limitation of his self-expenditure, I believe that invoking Nietzsche's analysis of sexual love encourages an alternative interpretation of Mellors' posture. According to Nietzsche:

> Woman wants to be taken, adopted as a possession, wants to be absorbed in the concept 'possession', 'possessed'; consequently, she wants someone who *takes*, who does not himself give or give himself away; who on the contrary is supposed precisely to be made richer in 'himself'—through the increase in strength, happiness, and faith given him by the woman who gives herself. Woman gives herself away; man takes more. (*GS* 363: 228)

As we have seen with Lawrence's rendering of Connie's complex feelings attending her erotic vulnerability, the novel undoubtedly complicates this vision of the woman's desire to be 'possessed'. Nevertheless, exploring Connie's conflicting affects, the novel valorises female submission, thus corroborating Nietzsche's conventional gender hierarchy: Connie's transfiguration is dependent on the overcoming of 'her hard bright female' will; the novel strongly associates the ubiquity of hurtful, instrumental sexual relations with the egoistic, appropriating female as several commentators have noted. What is more, according to Nietzsche's view of this exchange dynamic, the woman's yielding confers on the male with an 'increase in strength, happiness, and faith'. In terms of the novel, the import of the male's appropriative flow, as I read this passage to apprehend Mellors' posture, cannot be overstated: Mellors is invigorated with the capacity to engender new meaning, new value. Otherwise put, this hierarchical erotic dynamic, as Nietzsche outlines it, is central to understanding the characters' capacity to overcome nihilism and constitute new significance.

While critics generally focus on Connie's more obvious transformation, attending to Mellors' parallel development is crucial. His transfiguration is particularly significant in marking the transition from a condition akin to Nietzsche's description of 'passive nihilism' to that of one exhibiting the capacity to constitute a newfound sense of agency through the creation of a new cognitive orientation or purpose. This critical oversight regarding the import of Mellor's transformation is suggested, for example, in Wayne Burns' assessment of the gamekeeper:

> Mellors is [...] Lawrence's idealized self-image. [...] Mellors is so perfect, from the beginning, that he cannot possibly develop or even change. He has all the right feelings, all the right ideas, and knows all the right answers. (Burns 1993: 86)

Kate Millett similarly views Mellors to embody a 'solid identity' and 'infinite assurance' (Kate 1992: 76). I disagree with these readings and instead find it significant that prior to meeting Connie Mellors 'did not know what to do with himself' and existed 'day to day, without connection and without hope' (Lawrence 2006: 141). He is conscious of his aimlessness and perceives his own solitary existence, which consists of raising game for the wealthy on the Wragby estate, to be characterised by a sense of 'futility, futility to the nth power' (142). He can thus be aligned with the general, indifferent and purposeless populace: he, too, embodies the 'apartness, and hopelessness' that characterises the epoch (153). Significantly, it is only 'when this woman had come into his life' and the affair begins that Mellors consciously reconsiders his need to find his purpose: having 'not cared nor bothered till now' about his lack of direction (142), he now ruminates that he has '"no business to take a woman into [his] life, unless [his] life does something and gets somewhere, inwardly at least"' (276). Moreover, Mellors' drive to articulate a new meaning and purpose intensifies following intercourse with Connie. His renewed striving for purposeful activity implies that he has benefited from the positive flow, or the 'increase in strength, happiness, and faith' conferred to him by the woman's yielding, as Nietzsche conveys it in his outline of sexual love. Suggesting the import of the erotic on these terms, the narrative voice refers to coition as 'the creative act that is far more than procreative' (279).

In an earlier theoretical work, *Fantasia of the Unconscious* (1922), Lawrence makes a series of claims that anticipate his depiction of the erotic and its relation to meaning constitution in *Lady Chatterley*. For instance, here Lawrence contends that, '[m]en, being themselves made new after the action of coition, wish to make the world new' (Lawrence 1971: 108). Echoing Mellors' awakened yearning to join with others to 'fight that sparkling electric Thing outside there' (Lawrence 2006: 120), to destroy the impersonal industrial order, Lawrence claims in *Fantasia* that, as a result of 'successful sex union', the man 'craves' for 'the hope of purposive, constructive activity […] or the hope of passionate, purposive *destructive* activity: the two amount religiously to the same thing, within the individual' (Lawrence 1971: 187). Lawrence's insistence on the drive to engage in 'purposive activity', whether creative or deconstructive, recalls Nietzsche's claim that 'any goal at least constitutes some meaning': 'even the development toward a state of universal annihilation', Nietzsche argues, permits one to reflexively experience oneself as a willing agent of deeds (*WP* 12 (A): 12). Lawrence follows Nietzsche in this discursive text, and by extension in *Lady Chatterley*, by insisting on the need for meaning, of a cognitive orientation to stimulate and direct one's purposeful willing.

At the centre of *Fantasia* is a dialectic of passional and cerebral modes of being. For instance, any 'ideal purpose' that emerges, Lawrence contends, must have 'roots in the deep sea of passionate sex' (Lawrence 1971: 187). This dialectic gestures towards the productive Dionysian-Apollonian dynamic Nietzsche describes in *The Birth of Tragedy* insofar as Lawrence stresses the need to arrive at a fine balance between passional and intellectual forces. Just as Nietzsche laments the degenerative shift towards an Alexandrian or theoretical mode of being at the expense of the Dionysian, on the one hand, so Lawrence claims that when 'purposiveness' is held 'as the one supreme and pure activity in life', and the erotic is consequently neglected, there is a 'drift into barren sterility' (110). In the novel, Connie's deterioration within her marriage, exemplifying the modern condition, would illustrate this point. On the other hand, however, just as Nietzsche evokes the pathos of nihilism that attends the Dionysian, Lawrence similarly holds that passional forces must be held in check: '[a]ssert sex as the predominant fulfilment, and you get the collapse of living purpose in man' (110).

Nietzsche's analysis of sexual love also serves to caution against the potentially nihilistic consequences of the erotic experience:

> The passion of a woman, in its unconditional renunciation of her own rights, presupposes precisely that on the other side there is *not* an equal pathos, not an equal will to renunciation; for if both should renounce themselves from love, the result would be—well, I don't know, maybe an empty space? (*GS* 363: 228)

According to Nietzsche, this 'eternally "immoral"' exchange is dependent on the male appropriative drive: if the male fully partakes in the expenditure of one's selfhood, and so fails to augment himself, there is only a mutual projection into nothingness (*GS* 363: 228). As Staten puts it, in the case of an equal, reciprocal love, according to Nietzsche, 'there would be nothing left, no one to preserve being as each spilled toward the other, both would cease to exist: *horror vacui*, the nausea of spilling into a void' (Staten 1990: 166). Lawrence's novel stresses the need for the male to preserve and replenish himself in the erotic relation; on such terms we may read Lawrence's valorisation of Connie's resolve to yield. Therefore, while this contact with the female other entails a Dionysian experience of self-loss, Mellors' resolve to retain his integrity in the erotic encounter gestures towards the male need to distinguish and strengthen himself in order to generate a new vision of purpose. The appropriating male must retain a degree of Apollonian self-presence: if the male is absolutely overwhelmed by sympathetic-erotic feelings, there is only a collective impoverishment and disintegration, a resultant failure to formulate purposeful significance. As Lawrence puts it, 'you get the collapse of living purpose in man'. This point, that the democratic erotic-affective exchange would see neither party contributing to the generation of new meaning, can also be related to Nietzsche's view that one's experience as an effective agent depends upon a hierarchical organising capacity: regarding the self (or society), a dominant drive must establish itself, giving form to the plurality of competing impulses, and impose its telos; in the absence of this 'tyranny' there would be only non-productive conflict and paralysis.[18]

The novel, commonly read as a celebration of sexual love, therefore crucially stresses the need for new meaning and purpose which, while rooted in erotic fulfilment, is also something that surpasses the erotic. Sex, Lawrence claims in *Fantasia*, may 'disintegrate society', and so it must be 'subordinated to the great dominating male passion of collective *purpose*'. In the novel Mellors seems to recognise that '[s]ex as an end in itself is a disaster' (Lawrence 1971: 110). For not only does Mellors celebrate the newfound peace of chastity at the novel's coda, but also, in a pivotal exchange with Connie, where she asks him if his existence '"will have less point"' living with her, he warns that he is '"not just [his] lady's fucker, after all"' (Lawrence 2006: 276). Relatedly, he informs her: '"[a] man must offer a woman *some* meaning in his life, if it's going to be an isolated life, and if she's a genuine woman.—I can't be just your concubine"' (276). Indeed, insofar as Lawrence implicitly registers the primary importance of possessing meaning and hope to ground the successful erotic-sympathetic relation, it can be contended that he diverges from his intended privileging of the body.[19] For the novel observes that feelings of despair bound to the absence of meaning or lack of faith regarding the possibility of realising one's goal preclude the erotic relation on which the very potential of generating new hope and meaning depend. Connie's consequent perception of Mellors' vacillation into hopelessness following intercourse illustrates this point: '[t]hat was the death of all desire, the death of all love: this despair that was like the dark cave inside the men, in which their spirit was lost' (206). This conundrum is anticipated earlier in the novel with Connie's apprehension of Michaelis' similar disposition: 'she felt the reflection of his hopelessness in her. She couldn't quite, quite love in hopelessness. And he, being hopeless, couldn't ever quite love at all' (29). Importantly, Mellors rouses himself from his gloom when Connie, for the first time in the novel, provokes him to formulate his significance.

Feminist critics have commented upon the novel's privileging of male leadership. De Beauvoir and Simpson connect this vision to Lawrence's elevation of male purposive activity (see de Beauvoir 1953: 228–9). However, what is absent in their respective critiques is sufficient consideration of Lawrence's preoccupation with nihilism and senseless suffering. That is, one must keep in mind that Lawrence's insistence on the male's bestowal of meaning is, like Nietzsche's, addressing the ever-present threat of a life-nauseating collapse of willing. Lawrence's portrayal of Connie's relationship with the dominant male characters evinces the novel's sexual ideology in these terms. For instance, as Connie anticipates the inevitable intrusion of the hostile world coming between her and Mellors, she exclaims, '[i]f only *he* would make her a world' (Lawrence 2006: 212). Moreover, Clifford is explicitly castigated for abnegating this responsibility. This arises at the point where he consents to Connie's proposal of finding a surrogate partner to provide an heir to Wragby. Clifford's response reinforces the apprehension of the absence of agency he suffers from: he asserts that the arrival of a child would provide him with '"something to strive for"' insofar as he could feel that '"one was building up a future for it"' (111–2). Bound to his condition of passive nihilism, he also assumes a selfless, subordinate stance as he informs Connie: '"I mean, but for you, I am absolutely nothing. I live for your sake, and your future. I am nothing to myself"' (111–2). As this declaration of 'private worship put her in a panic', Lawrence conveys Connie's 'deepening dismay and repulsion' in gender terms:

> It was one of the ghastly half-truths that poison human existence. What man in his senses would say such things to a woman? But men aren't in their senses. What man with a spark of honour would put this ghastly burden of life-responsibility upon a woman, and leave her there, in the void? (112)

As Spilka observes, Connie's 'chronic' and 'basic problem' in the novel is '"the ghastly burden of life-responsibility" which Clifford puts upon her' (Spilka 1978: 202). Clifford, as previously noted, is initially attracted to Connie's 'assurance' and her sense of purpose. Now it is possible to fully see that his derision of existent values and hierarchies at the novel's opening does not lead to the construction of new meaning. He is in the throes of passive nihilism as those hitherto dominant values disintegrate. As demonstrated, his determinedly ascetic, cerebral existence intensifies the nihilistic conundrum, foreclosing the potential of generating a new significance.

Mellors' courage to express a new meaning diverges from Clifford's self-destructive, ascetic force and Michaelis' embittered disillusionment. Furthermore, Mellors' determination to preserve his integral selfhood during coition not only stands in opposition to the majority of men who 'insisted on the sex thing like dogs' but also contrasts to Clifford's extreme self-abandonment to Mrs Bolton (Lawrence 2006: 7). Clifford's perversity can now be fully apprehended: devoured by the appropriating female, this illustration of excessive male self-surrender signals the complete collapse of the possibility of meaning-generation and the overcoming of nihilism. Nevertheless, Lawrence subtly undercuts the male's exalted position, thus eroding the gendered binary distinction that the novel's ideology depends upon. That is, as I have largely presented it, the Mellors-Connie relation supports the standard feminist position voiced, for instance, by Judith Ruderman: 'the phallus always demands annihilation in the sense of complete capitulation of woman to man' (Ruderman 1992: 113). This gender hierarchy, where 'the man is the teacher (and preacher) and the woman his pupil', is given new emphasis in the final version of the novel as Sheila Macleod notes (Macleod 1987: 240).[20] Focussing, however, on the import the novel places on the dynamic of meaning constitution problematises the active-passive binary that such readings rest upon. This point is evinced in chapter XVIII where Connie challenges Mellors, for the second time in the novel, as to the '"point of [his] existence"' (Lawrence 2006: 277): Mellors not only fails to articulate this, but he also acquiesces to Connie's offer to formulate his purpose: '"[i]t's the courage of your own tenderness"', she tells him, '"that will make the future"' (277). That Mellors endorses Connie's explicit articulation of his personal significance cannot be understated: Lawrence argues in his 1925 essay, 'Blessed are the Powerful', that 'the real *exercise* of power' consists in determining or formulating the future orientation of one's life; as noted throughout this study, the capacity to impose a singular interpretation of one's life, to posit a goal, comprises the highest expression of the will to power according to Nietzsche (Lawrence 1979: 507).[21] Considering Connie's active, reciprocal role here, encouraging Mellors to reaffirm his inchoate and fragile sense of purpose, serves to complicate views holding Lawrence to be merely depicting the feminine in 'compliance to masculine direction and prerogative' (Millett 1992: 73). To reinforce this reading of Connie as a dynamic, leading force within this relationship I shall further scrutinise the problem of 'senseless suffering' afflicting the protagonists.

AN AFFIRMATION OF SUFFERING?

As Ludwigs points out, the word 'tenderness' itself is closely tied to notions of pain (Ludwigs 2011: 5). As I have implied above, suffering is integral to the novel's vision of self-transcendence: the novel's action confirms the painful need to squander one's egoistic security to enable one to potentially grow and flourish. Mellors and Connie thus develop from respective conditions of defensive recoil, defined by their past grievances, to become porous and dynamically engaged with the other in the erotic relation. This manoeuvre cannot be thought of without an intensification of suffering. Thus Mellors' articulation of his apprehension of the need to relinquish his self-contained identity, which is formulated as he anticipates the inevitable '"complications"' that will attend the affair, exemplifies the novel's ideology: '"It's life. [...] There's no keeping clear. And if you do keep clear, you might almost as well die. So if I've got to be broken open again, I have"' (Lawrence 2006: 117–8). The protagonists are clearly defined in opposition to the populace at large, and to the intellectual elites who evince a similar self-preservative aversion to difficulty and pain. Simply put, the novel's paradigmatic relationship illustrates Nietzsche's point that 'all becoming and growing—all that guarantees a future—involves pain' (*TI* X 4: 120).

Critical responses to the text nevertheless suggest that the novel's affirmative vision involves an overcoming of, or an amelioration of, pain. For example, T. H. Adamowski claims that, in the depictions of Connie's orgasmic fulfilment, Lawrence is 'imagining a miracle' (Adamowski 1985: 49) whereby the sexual encounter ultimately brings 'stability, recurrence, and coherence—an existence that is providing itself with a foundation' (47). Other critics echo Adamowski's view of Lawrence's utopian erotic in which the self attains 'a calm totality in full possession of itself' (49–50). For example, Koh contends that:

> Connie's choice is to yield up herself to 'new life' to heal her psychic trauma and to seek the tenderness of life. Her giving up of conscious control over herself leads her to a fuller and more fulfilling life. (2007: 177)

Note Koh's use of 'heal' here, subtly suggesting that the telos of the novel lies in the overcoming of suffering and the attainment of happiness. Michael Squires offers a similar reading by arguing that 'Connie eases the pain of life in the great outer world by escaping to the wood' (Squires 1975: 200). Thus, according to Squires, 'Connie and Mellors discover peace of mind' in the pastoral sanctuary (201). Ludwigs goes further and suggests that Connie's resolve to yield to Mellors enacts a utopian, democratic relation: '[T]he zero-distance model of love that the novel promotes, that of a tender touch that reaches the core of the other, overcomes the problem of separateness, alienation, mutual misunderstandings, and competing interests' (Ludwigs 2011: 15).

To assert, however, that Lawrence depicts a vision in which suffering is overcome, or aims at the palliation of pain, would situate the novel with the optimistic vision Nietzsche associates with both Alexandrian culture and with the ascetic ideal. From these cognate perspectives suffering 'counts as an objection to life' (*WP* 1052: 543). Given that I have argued that Lawrence presents the protagonists' transformation in opposition to the self-preservative pursuit of happiness associated with these related cultural forms, I shall turn now to challenge and complicate these interpretations of the novel.

Firstly, to contest those readings stressing the novel's depiction of a 'harmonious sex relation', I shall expand upon a claim alluded to above: namely that the protagonists are fully conscious of the fact that entering the relationship itself will entail an intensification of suffering (Daleski 1965: 286). For example, aware of the inevitable entanglement with Clifford, and of the gossip that will proliferate and engulf them, the couple nevertheless determine to embrace the relationship even as Mellors concedes that he was no longer '"buoyant"' and that '"[e]very bitterness and every ugliness would hurt him: and the woman!"' (Lawrence 2006: 148). More importantly, the couple also realise that greater suffering shall arise from internal, emotional sources. In contrast to Connie's sister, Hilda, who 'wanted no more of that nasty sex business' (239), the couple acknowledge that they are '"a couple of battered warriors"' who are '"returning to the fray"' (213). The confrontation with one's previous emotional wounds presents the greatest challenge to their capacity to affirm the pain of '"being broken open"' again.

Furthermore, as the preceding discussion has suggested, Lawrence paints a far more complex picture of the sexual experience than that of the self arriving at a point of absolute 'calm' self-possession or 'peace of mind'. This includes the strain observed above in relation to the individual's desire for self-control on the one hand, and the conflicting drive for sympathetic communion on the other. The suffering experienced from a state of heightened self-division is thus integral to the erotic-sympathetic and regenerative relationship. Furthermore, regarding Ludwigs' contention that the couple attain a 'zero-distance' resolution, I would argue that, on the contrary, the novel repeatedly insists upon the ontological isolation of the individual. Indeed, this sense of separateness is perhaps most evident particularly at the height of sexual intimacy, thus accounting for the self's greater sense of vulnerability at this moment. For instance, in the second sexual encounter in the Connie-Mellors' relation, Connie is grieved by her cognisance of detachment, that 'she was left out, distant', while Mellors comes to climax. He, however, is unaware of her tears and 'thought she was there with him'; for Connie, this unconnected other is a '[s]tranger' and thus '[s]he even resented him a little' (126).

The lack of sympathy between the couple in such instances can also be explained by Mellors' attestation that his tender feelings come and go.[22] That is, once a deep sympathetic connection is established it is not fixed and permanent. Rather, as Bell observes with regards to Lawrence's work in general, any emotional resolution is episodic, rather than absolute (Bell 2004: 55). The fluctuating sympathetic bond between the couple is illustrated, for instance, by Connie's reaction to the news she receives, while in Venice, of the scandal unfolding around Mellors and his estranged wife. Having determined that 'she musn't let go' 'in her inner consciousness' of their shared tenderness while apart, realising that she would be consequently 'lost, lost utterly in this world of riff-raffy expensive people and joy-hogs', Connie nevertheless recoils from the 'nasty blow' of the scandal threatening to implicate her: she contemplates abandoning her lover (Lawrence 2006: 256). While Connie ultimately dispenses with these thoughts, they nevertheless testify to the fragility of the relation. Furthermore, on her return she is startlingly insensitive to Mellors' distress, compounding his humiliation by relaying Clifford's derogatory judgment of him as a '"dog with a tin can tied to its his tail"' (275); Mellors suppresses his indignation towards Connie's cruelty, and so '[s]he never knew the fierce bitterness with which he resented the insult' (275). The other is again presented as detached or opaque, and Lawrence seems to be conveying a fundamental solitude of the individual. Indeed, Lawrence's use of free indirect discourse itself contributes towards this sense of the self's opacity, for the reader cannot absolutely determine whether one is entering the consciousness of the narrator or of the focalised character throughout the novel.

The fragility of the relation is also evident regarding the novel's infamous sodomy scene in Chapter XVI. According to Spilka, this scene is 'doctrinally insistent, at the expense of honest and dramatic context, about the value of purging Connie of organic shame' (Spilka 1978: 208). The dramatic context points to Mellors' sense of inadequacy and compensatory spitefulness arising from Connie's decision to go to Venice: while Connie comes to acknowledge with some 'mis-giving' that she was 'giving her man the go-by', her departure signals her shame at the source of her pregnancy (Lawrence 2006: 237). Spilka attends to this emotional context to contend that Lawrence 'conveniently forgets that Mellors needs to be purged of excessive fear and anger and of the self-doubt that implies' (Spilka 1978: 208–9). The ideological intent of the scene, then, in which Lawrence presents Mellors in the 'fearless role of phallic hunter', occludes Mellors' 'excessive fear and anger': Mellors' predatory domination of Connie expresses a profound bitterness and vulnerability (208–9). Graham Hough's assessment of the relationship is therefore germane: the couple 'are deeply injured and unhappy people: what they find in each other is the almost desperate satisfaction of desires that have long been cramped and distorted. And that is not at all like the simple flowering of natural passion and tenderness which Lawrence wishes to recommend' (Hough 1975: 166).

In the previous chapter I noted the fragility of Nietzsche's affirmative project; *Lady Chatterley's* affirmative vision appears similarly brittle. This is evident when one examines the potency of those reactive, vindictive sentiments that the protagonists struggle to overcome. The appearance of these feelings signals their respective incapacities to assimilate or redeem previous grievances. It is relevant to note that Connie incites her lover to recall his relationship with his wife, and thus '"his big wound"', particularly at the height of affirmation (Lawrence 2006: 88). Making this connection, I wish to equate Mellors' confrontation with his past with Nietzsche's ideal of '*amor fati*', love of one's fate: '[m]y formula for greatness in a human being is *amor fati*: that one wants nothing to be other than it is, not in the future, not in the past, not in all eternity' (*EH* II 10: 37). David Owen points to the 'experiential character' of this thought, noting that Nietzsche conceived it in a moment of 'overflowing joy' (Owen 1995: 107). Consequently, it can be seen to serve as a test of one's capacity to reinterpret and thus affirm one's past grievances from one's present vantage point. As Owen puts it, from such a position 'one would suffer all the frustration, despair, etc., again as a condition of possibility of this rapturous moment' (108). In a relevant notebook entry Nietzsche refers to this as performing a 'Dionysian affirmation of the world as it is, without subtraction, exception, or selection' (*WP* 1041: 536). To further clarify the weight placed on one's present moment towards one's interpretative activity, Kathleen Marie Higgins observes that, '[o]ne's activity in the present has impact on the entirety of time anyway, even disagreeable moments in the past. One's activity in each moment reweighs the entire causal nexus in which one exists' (Higgins 2008: 70). From Mellors' position of relative potency and affirmation, the recollection of his bitter experiences can therefore be viewed as an emotional-psychological test in which he can examine his ability to redeem or appropriate his previous suffering. Insofar as Mellors stands in contradistinction to those who populate the world of the novel, the workers and the elites who share a similar desire to repress previous wounds that remain raw, this episode signals a tentative progressive vision. However, it is clear that Mellors fails to perform what Nietzsche's Zarathustra would call a translation of "'[i]t was'" into an "'I wanted it thus!'" (*TSZ* II 20: 163), the reinterpretation necessary to surmount a retaliatory rage against the irreversible past: Mellors, who has insisted throughout that he has a "'[b]ellyful of remembering'" (Lawrence 2006: 204) and that he doesn't "'quite digest [his] bile'" (168), declares that he "'could wish the Clifford and Berthas all dead'"; he regrets that he had not shot Bertha and "'ended the whole misery!'" (280). Rather than construing Mellors to have 'all the right feelings', it is apparent that he, too, incarnates the vindictive rage permeating the fictional landscape of the novel. Moreover, it is this underlying, consuming rancour that thwarts him from articulating his own sense of significance. That is, regarding the aforementioned crucial scene where Connie challenges Mellors to declare his purpose, he concedes that while he "'can feel something inside'" him, he cannot express this: it is "'all mixed up with a lot of rage'" (Lawrence 2006: 277). Importantly, where he had previously roused himself from despair to gratify Connie's initial demand to articulate his personal sense of significance, now this emotional dissonance engendered by this provocation of unassimilated distress precludes him from discerning and expressing this vision. That Connie is able to articulate their shared meaning, contest his denunciations of his former lovers, and rebuke his exterminatory exclamations suggests not only her greater emotional resilience but also indicates the couple's potential to surmount these debilitating reactive sentiments.

Mellors' use of digestive metaphors to convey his emotional-erotic suffering evokes, and yet stands in opposition to, Nietzsche's image of the 'strong and well-formed man' who 'digests his experiences (including deeds and misdeeds) as he digests his meals, even when he has hard lumps to swallow' (*OGM* II 16: 101).[23] Mellors' annihilatory proclamation, signifying his repudiation of those unpalatable aspects of his life, rather recalls Clifford's restrictive economy: Mellors displays an incapacity to attain self-mastery through the assimilation of his past grievances. Mellors, it would seem, fails to synthesise these refractory experiences and, coming across a blockage to his interpretative will to power or mastery, is beset by resentful impotence that forecloses his possibility of generating new meaning. Thus, paralleling my earlier analysis of Connie's bitter indignation towards Clifford, Mellors' annihilatory proclamation can be viewed as a continued expression of a vindictive sensibility: his suffering remains senseless and his consuming indignation is only placated by the imaginary thought of a vengeance perpetrated against the identified culprits.

Lawrence aligns Connie and Mellors with Clifford to register the potency of these reactive desires and the depth of their respective grievances. Notably, this alignment, in conjunction with the observation of the characters' shared defensive postures, complicates the apparent binary structure of the novel's characterisation (see Daleski 1965: 265). Rather, Lawrence is highlighting his characters' respective capacities to self-regulate undigestible grievances and thus the degree to which these reactive sentiments consume them. Pointing to the modernists' engagement with 'unassumable' suffering, these reactive feelings also feature heavily in Kafka's *The Trial* (1925) and Beckett's *Endgame* (1957), texts that similarly focus upon powerless subjectivities. Clifford, as I have implied throughout, is repeatedly portrayed in terms of impotence, and often his ineffectualness is closely associated with vindictiveness. For example, his stories are conveyed as 'meaningless' and 'rather spiteful', 'very personal stories about people he had known' (Lawrence 2006: 16). Moreover, Clifford's reactionary response to Connie's disclosure of the affair at the novel's denouement evinces an exterminatory desire that can be apprehended in terms of his feelings of powerlessness: the narrator comments upon Clifford's 'sheer, unspeakable, impotent hate' when he exclaims that Connie '"ought to be wiped off the face of the earth!"' (296). And juxtaposing Clifford's restrictive economy, of the defensive posture of denying and rejecting the refractory, with these destructive sentiments, the narrator observes that Clifford 'couldn't even accept the fact' of Mellors' existence (296).

Lawrence follows Nietzsche in depicting morality as the instrument of the wounded and powerless to condemn the other. For instance, earlier in the novel when Connie failed to kiss Clifford goodnight 'after he had spent an evening reading to her', Clifford invokes the traditional virtue of selflessness to denounce Connie's egoism: '[s]he was callous, cold and callous to all that he did for her. He gave up his life for her, and she was callous to him' (139–40). Injured by what is seemingly a minor occasion of self-loss, of a lack of return for his reading, he inflames his sense of moral indignation by contrasting his total and righteous self-sacrifice to Connie's selfishness, her contravention of the 'formalities that life depends' on (139). As aforementioned, this proclaimed posture of selflessness stems from feelings of impotence, from an incapacity to master himself and posit his own meaning. At the novel's denouement Lawrence again juxtaposes morality with retribution as Clifford appeals to Connie's sense of duty to insist that she fulfil her obligation or promise to return to Wragby from Venice: Mellors presciently warns, '"[h]e wants to begin his revenge on you'" (292). Furthermore, Clifford's recourse to conventional moral binaries to demonise the other suggests his incapacity to exact an actual revenge: '[s]uddenly he had become almost wistfully moral, seeing himself the incarnation of good, and people like Mellors and Connie the incarnation of mud, of evil' (296). Mirroring Nietzsche's account of the slaves' appeal to morality to exercise retribution, Clifford's reactionary, exterminatory desire becomes more refined, less explicit, as he denounces Connie's immoral affair with the bestial Mellors.

Indeed, Mellors' attempt to vindicate his exterminatory logic is grounded upon his identification of Clifford's and Bertha's shared retributive drives. That is, Mellors' view of the novel's antagonists resonates with Nietzsche's identification of impotence and vengefulness: for Lawrence's protagonist claims that Bertha and Clifford '"can't live"' and '"[t]heir souls are awful inside them"'; they consequently '"only frustrate life"' (280). This view can be read alongside Nietzsche's contention that 'one thing is needful: a human being should *attain* satisfaction with himself [...] Whoever is dissatisfied with himself is continually prepared to avenge himself for this' (*GS* 290: 164).

Mellors' rationalisation of his desire to annihilate Bertha and Clifford also reverberates with Nietzsche's own reactionary defensiveness. That is, Mellors' murderous fantasy recollects my argument from the previous chapter that Nietzsche assumed similar reactive sentiments towards 'the sick'.[24] Among several such comments that I alluded to, Nietzsche declared that 'everything weak, sick, ill-constructed, suffering from itself [...] *ought to perish*' (*EH* XIV 8: 104). To repeat: what must be kept in mind regarding both Nietzsche's generous, expansive visions and these restrictive, defensive announcements, is that the overcoming of feelings of suicidal nihilism remains his central preoccupation: this dominating concern inflects such pronouncements. Here, then, in one such exclusionary declaration the philosopher claims that the pathos of distance between the healthy and the sick 'ought to be the chief concern on earth': for the healthy 'alone are *guarantors* of the future' (*OGM* III 14: 97). In terms of Lawrence's novel, which I have argued is similarly preoccupied with surmounting the threat presented by an endemic depressive loss of willing and nausea with life, it is the protagonists who can be perceived solely in the role of '*guarantors* of the future': in a 'worn-out' world succumbing to 'hopeless inertia' (Lawrence 2006: 254), Connie and Mellors exemplify a tentative but courageous self-overcoming and, as such, together they constitute a fragile new meaning (70). Nevertheless, having made the point that Mellors' vindication of his exterminatory logic may imply the need to protect the novel's '*guarantors* of the future' against the vindictiveness of the wretched and the sick, I maintain that this reactive posture simultaneously undermines the novel's expansive vision and underlines its brittleness.

Perhaps, then, as Lawrence's protagonists seek to fulfil their vision of tenderness and so surmount these consuming vindictive sentiments, Connie's resolve to detach herself from Clifford suggests the limits of Lawrence's centrifugal vision. A full affirmation of the other, a non-exclusionary 'Dionysian affirmation' of all, particularly of the sick and vindictive who threaten the self's flourishing, remains beyond the protagonists' reach. Here, echoing Nietzsche's suggested acknowledgement of his own digestive limits as he resolves to 'let *looking away* be [his] only negation' (*GS* 276: 151), Connie similarly determines that, regarding Clifford, '[s]he didn't want to hate him. She didn't want to be mixed up very intimately with him in any sort of feeling' (Lawrence 2006: 194). This normative position, suggesting the 'pathos of distance' that Nietzsche repeatedly privileges, illustrates Connie's determination not only to direct her flow of feeling away from 'things gone dead', but also exemplifies an ability to regulate extreme, negative feelings.

Lawrence's depiction of the self struggling to control the vindictive emotions arising from unredeemed suffering and feelings of impotence corroborates my view of Lawrence's continued engagement with Nietzschean themes in *Lady Chatterley's Lover*. And while I have also highlighted the novel's treatment of the primary need to confer meaning, or a goal, in order to avert the pathos of suicidal nihilism, it is clear that the constitution of meaning is entwined with the need to assimilate or digest one's experience of useless suffering. Here, then, lies the overlooked importance of Nietzsche to Lawrence's final novel. I shall now turn to examine Kafka's *The Trial*, a text that places similar emphasis upon the potency of vindictive sentiments arising from one's failure to interpretatively appropriate and affirm one's suffering.

NOTES

1. Others observing extreme, direct influence include Geoff Dyer: Lawrence was 'not so much transformed as formed by Nietzsche'. Geoff Dyer, *Out of Sheer Rage: In the Shadow of D. H. Lawrence* (London: Little, Brown and Company, repr., 2009), p. 186; John Carey calls Lawrence 'the major English disciple of Nietzsche'. John Carey, *The Intellectuals and the Masses:*

Pride and Prejudice Among the Literary Intelligentsia, 1880–1939 (London: Faber and Faber, 1992), pp. 10–1. H. Steinhauer claims: 'Lawrence espouses Nietzsche's irrationalism to a degree that would have embarrassed his master'. H. Steinhauer, 'Eros and Psyche: A Nietzschean Motif in Anglo-American Literature', *Modern Language Notes*, 64 (1949): 221. John B. Humma contends 'there could hardly be a more strikingly complete anticipation of one author's ethic by another's than in the way Nietzsche's ethic anticipates that of Lawrence'. John B. Humma, 'D. H. Lawrence as Friedrich Nietzsche', *Philological Quarterly*, 53 (1) (1974): 120.

2. For example, see Green, Eleanor H., 'Blueprints for Utopia: The Political Ideas of Nietzsche and D. H. Lawrence', *Renaissance & Modern Studies*, 18 (1974): 141–61 (159).

3. See Chapter 1, pp. 9–12.

4. In *A Propos of "Lady Chatterley's Lover"* Lawrence describes the larger cultural malaise, which has its roots in a hedonically orientated pessimism, in similar terms: 'Today is already the day after the end of the tragic and idealist epoch. Utmost inertia falls on the remaining protagonists. Yet we have to carry on'. D. H. Lawrence, 'A Propos of "Lady Chatterley's Lover"', in D. H. Lawrence, *Lady Chatterley's Lover* (London: Penguin, repr., 2006), p. 330.

5. See Chapter 2, pp. 36–7.

6. See Chapter 2, pp. 26–31.

7. See Chapter 2, pp. 29–30.

8. See Chapter 1, p. 11.

9. See Chapter 1, pp. 11–12.

10. See *TSZ* Prologue 5: 46; see Chapter 2, pp. 56–7.

11. See Chapter 2, p. 27.

12. See Chapter 2, pp. 39–40.

13. See *OGM* III 25 and *OGM* III 27.

14. See Chapter 2, pp. 42–3.

15. I am indebted to Michael Bell for this point regarding Constance's name and its significance. Michael Bell, *D. H. Lawrence: Language and Being* (Cambridge: Cambridge University Press, 1992), p. 215.

16. See Chapter 2, pp. 27–8.

17. See Chapter 2, pp. 28–30.

18. See Chapter 2, pp. 31–2, on the 'disgregation' of the will; see also *BGE* 19.

19. On Lawrence's favouring of the corporeal see his letter to Earl and Achsah Brewster, April 1928: "As I say it's a novel of the phallic Consciousness: or the phallic Consciousness versus the mental-spiritual Consciousness: and of course you know which side I take. The *versus* is not my fault: there should be no *versus*. The two things must be reconciled in us. But now they're daggers drawn". Quoted in Mark Kinkead-Weekes, 'Eros and Metaphor: Sexual Relationship in the Fiction of Lawrence', in *Lawrence and Women*, ed. by Anne Smith (London: Vision Press, 1978), pp. 122–35 (p. 117).

20. For considerations of the relation between *Lady Chatterley's Lover* and the two previous versions of the novel see, for instance, John Worthen, *D. H. Lawrence and the Idea of the Novel* (London: MacMillan, 1979).
21. D. H. Lawrence, 'Blessed are the Powerful', in *D. H. Lawrence: A Selection from Phoenix*, ed. by A. A. H. Inglis (Harmondsworth: Penguin, 1979), pp. 505–13 (p. 507). 'Living consists in doing what you really, vitally want to do: what the *life* in you wants to do, not what your ego imagines you want to do. And to find out *how* the life in you wants to be lived, and to live it, is terribly difficult. Somebody has to give us a clue. And this is the real *exercise* of power.'
22. See Lawrence 2006: 289. Mellors informs Connie: '"Ay! [tenderness] comes an' goes, like in me."' Also see Lawrence 2006: 207.
23. See Chapter 2, pp. 52–3.
24. See Chapter 2, pp. 62–3.

References

Adamowski, T. H., 'The Natural Flowering of Life: The Ego, Sex, and Existentialism', in *D. H. Lawrence's 'Lady': A New Look at Lady Chatterley's Lover*, ed. by Michael Squires and Dennis Jackson (Athens: University of Georgia Press, 1985), 36–57.

Bell, Michael, *D. H. Lawrence: Language and Being* (Cambridge: Cambridge University Press, 1992).

———, 'Reflections on Violence: Writing and/as Violence in Lawrence', *Etudes Lawrenciennes*, 31 (2004): 49–64.

Burns, Wayne, '*Lady Chatterley's Lover*: A *Pilgrim's Progress* for Our Time', in *D. H. Lawrence: Critical Assessments Vol. 3, the Fiction (2)*, ed. by David Ellis and Ornella De Zordo (Mountfield: Helm Information, 1993), 84–102.

Daleski, H. M., *The Forked Flame* (London: Faber and Faber, 1965).

de Beauvoir, Simone, *The Second Sex* (London: Jonathan Cape, 1953).

Dollimore, Jonathan, *Death, Desire and Loss in Western Culture* (London: Penguin, 1998).

Fernihough, Anne, *D. H. Lawrence: Aesthetics and Ideology* (Oxford: Oxford University Press, 1993).

Foster, John Burt, *Heirs to Dionysus: A Nietzschean Current in Literary Modernism* (Princeton, NJ: Princeton University Press, 1981).

Garrard, Greg, 'Nietzsche Contra Lawrence: How to Be True to the Earth', *Colloquy: Text Theory Critique*, 12 (2006): 11–27.

Green, Eleanor H., 'Blueprints for Utopia: The Political Ideas of Nietzsche and D. H. Lawrence', *Renaissance & Modern Studies*, 18 (1974): 141–61.

Higgins, Kathleen Marie, 'Suffering in Nietzsche's Philosophy', in *Reading Nietzsche at the Margins*, ed. by Steven V. Hicks and Alan Rosenberg (West Lafayette, IN: Purdue University Press, 2008), 59–72.

Hough, Graham, *The Dark Sun* (Aylesbury: Duckworth, repr., 1975).

Koh, Jae-kyung, *D. H. Lawrence and the Great War: The Quest for Cultural Regeneration* (Oxford: Peter Lang, 2007).

Lawrence, D. H., 'We Need One Another', in *Phoenix: The Posthumous Papers of D. H. Lawrence*, ed. by Edward D. McDonald (London: Heinemann, repr., 1961), 188–95.

——, *Fantasia of the Unconscious and Psychoanalysis and the Unconscious* (London: Penguin, repr., 1971).

——, 'Blessed are the Powerful', in *D. H. Lawrence: A Selection from Phoenix*, ed. by A. A. H. Inglis (Harmondsworth: Penguin, 1979), 505–13.

——, *Study of Thomas Hardy and Other Essays*, ed. by Bruce Steele (Cambridge: Cambridge University Press, 1985).

——, 'A Propos of "Lady Chatterley's Lover"', in D. H. Lawrence, *Lady Chatterley's Lover* (London: Penguin, repr., 2006), 305–35.

——, *Lady Chatterley's Lover* (London: Penguin, repr., 2006).

Ludwigs, Marina, '"A Democracy of Touch": Masochism and Tenderness in D. H. Lawrence's *Lady Chatterley's Lover*', *Anthropoetics: The Journal of Generative Anthropology*, 16 (2011): 1–22.

Macleod, Sheila, *Lawrence's Men and Women* (London: Paladin Books, 1987).

Martin, Kirsty, *Modernism and the Rhythms of Sympathy* (Oxford: Oxford University Press, 2013).

Millett, Kate, 'D. H. Lawrence (*Lady Chatterley's Lover*, *The Plumed Serpent*, "The Woman Who Rode Away")', in *D. H. Lawrence*, ed. by Peter Widdowson (Burnt Mill: Longman, 1992), 69–89.

Milton, Colin, *Lawrence and Nietzsche: A Study in Influence* (Aberdeen: Aberdeen University Press, 1987).

Muller-Lauter, Wolfgang, *Nietzsche: His Philosophy of Contradictions and the Contradictions of His Philosophy*, trans. David J. Parent (New York: University of Illinois Press, 1999).

Nietzsche, Friedrich Wilhelm, *The Will to Power*. trans. Walter Kaufmann and R. J. Hollingdale (New York: Vintage Books, 1968).

——, *Beyond Good and Evil: Prelude to a Philosophy of the Future*. trans. R. J. Hollingdale (Harmondsworth: Penguin, repr. 1990).

——, *Ecce Homo: How One Becomes What One Is*. trans. R. J. Hollingdale (London: Penguin, repr. 1992).

——, *The Birth of Tragedy*. trans. Shaun Whiteside (London: Penguin, 1993).

——, *On the Genealogy of Morality*. trans. Carol Diethe (Cambridge: Cambridge University Press, 1994).

——, *The Anti-Christ* in *Twilight of the Idols* and *The Anti-Christ*. trans. R. J. Hollingdale (London: Penguin, repr. 2003).

——, *The Gay Science: With a Prelude in German Rhymes and an Appendix of Songs*. trans. Josefine Nauckhoff and Adrian Del Caro (Cambridge: Cambridge University Press, repr. 2003).

——, *Thus Spoke Zarathustra*. trans. R. J. Hollingdale (London: Penguin, repr. 2003).

————, *Twilight of the Idols* in *Twilight of the Idols* and *The Anti-Christ*. trans. R. J. Hollingdale (London: Penguin, repr. 2003).

————, *Daybreak: Thoughts on the Prejudices of Morality*. trans. R. J. Hollingdale (Cambridge: Cambridge University Press, repr. 2007).

Nussbaum, Martha C., 'Pity and Mercy: Nietzsche's Stoicism', in *Nietzsche, Genealogy, Morality: Essays on Nietzsche's Genealogy of Morals*, ed. by Richard Schacht (Berkeley: University of California Press, 1994), 139–67.

Owen, David, *Nietzsche, Politics and Modernity: Critique of Liberal Reason* (London: Sage, 1995).

Phillips, Adam, and Barbara Taylor, *On Kindness* (London: Penguin, 2010).

Ruderman, Judith, 'The Symbolic Father and the Idea of Leadership', in *D. H. Lawrence*, ed. by Peter Widdowson (Burnt Mill: Longman, 1992), 103–18.

Sallis, John, 'Dionysus—In Excess of Metaphysics', in *Exceedingly Nietzsche: Aspects of Contemporary Nietzsche Interpretation*, ed. by David Farrell Krell and David Wood (London: Routledge, 1988), 2–7.

Sanders, Scott R., 'Lady Chatterley's Loving and the Annihilation Impulse', in *D. H. Lawrence's 'Lady': A New Look at Lady Chatterley's Lover*, ed. by Michael Squires and Dennis Jackson (Athens: University of Georgia Press, 1985), 1–16.

Schneider, Daniel J., *D. H. Lawrence: The Artist as Psychologist* (Lawrence, KS: University Press of Kansas, 1984).

Shiach, Morag, 'Work and Selfhood in *Lady Chatterley's Lover*', in *The Cambridge Companion to D. H. Lawrence*, ed. by Anne Fernihough (London: Cambridge University Press, 2001), 87–102.

Simpson, Hilary, *D. H. Lawrence and Feminism* (London: Croom Helm, 1982).

Spilka, Mark, 'Lawrence's Quarrel with Tenderness', *Critical Quarterly*, 9 (4) (1967): 363–77.

————, 'On Lawrence's Hostility to Wilful Women: The Chatterley Solution', in *Lawrence and Women*, ed. by Anne Smith (London: Vision Press, 1978), 189–211.

Squires, Michael, *The Pastoral Novel: Studies in George Eliot, Thomas Hardy and D. H. Lawrence* (Charlottesville: University Press of Virginia, 1975).

Staten, Henry, *Nietzsche's Voice* (Ithaca, NY: Cornell University Press, 1990).

Wallace, Jeff, *D. H. Lawrence, Science and the Posthuman* (Basingstoke: Palgrave Macmillan, 2005).

Warren, Mark, *Nietzsche and Political Thought* (Cambridge, MA: MIT Press, 1988).

Widmer, Kingsley, 'Lawrence and the Nietzschean Matrix', in *D. H. Lawrence and Tradition*, ed. by Jeffrey Meyers (Amherst: University of Massachusetts Press, 1985), 115–31.

Worthen, John, *D. H. Lawrence and the Idea of the Novel* (London: MacMillan, 1979).

CHAPTER 4

Franz Kafka's *The Trial* and the Interpretation of Suffering

Introduction: Kafka and Interpretation

The fragmentation of the protagonist's orderly universe is signalled in the first sentence of *The Trial* (1925), with the announcement of Josef K.'s arrest: '[s]omebody must have made a false accusation against Josef K., for he was arrested one morning without having done anything wrong' (Kafka 2000: 1). Assuming that someone has reported him to the authorities, K. consequently seeks to establish the grounds for the criminal proceedings brought against him. The plot of the novel revolves around this preoccupation. The critic Thomas M. Kavanagh thus notes: '[i]t is as the *inexplicable* breaks in upon his world that we, as readers, begin to follow the unfolding of his odyssey' (Kavanagh 1976: 92). As is well known, the reason for K.'s arrest remains beyond his and the reader's ken for the novel's entirety: the court's processes appear capricious, arbitrary and pernicious. K. confronts a world of impenetrable and empty signifiers. Invoking the motif that I have been applying throughout, I will argue that K.'s continuous incapacity to assimilate his experience amounts to an encounter with excessive or 'senseless' suffering: K.'s quest is one that is impelled by the need to render his persecution meaningful, to interpretatively master his suffering. The crucial role of interpretation in *The Trial* cannot be overstated: K.'s very existence hinges upon exegetic activity.

© The Author(s) 2018
S. Smith, *Nietzsche and Modernism*,
Palgrave Studies in Modern European Literature,
https://doi.org/10.1007/978-3-319-75535-9_4

As the narrative focalises through K.'s experience, the reader's engagement with the novel to a large extent mirrors Josef K.'s hermeneutic impasse. Added to this exegetical challenge, however, the reader must negotiate K.'s unreliability, apparent from his confused and partial view, his misinterpretations of events and characters, and his repeated patterns of assertions and negations. Furthermore, not only is the voice of the third person narrator similarly limited and undependable, but the narrative device of free indirect discourse compounds the reader's confusion. Interpretative activity and interpretative difficulty is thus central to the novel, for both the reader and the characters inhabiting this radically indeterminate world.

While interpretation is central to all literary and cultural discourse, the very constitution of Kafka's *The Trial* underscores the primacy of exegesis. A number of scholars have drawn attention to the novel's incompleteness and thus to the necessarily provisional nature of all interpretative claims regarding *The Trial*. Following Ritchie Robertson, Annie Ring points out that '*Der Proceß* has itself never hung together as a totality. Rather, it is made up of scattered chapters that were put together after his death in an order that Kafka scholars consider questionable' (Ring 2012: 319). Theodore Ziolkowski similarly notes that '*The Trial* has a definite beginning and end' with everything else 'left in a state of confusion', engendering various interpretations (Ziolkowski 1997: 227). Added to this conundrum, the scale of the Kafka critical industry itself, or what the novelist Milan Kundera refers to as '*Kafkology*', suggests the impossibility of arriving at any comprehensive, totalising position.

Nevertheless, it is useful to point to two dominant trends in Kafka scholarship with regards to readings of *The Trial*. First, as Robertson notes, '[m]uch contemporary Kafka criticism [...] argues that Kafka intended only to urge upon the reader the ultimate absence of meaning both in his own writings and in the surrounding world' (Robertson 1985: 89–90). This proclivity, to claim that Kafka 'designed to provoke and then frustrate the reader's desire for an intelligible meaning', can be seen as a corollary of the text's resistance to any univocal meaning, of the profusion of textual interpretations (ix). Robertson contests this 'mystificatory' or nihilistic interpretation of the novel, one that urges a cognisance of meaninglessness. Indeed, the reading he proffers, pointing to the protagonist's inherent guilt, characterises the alternative dominant construal of the novel. That is, as Kundera has observed, there is a traditional reading of the novel, beginning with Kafka's friend Max Brod and continuing to contemporary commentaries, which, in one way or another, locates the source of guilt in the accused himself (see Kundera 1995: 204–6).

Ring follows Kundera in pointing out that this interpretation of K.'s culpability is usually corroborated by adducing biographical evidence. Noting that 'it is the biographical reading that has carried the most weight in the late twentieth and early twenty-first centuries', Ring sums up this tendency:

> Biographical accounts of *Der Proceß* stress the similarities between Kafka and his beleaguered protagonist: they refer to the author's engagement of Felice Bauer, which ended just weeks before Kafka began writing the novel in a dramatic scene that he perceived as a tribunal. Alongside the drama with Bauer, Kafka's relationship to his father surfaces regularly in the interpretations of the text. (2012: 308)

Such accounts point to Kafka's sense of failure, and hence guilt, in light of the termination of his unorthodox relationship with Bauer; these readings also emphasise his persistent sense of inadequacy with regards to his domineering father. For instance, contending that most readings 'do not sufficiently point to the personal anguish' from which Kafka's 'sense of shame and guilt' stemmed (Friedländer 2013: 5), Saul Friedländer has recently offered an interpretation of Kafka's oeuvre on the premise that 'Kafka's fiction was but a more or less heavily disguised autobiography' (10).

In opposition to this biographical approach, however, Kundera exhorts that one read *The Trial* first and foremost 'as a novel' (Kundera 1995: 206). Doing so entails the relegation of the import of the biographical evidence adduced by so many. Instead Kundera stresses the need to identify with K.'s situation, one that recognises his persecution. Not only do I heed Kundera's admonition in my reading of the novel, but I shall also take Kundera's broader praise for the novel genre in the same text to offer an insight into this critical proclivity to find K. guilty: Kundera's claim that the novel allows for the temporary suspension of 'the ineradicable human habit of judging instantly, ceaselessly, and everyone' suggests the persistence of a particularly moral construal of events and behaviour (7). What I wish to suggest through my reading of *The Trial* is that I see the tendency to find K. himself culpable as exemplifying this 'ineradicable habit' of judging. As I have suggested in Chapter 2, this has its roots in the exegetical tradition Nietzsche identifies with the Christian ascetic ideal.

What is more, I shall illustrate in the course of this chapter that this 'ineradicable habit', or need, is most evident when one is confronted with that which apparently defies our interpretative capacity. Invoking Nietzsche's notion of the will to power to contend that we have a primary, 'ineradicable' need to confer meaning, I shall demonstrate that K.'s recourse to guilt, his exercise of a condemnatory self-judgement, reflects a powerlessness to bestow his experience with personal significance. Suggesting our immersion in the text's exegetical conundrum, the dominant readings of the novel somewhat mirror K.'s response to the court's indeterminacy: as we encounter a text that resists univocal interpretation, we decide upon its indecipherable meaninglessness, on the one hand; dissatisfied with this unpalatable realisation of the text's senselessness and the concomitant frustration of our exegetical activity, there is a turn to the most common interpretative port of call, to find the defendant guilty, on the other. Otherwise put, these dominant critical perceptions of the novel speak directly to Nietzsche's preoccupation with nihilism and the problem of 'senselessness of suffering'.

In holding Kafka's text as particularly amenable to a Nietzschean reading I stand opposed to Brod, whom Kundera refers to as the founding father of '*Kafkology*' (See Kundera 1995: 40–42). Brod rejected any connection between Kafka and Nietzsche:

> Nietzsche is Kafka's antipode with almost mathematical exactitude. Some Kafka interpreters only demonstrate their lack of instinct when trying to bring together Kafka and Nietzsche on one level of analysis—as if there existed even the vaguest ties or comparisons and not just pure opposition.[1]

Several studies have since refuted Brod's absolute dismissal of Nietzsche's relevance to Kafka. However, despite noting points of continuity, critics such as Benno Wagner and Peter Heller, for example, somewhat echo Brod's view by stressing Kafka's departure from the philosopher: Wagner focuses upon Zarathustra's ideal of squandering in order to chart Kafka's antithetical concern with insurance (Wagner 2006: 84); Heller ultimately aligns Kafka with the life-negating asceticism of Nietzsche's educator and antipode, Arthur Schopenhauer (see Heller 1971). Others tracing the affinities between the pair tend to offer broad discussions of Nietzschean motifs present in Kafka's work, while Lewis W. Tusken considers the relevance of Nietzsche's thought on suffering to Kafka's short story, 'In The Penal Colony' (see Tusken 1989).[2] Patrick Bridgwater offers the most extensive discussion of the relationship of the two figures in his *Kafka and Nietzsche* (see Bridgwater 1974). However, as Reinhold Grimm notes, Bridgwater's analysis of Nietzsche's relevance to Kafka remains rather loose and general (Grimm 1979: 41).[3] Indeed, with regards to *The Trial*, Bridgwater argues that Kafka's 'main source for this second novel was surely Kant's description of the workings of the Conscience' (Bridgwater 1974: 67). Furthermore, given that Bridgwater's reading of Nietzsche and Kafka is based on the premise that they 'were agreed in rejecting materiality in favour of inner, spiritual reality', I shall seek to overturn this problematic assessment (29). Again drawing on biographical sources, this assumption has implications for the reading of *The Trial*: K.'s guilt is *a priori*, and his trajectory acts as 'proof and product' of Kafka's 'asceticism' (44). For Bridgwater, K. accordingly comes to the realisation that man is guilty of living in the world.

Rejecting Bridgwater's biographical approach and his reading of K.'s inherent guilt, I shall remain attentive to K.'s actual experience of senseless persecution. I shall illustrate that K.'s incapacity to assimilate his experience, or to render his suffering as meaningful, provoke what I have been referring to as the physio-psychological experience of nihilism, the feelings of affective fatigue attending the thought that life is not worth living, that all is 'in vain' (*WP* 55: 35). By arguing that his recourse to guilt signifies a powerlessness to render his distress as purposeful and valuable, I shall thus draw upon Nietzsche's powerful insight of the human condition to apprehend K.'s trajectory: '[m]an, the bravest animal and the most prone to suffer, does *not* deny suffering as such: he *wills* it, he even seeks it out, provided he is shown a *meaning* for it, a *purpose* for suffering' (*OGM* III 28: 127).

A Senseless Invasion

As aforementioned, from the first sentence until the last action, the nature of the charges brought against Joseph K. remain undisclosed. Yet while this secretive aspect of the legal process may confound Anglophone readers, Ziolkowski points out that this is 'perfectly routine according to the Austrian Code of Criminal Procedure' (Ziolkowski 1997: 233). Ziolkowski therefore claims:

> [Kafka] is describing the normal procedures of civil-law courts, where the investigation remains private and confidential as long as it is in the hands of the examining magistrate, and becomes public only when that official turns it over to the prosecutor with the recommendation of a trial. Not until this point does the defense become formally involved. (230–1)

Ziolkowski similarly notes that the translation of the title *Der Proceß* into English misleadingly suggests that K.'s case culminates in an actual trial. However, K.'s case does not in actual fact go beyond the preliminary hearing stage. What is more to the point is that Kafka's narrative technique, together with the characters' responses to these institutional processes, serve to render such practices as alien and absurd from the perspective of the accused: the court's unfathomability and capriciousness is achieved by Kakfa's techniques of estrangement, permitting the reader to identify with K.'s experience of bewilderment. Indeed, the sovereignty of the court rests upon its capacity to confuse the accused, to frustrate the defendant's capacity to know. Thus, Michel Foucault's comment on the classical model of criminal procedure is pertinent: '[t]he secret and written form of the procedure reflects the principle that in criminal matters the establishment of truth was the absolute right and the exclusive power of the sovereign and his judges' (Foucault 1991: 25). Enduring elements of this classical model remained in practice in Kafka's day. Moreover, as an insurance lawyer, and previously as a student of law, Kafka was familiar both with these previous codes and with contemporaneous developments and debates that surrounded the transition to the modern, enlightened code of criminal law. For instance, as a student Kafka attended lectures given by Hans Gross. Neil Allen therefore notes that, 'Gross's psychological hypothesis (loosely derived from Brentanian theory) suggested that, in their ignorance of the charge, defendants would be more likely to divulge (involuntarily) evidence of their culpability' (Allen 2005: 158). Allen continues to observe that:

> The court's procedure is reminiscent, simultaneously, both of lack of any defendants' rights in the earlier system of justice, and of Gross's notion that the accused's ignorance of the charge would aid the progress of the investigation by obfuscating psychological defence mechanisms. (159–60)

Insofar as the court's mysterious operations serve to inflict on the accused an experience of radical indeterminacy, this constitutes K.'s primary experience of persecution. For instance, as the supervisor informs K. that "'I am absolutely unable to tell you that you stand accused, or rather I don't know if you are'" (Kafka 2000: 9), K.'s repeated refrain is to declare the "'senselessness'" of his arrest (see 10, 63). Again, this time at his first tribunal, having initially been mistakenly identified as an interior decorator, he argues that "'the purpose'" of the institution was to start proceedings "'which are pointless and mostly, as in my case, inconclusive'" (36). The court's intrusion thus operates to destroy K.'s logical interpretation of existence. K. registers the violence of the disturbance as he denounces the arbitrariness of his persecution: "'even Frau Grubach was intelligent enough to see that such an arrest has no greater meaning than an attack in the street by undisciplined young thugs'" (34–5).

Given this inexplicable disturbance of K.'s world, Cyrena N. Pondrom observes that 'K. sets clarity as his first goal. Only then is useful action possible' (Pondrom 1976: 73). This is key. K.'s overriding need to interpretatively master his situation is highlighted:

> [T]he right which he still possessed to dispose of his things did not rank high in his estimation; to him it was much more important to understand his position clearly, but in the presence of these people he could not even think. (Kafka 2000: 3)

At this juncture it is worth recalling a central argument from Nietzsche's *On the Genealogy of Morality* (1887), namely that the will to power can be apprehended primarily as an urge to impose form. This is simultaneously a drive to interpret. For instance, Nietzsche highlights the import of heuristic activity by claiming that 'the essence of life, its *will to power*' is constituted by 'spontaneous, aggressive, expansive, re-interpreting, re-directing and formative powers' (*OGM* II 12: 55). What is suggested here is that life itself is a process of creative interpretation, entailing the supplanting of existent interpretations *ad infinitum*. Alan D. Schrift's comment is helpful, as he ties the notion of the will to power to exegetical activity: '"will to power" operates through the interpretive imposition of meaning and is in Nietzsche's view nothing other than a name for the active process of interpretation itself' (Schrift 1990: 184). Simon May also succinctly captures the import of interpretative activity in Nietzsche's thought: '[i]n sum, "will to power" denotes the securing of power over the world, and to that extent, it is expressed through the valuing and interpretation which capture all (human) life' (May 1999: 12). Interpretation is constitutive of the subject's capacity to secure its place in the world, that is, to establish its conditions for the 'preservation and enhancement of the power' of a certain mode of life (*WP* 567: 305). From a Nietzschean perspective, the pathos of power is inseparably bound to the self's capacity to interpretatively master its place in the world: the experience of efficacious agency and one's interpretation are intertwined. Thus, as David Owen notes, '[f]or a human being to experience his or her *self* as powerful requires that s/he experience being in the world as meaningful' (Owen 1995: 43). One's Interpretation is bound to one's capacity to act in the world, to feel oneself as an agent of deeds. Thus, as one's interpretation of oneself and the world is expressive of one's power, so the loss or failure of one's interpretative capacity is attended by paralysis, a feeling of depressing lethargy.

The need for, and yet lack of, interpretative mastery is emphasised throughout the novel. This is particularly the case given that the court not only deliberately withholds the nature of the charge brought against the accused but the court's multi-stratified hierarchy also operates at every level to obfuscate its own proceedings. For instance, the novel's narrative voice declares that '[t]he hierarchical structure of the court was endless and beyond the comprehension even of the initiated' (Kafka 2000: 94). Its procedures induce uncertainty, frustration and resignation for its own servants and functionaries: without an awareness of the origins or the ends of the cases they 'were allowed to concern themselves with', the minor officials 'fell into the depths of despair when they encountered obstacles they could not overcome because of their temperament' (94). Thus, while Nietzsche stresses the need for 'enclosing oneself within a bounded horizon', for directing one's willing by positing or holding a telos, the court's processes thwart its officials from realising themselves as meaningful and autonomous goal-bound agents. (Muller-Lauter 1999: 28). Rather, when an official did work 'with any degree of success' with a case it 'was suddenly removed from them' (Kafka 2000: 96). The removal of the case, which denies the officials the experience of striving towards its completion, constitutes 'the worst that could happen for an advocate' (96). Their work seems in vain, senseless and fragmentary: 'one knew nothing more about the case and would learn nothing more about it' (97). Echoing Nietzsche's view that '[m]an is often fed up, there are whole epidemics of this state of being fed up', which he apprehends in terms of feelings of suspended agency (*OGM* III 10: 94),

Kafka's narrative voice comments on the court officials: '[o]f course there were depressing periods, such as everyone experienced, when one could believe nothing had been achieved' (Kafka 2000: 96). Relatedly, while Nietzsche claims that 'happiness' signifies the 'feeling that power *increases*—that, a resistance is overcome', the officials exemplify his insight that feelings of powerless hatred arise when one confronts overwhelming obstacles (*AC* 2: 127).[4] Attending their thwarted attempts to interpretatively master the fragments of cases that 'simply appeared in their orbit', these officials experience debilitating feelings of frustrated impotence that manifest in their everyday comportment: '[a]ll officials were irritable even when they seemed to be calm' (Kafka 2000: 94); '[o]ften they could be so offended by trivial things' (95); exhausted officials violently discharge their anger on their colleagues (see 94).

Defendants perceive the court's processes as an interminable movement of constant deferral without conclusion. Consequently, the defendants, like the court's officials, are denied the necessary telos, or goal, to stimulate their willing, to realise themselves as effective agents. As argued in Chapter 1, Nietzsche repeatedly emphasises the human need to constitute oneself as a goal-bound being. For instance, Nietzsche surmises in one notebook entry, '"[w]illing": means willing an end' (*WP* 260: 150). Relatedly, Nietzsche characterises 'passive nihilism' in terms of an absence of a goal: 'we are *weary* because we have lost the main stimulus', he contends concerning the demise of the ascetic ideal (*WP* 8: 11).[5] In the novel, the court's processes frustrate the defendants from holding the realisable goal of obtaining knowledge of their charges; this impedes them from constituting themselves as agents impacting the world they find themselves in: they are impotent with regard to constructing a defence; any thought of active intervention is nullified by the awareness that the interminable process does not promise any resolution, or the arrival at an actual trial. This precipitates the defendants' fall into despair. The merchant Block's story resembles K.'s trajectory: Block first appears to K. as assertive and defiant and, unlike the other submissive and herd-like defendants, he is actively engaged in the pursuit of the truth about his case, to discover the nature of the charges brought against him. Having hired several advocates to advance the proceedings, he informs K. that he '"wanted to see tangible progress, the whole thing ought to be working towards a conclusion or at least advancing in regular stages"' (Kafka 2000: 138). Foreshadowing K.'s decline, Block's subjugation is a corollary of his incapacity to interpret any sign of development in his case.

It is worth exploring the point that the incapacity to articulate one's charges signals an inability to determine oneself as an efficacious agent. As the court continually withholds defining the defendants' charges, this prevents the defendants from conceiving of an endpoint, namely the arrival at an actual trial, or of realising the attendant progress of giving form to one's defence. The court's perpetual deferral of disclosure also thwarts the defendants from establishing a startpoint, an origin from which they may self-reflexively experience themselves moving towards a telos. Paralysis ensues: one has lost all orientating points to guide one's willing. Hence the defendants must pursue the goal of establishing knowledge of one's charges in order to attain the feeling of striving, willing being and not collapse in resentful despair. The court's characteristic strategies of obfuscation and postponement, however, repeatedly impede the defendants from positing knowledge of one's charges as an obtainable goal. The absence of expressed charges hence frustrates the defendants' need to cognitively assimilate their respective experiences and so accelerates feelings of resignation and powerlessness: they are subject to an overwhelming experience of 'senseless suffering'. For instance, when K. quizzes 'a man of the world who in any other circumstances would be completely in command of himself' as to why he is waiting in the corridor, not only is this man incapable of completing his sentence, but he 'looked at the others as if it was their duty to help him' (50). Turning to others, or to external interpretative frameworks, to apprehend one's situation is suggestive of the defendants' inability to bestow their experiences with personal significance. Block corroborates this view as he divulges to K.:

> You must remember that in this business many things are constantly coming up for discussion which are beyond the range of the intellect; people are just too tired and distracted to cope with a lot of things and so take refuge in superstition. (136)

Collectively imprisoned in the indefinite and indeterminate proceedings, the weakened defendants do not have the strength to confer a rational or individual explanation of their suffering: they '"take refuge in"' an irrational, collective interpretation that seems to '"propagate"' itself (136–7).

Several commentators have noted K.'s persistent reliance on logic.[6] However, many overlook the fact that his absolute recourse to logic is entwined with his obvious need to discover the legal rationale behind his charge. In line with this rational pursuit of the cause of the proceedings, Nina Pelikan Strauss thus notes that '[t]o discover the Authority who has authorized his arrest is K.'s goal, a goal any reader with a modern concept of justice can identify as sane' (Straus 2007: 384). Invoking Nietzsche to perform a more abstract level of analysis sheds further light upon K.'s hyperlogical exegetical activity: the appeal to causality, Nietzsche observes, allows one to appropriate and domesticise the unfamiliar and the distressing. Nietzsche outlines this self-preservative hermeneutical activity in the following passage:

> To trace something unknown back to something known is alleviating, soothing, gratifying and gives moreover a feeling of power. Danger, disquiet, anxiety attend the unknown—the first instinct is to *eliminate* these distressing states. First principle: any explanation is better than none. [...] The cause-creating drive is thus conditioned and excited by a feeling of fear. The question 'why?' should furnish, if at all possible, not so much the cause for its own sake as a *certain kind of cause*—a soothing, liberating, alleviating cause. [...] Thus there is sought not only some kind of explanation as cause, but a *selected* and *preferred* kind of explanation, the kind by means of which the feeling of the strange, new, unexperienced is most speedily and most frequently abolished. (*TI* VI 5: 62)

Accordingly, K. aims to avert his experience of senseless suffering by attributing to it a cause or origin. He seeks to comprehend the court's distressing invasion by firstly appealing to the most readily familiar sources: he reckons that his landlady, Frau Grubach, must be able to offer an explanation, that she is somehow responsible; he then considers the intrusion as an elaborate prank, 'for some unknown reason', carried out by his colleagues at the bank to mark his thirtieth birthday (Kafka 2000: 3).

Nietzsche's discussion of the 'cause-creating drive' recalls his notion of the self's digestive-appropriative capacity, alluded to in previous chapters[7]: Nietzsche argues that the mind operates to 'make the new like the old, to simplify the many-fold, to overlook or push away the completely contradictory' (*BGE* 230: 160). Laurence Lampert thus claims that, for Nietzsche, '[t]he basic will of the human mind inclines it powerfully to cosmetics, to lying surfaces' (Lampert 2004: 228). Lampert's comment also gestures towards Nietzsche's notion of Apollonian appearances as he presents it in *The Birth of Tragedy* (1872). Regarding Kafka's novel, K. resembles Nietzsche's figure of the Alexandrian man who fetishises reason and Apollonian appearances to an extreme degree: for

K. the world is inherently rational, everything is explicable and amenable to the application of logic. K. thus possesses what Nietzsche refers to in *The Gay Science* (1882–1887) as 'faith in a world that is supposed to have its equivalent and measure in human thought, in human valuations—a "world of truth" that can be grasped entirely with the help of our four-cornered little human reason' (373: 238). Correspondingly, it is possible to read the court's seemingly meaningless invasion as an eruption of the Dionysian chaos that shatters K.'s logical colonisation of existence: the court represents 'the essential, indifferent [...] comings and goings of the contingent world' (Pondrom 1976: 80). K.'s primary drive, then, is to assimilate this experience, for the senselessness to be interpretatively integrated. He thus seeks to restore order, or to recuperate the Apollonian veil of illusion: once 'order was restored, then every trace [of the arrest] would be eliminated and everything would resume its old course' (Kafka 2000: 14).

Furthermore, just as Lawrence depicts the populace in *Lady Chatterley's Lover* (1928) in terms of the pursuit of pleasure and aversion to pain, K. similarly resembles Nietzsche's 'Last Man'[8]:

> After all, K. lived in a country which enjoyed law and order; there was universal peace; all the laws were upheld; so who dared to pounce on him in his own home? He had always been inclined to take everything as easily as possible, to believe the worst only when the worst happened, not to worry about the future even when everything seemed threatening. (3)

K.'s interpretative perspective operates to ensure that he inhabits what Nietzsche refers to as a 'narrower, abbreviated, simplified world' (*WP* 15: 15). Another Nietzschean passage, alluded to above, comes to mind in line with K.'s optimistic perspective:

> Most men tolerate life without grumbling too much and *believe* thus in the value of existence, but precisely because everyone wills himself alone and stands his ground alone, and does not step out of himself as do those exceptional men, everything extrapersonal escapes his notice entirely, or seems at most a faint shadow. (*HAH* 33: 36)

K. seeks to maintain this simple, 'narrow' perspective of life: we learn that he had never visited the squalid suburbs until his first tribunal; he consoles himself in adversity that he would not have suffered '[i]f he stayed at home and led his normal life' (Kafka 2000: 46). His thought and behaviour are repeatedly characterised by a desire to minimise his distress. Applying Nietzsche's observation, K. 'wills himself alone and stands his ground alone' in order not to be exposed to others' pain (*HAH* 33: 36). However, one consequence of K.'s habitual denial of struggle and difficulty is an 'excessive sensitivity' towards suffering: K. evokes Nietzsche's argument that, as a consequence of 'the poverty of real experience of pain' in the comfortable, modern world compared to past ages, 'pain is hated much more than formerly' (*GS* 48: 61). For according to Nietzsche, the modern age is characterised by such 'refinement and ease' that 'one can hardly-endure the presence of pain' (61). The weight to this argument is achieved as Nietzsche claims that 'excessive sensitivity [...] seem[s] to me to be the real "distress of the present"' (61). As a result of the court's persecutory intrusion, K. is propelled into a world of pain and senseless distress, as Karl J. Kuepper observes: '[h]umiliation and pain are such integral components of all procedures of the trial, that the stooping posture seems like the distinguishing mark of everyone connected or involved with the trial authorities' (Kuepper 1976: 66). In this world K. repeatedly exemplifies Nietzsche's point on this modern sensitivity to distress. For instance, as K. becomes aware that Block's appearance is reflective of the hardship that the merchant has endured, he commands Leni to take Block away: for he 'could not stand the sight of the merchant any longer' (Kafka 2000: 142). Furthermore, while a host of readings of the lumber room scene have been proffered, one may also conjecture that K. offered to be whipped in place of the guards due to an incapacity to stomach the sight of others' distress.[9]

By illustrating K.'s hypersensitivity I wish to augment the point that prior to the court's intervention K. has minimal encounters with others. Indeed, for James Hawes it is precisely this absence of contact with others that constitutes K.'s guilt:

> Guilt (if it merits the title) that comes from inaction is incurable. This may be the hidden logic in the opening line of the novel. Josef K. has done nothing bad to anyone. He has actually 'done' nothing at all to anyone, he has not functioned interpersonally. (1988: 145–6)

K. is primarily characterised by a desire to avoid contact with the court. I would add to Hawes' reading that K.'s experience of others, since the initiation of the process at least, would seem to justify such recoil:

others appear to be hostile forces, working against him from the moment that the court intervenes in his life. Indeed, as Kundera notes, everyone readily assumes K's guilt (Kundera 1995: 209).[10] His enduring desire for detachment may be reflective of an unconscious awareness that becomes increasingly conscious with the novel's movement, namely that '[e]verything belongs to the court' (Kafka 2000: 118).

Furthermore, it is key to note that K. reads his relations with others on a contractual basis, one that consists of the identification of obligations, debts and compensation.[11] By tracing K.'s comportment through this heuristic lens, it may be argued K.'s desire not 'to be obliged to anyone' reflects his fear of further suffering given the particularly retributive nature of social relations that he witnesses and experiences (27). The narrator's mediation of the advocate Huld's account of the court, for example, suggests that 'the great organism' can be seen as a creditor seeking recompense for an injury suffered. On this understanding, the primary affect instilled by the court on the populace and the defendants is one of fear, and hence paralysis. Reinforcing K.'s apprehension and anxiety, this analysis of the court serves to deter K. from active intervention, of 'doing oneself immeasurable harm through attracting the particular attention of a bureaucracy which was always vengeful' (Kafka 2000: 95):

> One had to keep quiet, even when this went against the grain! And try to see that [...] the great organism itself compensated for the slight disturbance by easily producing a replacement at another point—everything was after all connected—and remained unchanged, assuming it did not become (and this was probable) even more secretive, even more observant, even more severe, even more malevolent. (95)

This account of the court evokes Nietzsche's hypothesis of primeval punishment in the *Genealogy*:

> Throughout most of human history, punishment has *not* been meted out *because* the miscreant was held responsible for his act, therefore it was *not* assumed that the guilty party alone should be punished:- but rather, as parents still punish their children, it was out of anger over some wrong which had been suffered, directed at the perpetrator, but this anger was held in check and modified by the idea that every injury has its *equivalent* which can be paid in compensation, if only through the *pain* of the person who injures. (*OGM* II 4: 43)

As Nietzsche scholar Aaron Ridley succinctly puts it, '[i]n injuring someone the culprit becomes a debtor—one who owes recompense to his creditor' (Ridley 1998: 31). The primitive logic of punishment thus appeals to the 'psychological trappings' of 'buying and selling', 'the oldest and most primitive personal relationship there is' (*OGM* II 8: 49). Moreover, Nietzsche stresses that:

> Through punishment of the debtor, the creditor takes part in the *rights of the masters*: at last he, too, shares the elevated feeling of despising and maltreating someone as an 'inferior'—or at least, when the actual power of punishment, of exacting punishment, is already transferred to the 'authorities', of *seeing* the debtor despised and maltreated. So, then, compensation is made up of a warrant for and entitlement to cruelty. (*OGM* II 5: 45)

Punishment, then, as Christopher Janaway expresses it, is 'a legitimization of cruelty' (Janaway 2007: 134). Echoing Zarathustra's pronouncement that 'man is the cruellest animal' (*TSZ* III 13: 235), here in the *Genealogy* Nietzsche contends that man has an instinctive disposition to inflict suffering upon others: '[t]o see somebody suffer is nice, to make somebody suffer even nicer—that is a hard proposition, but an ancient, powerful, human-all-too-human proposition' (*OGM* II 6: 46). Nietzsche claims that these aggressive drives are permanent human traits, although they may have altered in form, having become spiritualised or sublimated. Kafka's novel, I would suggest, parallels Nietzsche's insights on the human condition, on the persistency of the 'human-all-too-human' pleasure of inflicting suffering; as I shall explore below, Kafka dramatises the Nietzschean insight that this pleasure extends to inflicting suffering upon oneself. Regarding the court, Allen notes that Kafka seems to be suggesting that 'the "modern", "enlightened" mode of justice is always capable of relapsing into the arbitrariness and "inhumanity" of apparently outdated procedures' (Allen 2005: 159). Tellingly from a Nietzschean perspective, the court's exercise of severe punishment suggests that it is a 'weakened or endangered' institution: Nietzsche argues that strength manifests in the exercise of mercy, of 'letting [one's] malefactors go *unpunished*', reflecting one's power to sustain an injury 'without suffering from it' (*OGM* II 10: 51). Accordingly, Nietzsche describes this disposition as 'the highest form of mastery to be had on earth' and idealises the capacity to forego the compensatory, appropriative gesture:

'[j]ustice, which began by saying "everything can be paid off, everything must be paid off" ends by turning a blind eye and letting off those unable to pay' (II 11: 53). Kafka's description of the court attaining return for any 'slight disturbance' is suggestive not only of the court's vulnerability or sensitivity, but also of its inability to endure any loss.

Corroborating this general overview of the court's functioning, Block describes particular individuals within the court as vengeful. For instance, Block warns K. of Huld's vindictiveness (Kafka 2000: 134), and the advocate's cruel subjugation of the merchant can be interpreted as punitive and compensatory: Block is made to pay for apparently betraying the advocate by hiring extra legal assistance. What is more, Huld punishes Block by systematically denuding him of his interpretative integrity: Huld firstly confuses Block as to whether he is to wait or to enter his room; the advocate subsequently compels the merchant to study abstruse legal documents beyond his comprehension, which Huld claims are "'only to give him an idea of how difficult the battle I'm waging on his behalf really is'" (Kafka 2000: 152). Moreover, Huld informs the merchant of news of his case which, however, is indecipherable: the advocate speaks unclearly throughout and informs Block that, "'[y]ou will know that various opinions pile up round every case like an impenetrable thicket'" (153). Adumbrating K.'s encounter with the priest in 'The Cathedral' chapter, Huld thus subdues Block by referring to an infinite proliferation of interpretations of his case: Block, like K., is subject to an indefinite deferral of the definition of the charge brought against him. The court and its officials thus exact cruel compensation for perceived disturbances by subjecting the identified debtor to an irresolvable indeterminacy and thus terrifying senselessness.

A VINDICTIVE PROCESS

Interpreting his case from his familiar banking perspective, that is, domesticising it in terms of debit and credit, allows K. momentary hermeneutic mastery: '[t]he case was nothing but a large business deal', he surmises (Kafka 2000: 99). Furthermore, as he recalls previous successes in his banking role, K. is temporarily buoyed and reassured of his capacity to triumph against the court. For K. it is primarily a matter of success or failure against an adversary, rather than that of moral guilt or innocence. For many critics this approach typifies K.'s failing, a failing that is marked by an inadequacy to look inward and recognise his own inherent culpability. For instance, Robertson among others points to K.s moral lack: hinting at the court's potentially benevolent role, Robertson claims that '[t]he Court has begun arousing him from previous moral indifference into the beginnings of self-awareness' (Robertson 1985: 104).[12] In this line of argument, K. is not guilty of any particular act of transgression, but rather of a more general ignorance of 'the moral law'. Robertson goes on to claim that '[r]igorous self-examination is the only means to overcome his "repressed moral awareness"' (118).[13]

It is evident in the novel, however, that the court's processes actually prevent any form of 'rigorous self-examination'. K. realises, for instance, as he contemplates transcribing and then scrutinising his personal history, that the continual inability to comprehend the actual charge brought against him outweighs any ameliorative manoeuvre, even that of self-examination:

> Without having a particularly apprehensive nature one could easily come to believe that it was impossible ever to get the plea ready. Not because of laziness or cunning (only the advocate could be hampered by these) but because in ignorance of the actual accusation and even of any further charges arising from it one had to recall the most trivial actions and events of one's life, present them and review them from every angle. (Kafka 2000: 100–1)

K. is aware that the lack of specific charge itself prevents any willed attempt at self-exculpation. The thought of embarking upon an endless and ultimately fruitless process of self-scrutiny, one that will inevitably fall short of attaining a totalising perspective, precipitates a depressing lethargy: having resolved to write his plea given that 'it would not be enough [...] to sit in the corridor like the others with his hat under the bench' (100), K. is now beset by weariness and despondency, for '[a]gain his thoughts were ending in lamentation' (101). The court precipitates resignation and paralysis, the pathos of nihilism, rather than moral self-scrutiny. Giles Deleuze and Felix Guattari's point on the court's perniciousness is pertinent: '[c]ulpability is never anything but the superficial movement whereby judges and even lawyers confine you in order to prevent you from engaging in a real movement, that is, from taking care of your own affairs' (Deleuze and Guattari 1986: 45).

Critics also hold K. culpable by adducing evidence of his immoral, instrumental behaviour in his relations with others. Robertson contends that '[i]n his dealings with other people, K. is aggressive and calculating' (Robertson 1985: 99). Hawes echoes this, and, 'doubting the moral soundness of Josef K.' (Hawes 1988: 140), adduces Roy Pascal's evaluation: '[s]exuality has a place in *Der Proceß* and *Das Schloss* chiefly as a means to acquire power over another person' (Pascal 1973: 240). I do not dispute K.'s moral ambiguity. However, I follow Ring's observation that, '[i]t appears as though the entry of the court into K.'s life unlocks a sadistic instinct in him: to preserve the law, and to extract enjoyment from enforcing it upon others' (Ring 2012: 312). That is, Ring's claim that 'K. begins to yield to the court's strange processes', having at first protested against his arrest, echoes my reading of K.'s development: having previously lived a sheltered, ascetic life, the court's intervention not only opens K. to various erotic encounters, but it also induces him to perpetrate cruelties against others, afflicting his victims with a similar sense of meaninglessness to which he is subjected (306). In the first instance, the court's malign influence can be illustrated by pointing out that K., in his business capacity, harms others unintentionally. These instances result from K. being both exhausted and distracted by the legal proceedings. Indeed, increasingly afflicted by a sense of self-division as the pursuit of knowledge regarding his charges overwhelms him, K. perceives this diversion from his business affairs itself as 'a torture sanctioned by the court as part and parcel of the proceedings' (Kafka 2000: 105). It is a 'torture' that afflicts and weakens his interpretative will to power. The effect of his growing neglect of bank business is to inflict his dependents with a similar sense of futility: K. refuses to see the clients 'who now appeared to have waited entirely in vain' (109); in no 'fit state to listen' to the manufacturer's financial request, he wonders 'when the manufacturer would eventually realize that all his words were useless' (102). K. increasingly resembles the court's officials: frustrated, exhausted, and subjecting others to feelings of powerlessness.

Moreover, I read further instances of K.'s collusion with the court's punitive structure to derive from his need to palliate his own pain through exercising a compensatory cruelty. That is, K.'s complicity with the court, or what Ring calls his 'paradoxical attraction to the regulation and retribution of the law', stems from his need to assuage his suffering (Ring 2012: 312). As noted above, the retributive drive is symptomatic of a condition of weakness. Again, Nietzsche's penetrating analysis of the psychology of the sufferer informs my reading. Nietzsche contends in the *Genealogy*, in his account of the development of slave morality, that 'every sufferer instinctively looks for a cause of his distress; more exactly, for a culprit, even more precisely for a *guilty* culprit who is receptive to distress' (*OGM* III 15: 99). The novel insists upon the characters' need to identify the nearest culprit, or debtor, to hold accountable for any perceived loss. Tellingly, *The Trial* emphasises the incongruity of such identifications. For instance, K. mistakenly holds his landlady accountable for his arrest and had 'even thought for a moment of punishing Frau Grubach by persuading Fräulein Bürstner to join him in giving notice' (Kafka 2000: 18). K.'s relationship with Fräulein Bürstner is similarly characterised by K.'s aberrant apportioning of blame. Debtor-creditor positions are highly unstable in this relationship, and the characters' discourse confuses conventional notions of transgression and accountability: immediately following K.'s misplaced reproach of the Fräulein for 'introducing disturbance and disorder', he seeks her forgiveness for the court officials' invasion into her room, which, he tells her, was '"done by strangers, against my will"'; insofar as Fräulein Bürstner '"can't find any trace of disorder"', she grants '"with pleasure the forgiveness"' that K. requests (Kafka 2000: 19). However, gesturing towards her own hypersensitivity, she instantly reproaches K. when she then notices the slightest of disturbances to her room. Given that he is not ultimately accountable for this almost imperceptible disruption, Kafka again portrays the characters' delicacy while highlighting their primary need to assuage any perceived injury.

Additionally, Paul Alberts' argument, suggesting that the court's incompetency compounds K.'s confusion in his social interactions, is relevant:

> The figure of K. struggles within himself, but also with social relations, and the rules of interaction, legal and extra-legal, that demand obedience. Human social relations for Kafka are not neatly enframed, regulated or enhanced by the legal system, but appear as too-often insincere, unreliable—threatening or driven by base needs that erupt irregularly. (Alberts 2013: 189)

As I read the novel, the 'base needs that erupt irregularly' include the fundamental, human-all-too-human need to bring relief to one's suffering. From this point of view, Alberts' comment suggests that there is an absence of a controlling, authoritative judiciary which would stabilise these outbursts of vindictive sentiments. Indeed, it may be surmised that the irregular court seems to operate immanently and insidiously. In effect, the disorderly nature of the court itself proliferates its own retributive structures on a micro, interpersonal level.[14]

What is also evident, as K. repeatedly misreads the roles of debtor and creditor, is that it is his position of powerlessness that propels K.'s drive to reproach the other. For instance, K. identifies the washerwoman as the culprit for interrupting his moment of grandiloquence at the tribunal despite the fact that it was 'not clear' whether she was to 'blame' for the shrieking (Kafka 2000: 36–7). Indeed, despite realising that it is the student, rather than the washerwoman, who is responsible for the offensive, distracting shrieking, K. continues to hold her culpable, suggesting that what is key is simply identifying a guilty culprit: there must be some form of restoration following a perceived loss. Furthermore, when he returns to the courtroom the following week, K.'s ineradicable need to find a guilty culprit, and his incapacity to surmount his grievances, are again illustrated when he belies his apparent magnanimity towards the washerwoman: despite claiming that the speech's interruption was "'all in the past, almost forgotten'", even though it had "'really infuriated'" him at the time, he immediately subverts this poise of equanimity to explicitly censure her (40). Kafka's characters, like Lawrence's, struggle to match Nietzsche's exemplars, the nobles who immediately discharge such poisonous feelings, or the strong man able to digest his grievances and perform an 'active forgetfulness' (*OGM* II 1: 38).[15]

Moreover, as the washerwoman subsequently exculpates herself by clarifying her situation and claiming that "'I am excused in the eyes of all who know me'", she points to K.'s limited perspectival knowledge and to the inappropriateness of his reproach (Kafka 2000: 37). This episode, highlighting K.'s incomplete knowledge, gestures to another key theme of the novel, namely, the finite and embodied nature of truth claims. This point evokes Nietzsche's doctrine of perspectivism: countering traditional epistemological notions of objectivity and disinterestedness, Nietzsche contends that '[t]here is only a perspective seeing, only a perspective "knowing"' (*OGM* III 12: 92). As he puts it elsewhere: 'every centre of force [...] construes all the rest of the world from its own viewpoint, i.e., measures, feels, forms, according to its own force' (*WP* 636: 338). Perspectivism is thus 'the basic condition of all life' (*BGE* Preface: 32). The novel corroborates Nietzsche's view that truth or knowledge claims are inextricably orientated by needs, or the individual's dominant drives and affects. That is, knowledge is guided by the feelings attending the individual's striving, or the activity or predisposition of the unconscious drives. Truth claims thus reflect the physio-psychological will to power of the individual. Nevertheless, several characters in the novel presume to hold a neutral, objective position, usually claiming to offer K. a supposedly detached and reliable overview of the court's operations.[16] The reader learns to be suspicious of such claims. And the reader's ironic detachment extends to K. when he promulgates similar views. At his first hearing, for instance, K. claims to possess a dispassionate, objective view of the court's proceedings. He purports to '"distance"' himself '"from the whole business"' of his arrest and so '"judge it calmly"' (Kafka 2000: 35–6). From this privileged standpoint, he promises to bequeath insights that are to the court's '"advantage"' and which will also provoke improvements. His purported perspectival distance is accompanied by an alleged stance of affective disengagement, as he informs the court:

> What has happened to me represents of course only one individual case, and as such it's not very important since I don't take it too seriously, but it's typical of the proceedings instituted against many people. I speak here for those, not for myself. (33)

Here, then, K. authoritatively passes judgement on the whole process to claim that his own experiences of distress, the '"public outrage"' of his case, will contribute towards the eradication of other unjust experiences (34). He thereby denounces the '"pointless"' distress perpetrated by corrupt officials against the innocent. Not only does this interpretation bestow significance on his own unredeemed suffering, but it also implicitly imbues all other senseless grievances with meaning. That is, K.'s attempt to take exegetic power over the senselessness of his past suffering, and of others' experiences of useless suffering, takes moral form and significance, evoking Henry Staten's powerful insight, which is here alluding to modern liberal engagements with the absurdity, senselessness and horror of the past: 'we draw an invisible line of rectitude through history and in this way take power over it. Against the awesome "Thus it was" of history we set the overawing majesty of "Thus it *ought to have been*"' (Staten 1990: 79).

Moreover, K.'s very 'interested' position becomes immediately apparent, primarily signalling his need to assuage his grievances. For his assertion, claiming to transcend his own suffering to selflessly represent others and redress the injustices perpetrated against them, is considerably undermined by his later concession to the washerwoman:

> I would never have got mixed up voluntarily in these things, and my sleep would never have been troubled by the need to make improvements in this judicial system. But because I was allegedly arrested—I am under arrest, in fact—I've been forced to intervene here, indeed in my own interest. (Kafka 2000: 40)

K.'s detailed articulation of his injuries, coupled with his delight at the ostensible disturbance to the examining magistrate's authority caused by his remonstrative speech, belie K.'s posture of equanimity to signal, rather, a deep drive for a compensatory retribution. This drive for revenge, however, cannot be actually fulfilled. Even K.'s apparent humiliation of the examining magistrate is ambiguous, and, like all events in the text, provisional and subject to one's interpretative perspective. K.'s only recourse is to have his suffering palliated by the thought of an imaginary or deferred vengeance against his more powerful adversary: he indulges in a fantasy of the magistrate's loss when he envisions abducting the washerwoman. Here K. brings to mind Nietzsche's characterisation of the powerless slaves who 'being denied the proper response of action compensate for it only with imaginary revenge' (*OGM* I 10: 21).[17]

Evoking Nietzsche's analysis of *ressentiment,* the characters' frequent vengeful imaginings are not only attended by a cognisance of impotence, but they involve the cruel spectacle of the other's violent punishment. For instance, the court usher acknowledges his actual powerlessness as he fantasises retaliating against the student who goes off with his wife, the washerwoman:

> If I were not so dependent on them I would have squashed that student against this wall long ago. Here, next to this notice. I dream about that all the time. Here, a little above the floor, he is pinned to the wall, arms stretched out, bandy legs in a circle, and streaks of blood all round. But so far that's only a dream. (Kafka 2000: 48)

In also being deprived of possession of the washerwoman, K. registers his 'first indubitable defeat' and resorts to a similar compensatory vision: K. 'pictured to himself the most ridiculous scene possible' whereby this 'pathetic student, this puffed-up child' would kneel by his mistress Elsa's bed 'and beg for mercy with hands clasped in prayer' (46). This image of the student's humiliation anticipates Block's subjugation and, by extension, K.'s own demise. Moreover, as I shall discuss below, Elsa's deification in this fantasy prefigures K.'s own execution scene: in both scenarios suffering is presented for the pleasure of the spectator; here, and at K.'s death, this spectator suggestively assumes divine status.

To recapitulate, *The Trial* alerts the reader to the fallibility of any objective, omniscient claims to knowledge. It continually highlights the provisional and interested, or motivated, nature of such claims, which, in K.'s case, are largely determined by his pathos of powerlessness and injury. Attending to these points to highlight Kafka's insistence upon the embodied nature of knowledge would seem to counter Bridgwater's claim that '[b]ecause he rejected material reality, Kafka sought to create wholly "spiritual" works that would have no reference back to the empirical world' (Bridgwater 1974: 44). In the following examination of the priest's parable of the man from the country, the perspectival, limited basis of truth claims are again highlighted. Turning to this passage, I shall depart from the critical tendency to privilege the parable solely as a philosophical or interpretative conundrum by remaining attentive to K.'s actual plight: interpretation is a site of agonistic conflict; K.'s subsequent paralysis must be read in light of the frustration of his actual and urgent need to actively bestow significance upon an inexplicable, indeterminate and overwhelming experience.

THE WILL TO INTERPRETATION

There are parallels between the advocate Huld's subjugation of the merchant Block and K.'s hermeneutical dispute with the prison chaplain in 'The Cathedral' chapter: in both cases there is a contestation of interpretations; the official's voice dominates the discourse, purporting to hold an authoritative, omniscient and unassailable standpoint; the seemingly endless proliferation of interpretations that the defendants are exposed to, signalling the perpetual deferral of the disclosure of the charges brought against them, subjects them to a hermeneutical impasse; the exegetical conundrum propels the defeat of the respective defendants. K.'s encounter with the priest amplifies his pathos of impotence: his incapacity to actively interpret his situation in relation to the priest's parable provokes an extreme deflation of his feelings of efficacious agency, accelerating his suicidal complicity in his execution.

Nietzschean echoes abound in 'The Cathedral' chapter. Robertson and Hawes point to the religious setting to suggest reverberations with Nietzsche's articulation of 'the death of God'[18]: K. is drawn to a man in the cathedral looking on at a picture of the burial of Christ (see Robertson 1985: 122; Hawes 1988: 135). As Hawes clarifies, the cathedral 'is literally a structure which has lost its rationale but still exists' (135). This cathedral setting acts as the background in which the priest narrates the parable of the man from the country, or the story of 'Before the Law'.[19] Critics have tended to privilege the import of the parable with regards to the novel as a whole: Robertson claims that '[i]t is perhaps the supreme moment in Kafka's writing' (Robertson 1985: 122–23); Ingeborg Henel argues that it is 'the key to the novel itself' (Henel 1976: 48). Robertson and Henel both focus upon the parable's final sentence to unlock the 'puzzle' of the novel. Robertson, for instance, argues that '[t]his peripeteia—the doorkeeper's information to the dying man that the door was all along intended for him and for him only—is an essential part of the story's meaning' (Robertson 1985: 123). As Henel puts it, '[t]he law in question here is the law of each individual' (Henel 1976: 48). Consequently, the individual must perform 'the act of self-judgment' (48). Henel thus claims that K.'s 'desire to lead a quiet life outside the trial have prevented him from hearing what the priest meant to tell him by means of the legend: that he should give up his evasions and confront his judge' (50).[20] For Henel, then, K. fails through weakness: as a perfect example of a Nietzschean Last or Ultimate Man, the character type to whom Nietzsche attributes the typical modern drive for comfort, peace and security, K. evades the arduous task of realising one's own individual responsibility, of fashioning one's own sense of autonomy. While this reading may be seductive, it invites disputation: firstly, one may challenge the assumed authority of the priest's discourse; secondly, it is important to remain attentive towards K.'s actual quest, that of discovering the nature of the court's charge, and so foreground the interpretative impasse that besets the protagonist. That is, K.'s experience remains, first and foremost, one of 'senseless suffering' at the hands of the court.

By contesting the priest's privileged position assumed by Robertson, Henel and others, I follow Allen who observes:

The priest is as much a functionary of the law as Titorelli, the Advocate, or the arresting officers, and thus his tale does not inevitably explain any more or less of the law than does that of any other character; it could be as much symptomatic as revelatory. (2005: 145)

To corroborate this argument, it is worth examining K.'s actual exchange with the priest. This is somewhat neglected in the aforementioned discussions. Here K. oscillates from a combative independence to a desire for conciliation that amounts to his capitulation. K.'s surrender is prefigured when he overrides his own empirical experience to place trust in the priest: his faith in the priest involves the repudiation of obvious signs of the priest's hostility. This is tantamount to a denial of his own embodied perspective, a relinquishing of his own interpretative integrity. Fatigued, and ultimately determined to achieve conciliation, he surrenders any remnant of autonomy that he possesses. Here K.'s movement parallels Block's trajectory: the merchant's transformation from proud defiance to a debased surrender, signified most apparently by his growing and humiliating dependence on Leni, the advocate's maid, is mirrored in K.'s newfound desire for an absolute and 'decisive' dependence upon the other:

> K. had no doubts about the priest's good intentions; it was not impossible that if he were to come down he would make common cause with him, it was not impossible that he might receive from him some decisive and acceptable advice. (Kafka 2000: 165)

Contrary to K.'s certitude, the figure of the priest remains ambiguous and radically indeterminate. The priest is thus similar to the other 'helpers' K. seeks and encounters. This becomes increasingly apparent when examining the discourse that ensues following the priest's narration of the parable, which itself highlights the role of exegesis: both K.'s and the priest's respective interpretations of the parable examine the interpretative capacities of both the man from the country and the doorkeeper. Central to the debate is the notion of truth and perspective: the reliability of each figure in the narrative and whether they have been deceived or not, either by the other or by their own respective, necessarily limited perspectives, comes to the fore.

For some, such as Jacques Derrida, what is crucial about this chapter is its demonstration of the endless proliferation of discourse: '[t]his entire chapter is a prodigious scene of Talmudic exegesis, concerning *Before the Law*, between the priest and K.' (Derrida 1992: 217).

For Derrida the discussion is paradigmatic of deconstructive practice, revealing the perpetual play or deferral of meaning. As he puts it elsewhere, '[t]he absence of the transcendental signified extends the domain and the play of signification infinitely' (1993: 110). In Nietzsche's terms, attending the devaluation of our hitherto highest values, the revelation that '"nothing is true" means '"everything is permitted"': freed from the enclosed horizon of an absolute notion of truth, posited by the ascetic ideal, every perspective is 'permitted' (*OGM* III 24: 118). Nietzsche undermines absolutised notions of truth by arguing for a multiplicity of perspectives: '[t]here are many kinds of eyes. Even the sphinx has eyes— and consequently there are many kinds of "truths", and consequently there is no truth' (*WP* 540: 291). As Schrift puts it, 'the assertion of a multiplicity of truths effectively deconstructs the epistemological standard of truth as single and univocal' (Schrift 1990: 154). In *The Trial*, the priest makes K. aware of the proliferation of interpretations surrounding the parable, suggesting a potential radical play of significance; he seemingly endorses an active heuristic engagement with the parable, implicitly encouraging K.'s interpretative agency when he rebukes him not to '"take somebody else's opinion without testing it"' (Kafka 2000: 167). With this enunciation, the priest here can be aligned with Nietzsche's attack on truth as a '*metaphysical* value' (*OGM* III 24: 119). Notably, however, the priest retains an authoritative stance, issuing injunctions to K. while seemingly espousing the necessity of one's own personal interpretative engagement with the text.

Moreover, the priest comes to repudiate K.'s reading of the text: the discourse of the parable is revealed to be primarily a site of interpretative power struggles. The priest, then, who dominates the discourse, subtly shifts his argument to foreclose any interpretative profusion. For instance, he chastises K. for having '"insufficient respect for the written record and [...] [for] altering the narrative"' (Kafka 2000: 168). Not only is the priest's authoritative voice prominent, but this claim presupposes privileged access to a transcendental signified that precludes interpretative variation. The strategy is repeated with his invocation of the law's absolute infallibility. Again, this manoeuvre seeks to undermine K.'s interpretation: as K. determines the doorkeeper's culpability for having deceived the man, the priest confers on the functionary a transcendent status, warning K. that '"to doubt his worthiness is to doubt the law"' (Kafka 2000: 168). Presenting the doorkeeper as infallible and beyond reproach, the priest's modulating position now clearly controverts

Nietzsche's pronouncement that the absolute, unconditional truth needs 'to be *called into question*' (*OGM* III 24: 120).

It is worth emphasising that the priest's authoritative appeal to an esoteric knowledge of a transcendent truth is accompanied by a persistent combative posture, manifesting in the repeated negation of K.'s interpretative capacity. For, having guided K. through a number of interpretative orientations, the priest argues: '"[a]t any rate, the figure of the door-keeper is thus interpreted in a way that differs from your opinion"' (Kafka 2000: 169). The priest's rhetorical strategies thus suggest a resemblance to Nietzsche's portrayal of the dogmatic ascetic ideal: this 'rejects, denies, affirms, confirms only with reference to *its* interpretation' (*OGM* III 23: 116). Highlighting the agonistic nature of exegesis, that interpretation is reflective of respective power positions and claims, this episode reveals that the text is not a site for the neutral, free play of discourse. Rather, the priest ultimately seeks to deter K. from interpretative engagement: '"I am only telling you the opinions which exist. You must not pay too much attention to opinions. The written word is unalterable, and opinions are often only an expression of despair"' (Kafka 2000: 169). The truth is fixated, absolutised, unassailable.

The priest's defamation of interpretative plurality recalls the advocate Huld's concluding comments to Block, which similarly operate to discourage the accused from active interpretative investment. As Block desperately awaits information on his case regarding the advocate's discussion with another judge, Huld informs him: '"[t]hat declaration by the judge has no significance at all for you [...]. You wouldn't understand them anyway, so it's enough for you to know there are lots of arguments against it"' (153). This comment accompanies and underscores Block's utter subjugation. Both Block and K. are presented with a plethora of interpretative positions. This plurality of interpretations is referred to in order to overwhelm their interpretative capacities while also rendering their own perspectives insignificant. On the other hand, the claim of a privileged, authoritative exegesis, articulated by the court's officials, denies the value of any such interpretative plurality and thereby rejects the validity of any personal interpretative investment.

To further illustrate the radical instability of authoritative positions, and thus the interpretative conundrum that K. is subject to, it is worth noting that the priest, at the conclusion of the discourse, again invites a Nietzschean reading. To substantially undermine K.'s exegesis of the parable, the priest simultaneously subverts the presupposition of an external, validating truth or authority by retorting, '"one does not have to believe everything is true, one only has to believe it is necessary"' (Kafka 2000: 172). Hawes points out that the priest's statement is 'almost verbatim a Nietzschean formulation' (Hawes 1988: 132): the priest's warning compels K., in Nietzsche's words, '[t]o recognize untruth as a condition of life' (*BGE* 4: 36). Reinforcing the Nietzschean flavour of this discourse, K. responds: '"[d]epressing thought. It makes the lie fundamental to world order"' (Kafka 2000: 172). To apprehend the shattering impact that the priest's concluding remark has upon K., it is necessary to explore Nietzsche's view that 'without a constant falsification of the world […] man could not live—that renouncing false judgments would mean renouncing life and a denial of life' (*BGE* 4: 35–6). Accordingly, it is through human interpretative activity that we have imposed order upon a world which is 'for all eternity chaos' (*GS* 109: 109): 'for all life is based on appearance, art, deception, point of view, the necessity of perspective and error' (*BT* 5: 8). Logic is one such lie, or anthropomorphism, by means of which humanity has preserved itself, performing a life-facilitating function: as a conventionally agreed form operating through the principles of equivalence and fixation, it does not correspond to reality as 'change, becoming, multiplicity, opposition, contradiction, war' (*WP* 584: 315); it is 'designed to maintain and increase human constructs of domination' by synthesising the incessant plurality of sensations and experiences (12 (B): 14), by reducing the dissimilar or antithetical to the similar, by establishing the 'essential, common and eternal' from the flux of becoming (*GS* 109: 109). Interpretative activity is the primary means of securing, preserving and enhancing man's feeling of power within a world that 'for all eternity' lacks 'order, organization, form, beauty' (109: 109).

In Nietzsche's thought, this disclosure of the fictive nature of truth may signal a celebration of our individual creative, interpretative capacity. That is, given that a necessary consequence of the devaluation of our hitherto highest values is that we can no longer hold onto the Christian unconditional truth to experience ourselves as powerful agents, we are impelled to generate new truths that correspond to this need. The liberating potential of this necessity is also an examination of our inventive strength:

> That it is the measure of strength to what extent we can admit to ourselves, without perishing, the merely *apparent* character, the necessity of lies.

To this extent, nihilism, as the denial of a truthful world, might be *a divine way of thinking*. (*WP* 15: 15)

Yet, as noted in Chapter 1, the negation of the 'old' truth firstly involves a characteristically extreme counter-reaction: from construing everything according to *the* interpretation, namely that of the ascetic ideal, now '"[a]ll is false"' (*WP* Outline 2: 7).[21] As James Miller points out, the revelation that the truth is illusory, or a 'kind of fiction', exposes us to the notion that 'everything we hold as solid and certain about the world is, on closer examination, demonstrably accidental, contingent, or false—laws, ideas, philosophies, religions, moralities, everything' (Miller 1990: 477). This 'insight', that 'there is no truth at all', that 'every considering-true is necessarily false' (*WP* 598: 325), Nietzsche holds, is 'the most extreme form of nihilism' (*WP* 15: 14).

In terms of Kafka's novel, the priest's disclosure shatters K.'s 'essential conviction' that the law is 'solid and certain'. Devastating his necessary (illusory) belief of discovering a just authority formulating a concrete charge, K. learns that the 'only functioning code is arbitrary' (Kavanagh 1976: 90). As Nietzsche observes, it 'is a precondition for every living thing' that 'that something must be held to be true' (*WP* 507: 276). The priest's claim operates to absolutise the 'lie': there is no definitive 'truth'; there is only a plurality of competing perspectives without decisive resolution. K., whose experience of persecution is perpetrated by an external authority, and who is impelled to render this experience significant by discovering the charges held by the 'rational' 'just' court, only discerns a chaotic and contradictory institution: no stable authority will definitively articulate the truth of the charges brought against him. The priest's revelation of the court's absolute indeterminacy, signalling the perpetual deferral of a substantive disclosure of his charges, now foregrounds the limits of the fatigued K.'s interpretative, synthesising capacity regarding his strength to render his experience meaningful.

The thoughts and imagery that dominate the close of the chapter reflect K.'s debilitating paralysis and anticipate his pending execution. He now resembles those passive, impotent defendants whom he had encountered in the corridors whose interpretative capacities were exhausted. Now K. similarly appears overwhelmed by things 'beyond the range of the intellect' (Kafka 2000: 136):

> He was too tired to follow all the deductions that could be drawn from the story; they led him into unaccustomed trains of thought, removed from reality and more suitable for academic discussion among court officials. The simple story had become perplexing, he wanted to be rid of it; and the priest, showing great delicacy of feeling, let him do this. (172)

K.'s psychological disorientation and dependence is symbolically represented: he becomes reliant on the priest to guide him out of the cathedral as he was unable 'to get his bearings in the dark. The lamp in his hand had gone out long ago' (172). Furthermore, K., who had previously eschewed others' compassion as degrading and debilitating, now invokes the priest's pity and remonstrates when the priest dismisses him as if he 'meant nothing' (172).[22]

For Straus, Kafka supersedes Nietzsche by exploring the social and psychological repercussions of the 'liberation from stabilized, hegemonic, essentialist, or metaphysical forms of discourse or belief': Kafka combats Nietzsche's apprehension of the consequent '"insouciance, cheerfulness, elegance, brightness of spirit"' (Straus 2007: 382). While I echo Straus's endorsement of Kafka's exploration of the modern nihilistic predicament, I have argued throughout that Nietzsche's thought is preoccupied with 'the trauma of nihilism', that his work reveals a deep sensitivity towards the negative social and psychological impact of nihilism (Straus 2007: 387). Indeed, Nietzsche's work offers a means to apprehend K.'s condition in ways which have hitherto remained unexplored: in line with Nietzsche's analyses of nihilism and its tie to experiences of 'senseless suffering', I read K.'s predicament to dramatise Nietzsche's view of the modern conundrum. The following passage captures Nietzsche's assessment of this nihilistic pathos:

> But the tragic thing is that we can no longer *believe* those dogmas of religion and metaphysics, once we have the rigorous method of truth in our hearts and heads, and yet on the other hand, the development of mankind has made us so delicate, sensitive, and ailing that we need the most potent kind of cures and comforts:- hence arises the danger that man might bleed to death from the truth he has recognized. (*HAH* 109: 78)

Nietzsche contends that we are now aware that 'for far too long we have interpreted [the world] falsely and mendaciously, [...] that is, according to a *need*' (*GS* 346: 204). That is, the honesty of the intellectual conscience fostered by Christianity itself has eroded credulity in the ascetic ideal and its metaphysical notions. The psychological '*need*' Nietzsche highlights involves imbuing suffering with significance. This '*need*' remains even though 'now we realize that the way of the world is not at all divine—even by human standards it is not rational, merciful, or just'; indeed, this '*need*' is rendered all the more pressing given that we have become 'so delicate, sensitive, and ailing', that we moderns have developed a particularly heightened sensibility towards suffering (*GS* 346: 204). As I have implied above, this analysis clearly resonates with Kafka's depiction of K.'s trauma: the hyperlogical and hypersensitive protagonist is exposed throughout, and particularly through the priest's discourse, to the realisation that the world, or the court, is 'not rational, merciful, or just'. 'The danger' from which K. 'might bleed to death', then, regards his experience of unbearable, senseless suffering.

As alluded to in Chapter 1, Nietzsche contends in one notebook entry that '[n]ihilism appears at that point, not that displeasure in existence has become greater than before but because one has come to mistrust any "meaning" in suffering, indeed in existence' (*WP* 55: 35). Ridley succinctly observes that with the decline in the ascetic ideal, which 'had succeeded for 2000 and more years in making existence and suffering bearable (by making them, at bottom, illusions)', 'we suddenly find ourselves without those resources which, hitherto, we had used to deal with' suffering. Nietzsche's work participates in the deconstruction of the Christian metaphysical picture and its absolutised notion of truth. However, Nietzsche remains cognisant of the ascetic ideal's historical worth in terms of the preservation of the human species: '[w]ithin it, suffering was given an interpretation; the enormous emptiness seemed filled; the door was shut on all suicidal nihilism' (*OGM* III 28: 127). Kafka's depiction of K. in the novel's final chapter is suggestive of modernity's predicament given the absence of, or 'mistrust' in, 'any meaning in suffering': K. confronts the senselessness of his trial, or rather the meaninglessness apparent in its failure to materialise as a trial; the door opens to suicidal nihilism. K. proceeds to the '*deed of nihilism*, which is suicide' (*WP* 247: 143).

A Spectacle of Suffering

Colluding in his execution, the novel's final chapter nevertheless stresses K.'s insistent need to validate himself, to confer meaning upon his existence. His final thoughts emphasise his need to interpretatively redeem his suffering:

the only thing I can do now is preserve my logical understanding to the end. I always wanted to grab at life, and not with the best of intentions either. That was not right; and am I to show now that not even these proceedings lasting a whole year could teach me anything? Am I to depart as an utterly stupid man? Are they going to say when I have gone that I wanted to end the case at the beginning and that now, at the end, I want it to begin again? I don't want people to say that. I'm thankful they've given me these stupid inarticulate companions for this journey and that they've left it to me to say what has to be said to myself. (Kafka 2000: 176)

While K.'s determination to remain logical appears constant, there are aspects of this rumination that reveal a marked shift in K.'s thought, signalling his resignation: he turns his attention outwards to how others will perceive him where previously he had been dismissive of those who had largely appeared hostile or indifferent; his self-reproach has become more general, more all-encompassing, as he censures himself for wanting '"to grab at life"'. For Heller and others stressing Kafka's depiction of the ascetic realisation of the 'futility of striving', such an admission may be construed as evidence of K.'s voluntary renunciation of willing, or desiring: K. is no longer deceived by life but is engaged in 'an effort to dissolve world and self [...] to achieve a state of non-volition' (Heller 1971: 76). My concern with this view is that it seems to be at odds with K.'s empirical experience of persecution and his persistent, though dwindling, resistance to this: K.'s sense of agency is not willingly relinquished but rather gradually eroded by the court's insidious and senseless operations; through a Nietzschean lens, K.'s constant need to experience himself as an active agent is apparent even at his moment of surrender. That is, the interpretation of his suffering remains his chief concern as he anticipates his execution and seeks to accord it a redemptive significance: to fulfil his interpretative will to power he desires to impose a teleological trajectory upon his experience and so discern that there has been some return, that he has grown through learning, that something has been '*achieved through the process*' (*WP* 12 (A): 12).

More telling, however, is that K.'s understandable rejection of the thought of the endless repetition of the court's proceedings, apparent in his need to impose an origin and an end to this experience, suggests his current position of weakness or life-negation in Nietzschean terms: K.'s ruminations evoke, and subsequently repudiate, Nietzsche's thought experiment of the 'eternal recurrence'. That is, as Nietzsche calls this experiment 'the heaviest weight' in *The Gay Science*, the notion of eternal recurrence equates to the greatest test of one's capacity to appropriate and affirm one's suffering. Nietzsche asks the bearer of this thought to examine his or her life with the view that 'everything unspeakably small or great in your life must return to you, all in the same succession and sequence—[…] innumerable times again' (*GS* 341: 194). Importantly, Nietzsche acknowledges in his notebooks that reflecting on 'existence as it is, without meaning or aim, yet recurring inevitably without any finale of nothingness' constitutes the 'most terrible' thought: it entails the potentially nauseating realisation that 'everything' is 'in vain' (*WP* 55: 35). With the seemingly extreme responses of despair or affirmation provoked by engaging with this notion, Nietzsche thus claims that, '[i]f this thought gained power over you, as you are it would transform and possibly crush you' (*GS* 341: 194). As only the strongest are capable of enduring such a thought for Nietzsche, K.'s repudiation of the possibility of an interminable, cyclical continuation of the court's processes is thus symptomatic of weakness, or a failure to attain the exemplary 'Dionysian affirmation of the world as it is, without subtraction, exception, or selection' that this notion of 'eternal recurrence' aims towards (*WP* 1041: 536). One may surmise that, as Nietzsche considers this notion as an examination of how 'well disposed' one is towards one's life, K.'s determination to deny the thought of an endless return of the same is reflective of his fatigued condition (*GS* 341: 194): being unable to posit personal significance within this indifferent, hostile world of the court, to conceive of its end, or to construe himself as a goal-bound agent, is symptomatic of and precipitates K.'s hopeless despair. According to the crucial teaching of Nietzsche's prophet, Zarathustra, as discussed in Chapter 2, K. fails to perform a synthesising interpretation of his experiences, evincing a lack of 'creative will' to transform '"[i]t was"' into an '"[b]ut I willed it thus!"', […] [t]hus shall I will it!' (*TSZ* II 20: 163).[23]

Exhausted and denuded of his own interpretative capacity, K.'s guilt, as Mark M. Anderson notes, is 'produced by accusation and the attendant persecution' (Anderson 1994: 155). As I read it, K. constitutes his own guilt in order to fulfil his impulse to interpret, to render his senseless suffering significant. Yielding to the court's unstable punitive logic allows him to comprehend his distress: he suffers as he has transgressed the law. Like Nietzsche's powerless slaves' heeding the teachings of the ascetic priest, K. can 'understand his suffering itself as a *condition of punishment*' (*OGM* III 20: 111). Nietzsche's apprehension of guilt further illuminates K.'s fatigued, impotent sensibility: '[t]o condemn oneself can also be a means of restoring the feeling of strength after a defeat' (*D* 140: 88). That is, the attribution of guilt permits 'the weak, humiliated and depressed' to show 'that they still have some strength left': instinctively, it provides 'a new excitation of the *feeling of power*' (88). K.'s recourse to finding himself culpable, as a guilty debtor who deserves his punishment, is evident at the novel's denouement.

Bernard Williams observes that 'feeling guilty involves the internalization of a figure who is an ideal "victim" or "enforcer"' (Williams 1993: 89–90). Notably, K. relinquishes his feeble resistance against his guards, and indeed begins to direct the procession towards his death, when a figure resembling Fräulein Bürstner 'appeared in front of them' (Kafka 2000: 175). Furthermore, 'K. was not at all concerned about whether it was Fräulein Bürstner or not': 'he wanted to keep her in sight as long as possible, but only because he wanted to keep in mind the reproach she signified for him' (175). That he projects the figure of Fräulein Bürstner, then, signals the presence of a 'victim' or 'enforcer'. With K.'s 'reproach' established, or internalised, K. and the guards cease following Fräulein Bürstner: for K. 'could do without her now' (176).

Projecting the figure of Fräulein Bürstner indicates K.'s awareness of having committed a transgression: '[g]uilt is occasioned only by *failing* to honour what we take to be an obligation', as May notes (May 1999: 59). The nature of the 'reproach' that 'she signified for him' is important: earlier in the novel, K. had committed a sexual, predatory attack on Fräulein Bürstner in which 'he seized her, and kissed her on the mouth and then all over the face like a thirsty animal' (Kafka 2000: 23). Fräulein Bürstner departs from K.'s embrace an exhausted, forlorn, defeated figure. There is a marked shift in K.'s interpretation of this assault: he moves from an initial innocent triumphalism, oblivious of any sense of transgression committed or injury inflicted, to one of considered self-reproach. This transformation attends his defeat at the hands of the court. Essential elements of the guilty sensibility are now evident: a victim has been harmed and, acknowledging his status as a debtor, K. is beset by feelings of failure. Furthermore, by invoking the figure of Fräulein Bürstner, K. finds his guilt irredeemable. K.'s previous failed attempts to contact the Fräulein reveal that his debt towards her has not been, and cannot be, discharged:

He tried to contact her in several different ways, but she always managed to avoid him. [...] Then he wrote her a letter addressed to her both at her office and at her apartment in which he tried once again to justify his behaviour, offered any satisfaction she might require, promised never to overstep any bounds she might set, and asked only to be given an opportunity to speak to her sometime. (59)

As May notes, the sense of failure that characterises guilt may arise as 'the creditor's terms are not known or even knowable, or because repayment has no conceivable terminus' (May 1999: 59). Thus, even though K. 'had promised to defer to her wishes in everything', there is no response, not even 'to tell him why she could not grant his request' (Kafka 2000: 59). K., who 'did not want to be obliged to anyone', has not repaid his dues and has not even attained clarity with regards to the gravity of his misdemeanour: Fräulein Bürstner does not 'appear' again in the novel until this point (27).

Indeed, recalling K.'s retribution fantasy discussed above, in which the apotheosised Elsa witnesses the punishment of the student, is suggestive of the elevated, deified status that Fräulein Bürstner's ghostly appearance now assumes for K. With this point in mind, the carnal, sexualised nature of the violation K. perpetrates takes on added significance in pointing to his irredeemable culpability. For there is a parallel with K.'s crime and Nietzsche's analysis of guilt in his discussion of the ascetic ideal: for the Christian, Nietzsche contends, it is the corrupt essence of carnal embodiment that forecloses the possibility of fully discharging one's debts before God, the pure, transcendent deity. Nietzsche argues:

> You will already have guessed *what* has really gone on with all this and *behind* all this: he seizes upon the ultimate antithesis he can find to his real and irredeemable animal instincts, he re-interprets these self-same animal instincts as guilt before God. (*OGM* II 22: 68)

Accordingly, man is comparatively corrupt and inferior, forever subject to being betrayed by his recalcitrant drives as he seeks to imitate or become one with the transcendent deity. Bound to inevitable failure, man is thus forever guilty. As Nietzsche argues, '[g]uilt towards *God*' allows man 'to feel the palpable certainty of his own absolute unworthiness' (*OGM* II 22: 68). Corroborating K.'s resolve to find himself worthless in

contradistinction to his own deified creditor, the novel repeatedly associates the sexual with depravity and decay as it depicts erotic encounters
through predatory, animalistic imagery.[24]

Furthermore, Nietzsche holds that guilt exemplifies the 'will to torment oneself, that suppressed cruelty of animal man' that has 'seized
on religious precepts in order to provide his self-torture with its most
horrible hardness and sharpness' (*OGM* II 22: 68). Critics such as Ring,
Anna Katharina Schaffner, and Margot Norris have investigated sadomasochistic themes in Kafka's oeuvre by appealing to thinkers such as Freud,
Kraft- Ebing, and Gilles Deleuze (see Schaffner 2011; Norris 1978; Ring
2012). By contending that civilised man is constituted by a sadomasochistic subjectivity, Nietzsche anticipates much of this field of thought.
Bringing Nietzsche's insights upon self-directed cruelty into this discussion offers further analytic tools to bring to Kafka's novel: for the beleaguered protagonist, not only does the perpetration of sadomasochistic
acts enable him to experience some form of a pathos of agency, but it
also, according to Nietzsche, fulfils the primary urge to inflict suffering.
I shall briefly contextualise these claims.

As noted in Chapter 2, Nietzsche hypothesises in the *Genealogy* that
the incipience of primordial, collective living entails the necessary repression of our primary aggressive and antisocial instinctive drives.[25] Brian
Leiter therefore observes that in Nietzsche's account 'instinctual energy
does not simply vanish: it must be continuously discharged somehow'
(Leiter 2002: 234). Thus, unable to freely discharge these aggressive
urges in the social sphere, Nietzsche contends that the 'internalization'
of these instincts is unavoidably traumatic. For an exceptional minority
the inward-turning of these drives provides a 'pregnant' potential for
future development: Nietzsche valorises the self-reflexive 'pleasure of
making suffer' in which the self discharges its cruel instincts in the project of giving 'form' to itself (*OGM* II 18: 64).[26] Yet while Nietzsche
embraces the self-violation integral to practices of self-cultivation, he is
ambivalent, however, about the development of guilt among the majority of sick, self-lacerating creatures: the priest may encourage the intensification of self-cruelty for 'the purpose of self-discipline, self-surveillance
and self-overcoming', on the one hand (III 16: 100); on the other, however, the absolute nature of guilt towards a deity is, for Nietzsche, where
self-terrorisation 'reached its most terrible and sublime peak' (II 18: 64).
Furthermore, guilt aims at life-denying as opposed to life-enhancing
ends: rather than seeking to integrate and harness our drives and affects,

the ascetic ideal encourages the extirpation of our 'irredeemable animal instincts' (II 22: 68).

Given that Nietzsche posits that man has indelible cruel instincts, and that civilisation is borne from the inward-turning of these drives, it is no surprise that Nietzsche argues that 'one should open one's eyes and take a new look at cruelty': there is 'an abundant, over-abundant enjoyment of one's own suffering, of making oneself suffer' (*BGE* 229: 159). In both life-denying and life-enhancing forms of self-inflicted cruelty, the masochist is 'split within himself' and is gratified by identifying with the perpetrator of suffering. In a passage from *Daybreak* Nietzsche apprehends the ascetic's self-directed cruelty as more sophisticated than the crude, externally-directed cruelty perpetrated by the barbarian:

> The triumph of the ascetic over himself, his glance turned inwards which beholds man split asunder into sufferer and a spectator, and henceforth gazes out into the outer world only in order to gather as it were wood for his own pyre, this final tragedy of the drive for distinction in which there is only one character burning and consuming himself—this is a worthy conclusion and one appropriate to the commencement: in both cases an unspeakable happiness at the *sight of torment*! (2007, 113: 68)

'Split off from him—or herself as the suffering object', there is possible pleasure in identifying with the inflictor of suffering, as Janaway notes (Janaway 2007: 126). The fundamental drive to inflict suffering is thus gratified. In the novel, K.'s masochistic proclivity is evinced at moments of great distress: K. inflicts, or considers perpetrating, suffering upon himself as a means to claim some form of agency when particularly threatened by a paralysing impotence.[27] K.'s self-incrimination thus permits him to fulfil the instinctive drive to perpetrate cruelty, albeit on himself, when his feelings of agency regarding his capacity to impact the world are diminished. Schaffner's comment is insightful: 'Kafka's characters resort to masochistic survival strategies, investing the menace with pleasure so as to regain a modicum of control over their lives' (Schaffner and Weller 2012: 85).

Nevertheless, this sensation of power seems to be ultimately denied K. at the moment of his greatest need, namely at his execution scene: K.'s absolute defeat is signalled as he fails to assume the position of perpetrator of his own suffering. The fatal blow is beyond K. and is performed by the guards:

> K. was perfectly aware it was supposed to be his duty to seize the knife as it hovered from hand to hand above him and drive it into himself. But he did not do this [...] He was not able to prove his own worth completely. (Kafka 2000: 177)

K.'s ignominy is confirmed by the final deprivation of his claim to agency. His interpretative power is similarly extinguished at the end, as it is the '"stupid inarticulate"' guards whose voice he last hears, denying him the final chance to impact his reception (177). Like Block's humiliation before Huld, K.'s wretched execution is similarly expressed: he dies '"[l]ike a dog!"' (177).

For Robertson, the novel's tragedy lies 'in the fact that Josef K.'s sense of shared humanity awakens only in the last minute of his life' (Robertson 1985: 129). Hawes shares this perception, claiming that K. similarly sees 'a vision of the human community he has failed so conspicuously to attain' (Hawes 1988: 146). Hawes in particular implies that at the final moment K. can understand his guilt. I agree with Ziolkowski's assessment, however: 'K. is summarily executed "like a dog" with no understanding or clarification of his guilt' (Ziolkowski 1997: 240). Rather, K.'s invocation of Fräulein Bürstner registers his own desperate attempt to clarify his guilt, to avert senseless suffering: K. constitutes his own guilt given the absence of an actual charge, underwriting Nietzsche's insight that man 'does *not* deny suffering as such: he *wills* it, he even seeks it out, provided he is shown a *meaning* for it, a *purpose* for suffering' (*OGM* III 28: 127). And K.'s concluding, desperate plea suggests that he remains uncertain, unconvinced of his complicity in this constitution of his guilt: '[w]ere there still objections which had been forgotten? Certainly there were. [...] Where was the judge he had never seen? Where was the high court he had never reached?' (Kafka 2000: 178). K.'s death is dismal, remaining uncodified by the court authority that now operates secretly, transporting him to an empty industrial wasteland. In my opinion, Robertson and Hawes are engaged in the 'human-all-too-human' project of conferring significance upon K.'s brutal and abject end: providing a redemptive inflection of K.'s execution seems at odds with the novel's insistence of the senselessness of the process, from K.'s point of view. That is, as suggested at his first tribunal, the process that induces K.'s suicidal execution may in fact be based on nothing more than that of mistaken identity. Thus, borrowing Deleuze and Guattari's words, the respective readings proffered by Hawes and

Robertson appear 'unsustainable on the basis of the novel's overall architecture and movement' (Deleuze and Guattari 1986: 44).

I would argue that K.'s preoccupation with, or his projection of, others at the scene of his execution does not indicate a belated awareness of his 'shared humanity', as Robertson contends, but is reflective of the very fact that he cannot escape cognisance of the very senselessness of his execution: overwhelmed by the meaninglessness of his suffering, and incapable of performing the fatal blow himself to reclaim some sense of agency, his final recourse is to consider his suffering as a cruel spectacle for others' pleasure. My argument derives from Nietzsche's claim that 'the primitive logic' that '"[a]ll evil is justified if a god takes pleasure in it" […] still penetrates into our European civilization!' (*OGM* II 7: 48). According to Nietzsche, the ancients shielded themselves from the nauseating truth of the pointless horror of existence by considering their suffering as a cruel spectacle for the Gods' enjoyment:

> In order to rid the world of concealed, undiscovered, unseen suffering and deny it in all honesty, people were then practically obliged to invent Gods and intermediate beings at every level, in short, something which roamed round in obscurity, which could see in the dark and which would not miss out on an interesting spectacle of pain so easily. With the aid of such inventions, life then played the trick which it has always known how to play, of justifying itself, justifying its 'evil'. (48)

Obscure, indeterminate figures appear in the murky twilight at K.'s actual moment of execution. Tellingly, K. had previously shunned any public exhibition of self-loss as shameful.[28] Yet, in contradistinction to his constant hostility towards the profusion of spectators who recurrently appear to witness his distress throughout the text, K. now protests at their absence: as he surveys the theatrically costumed executioners, he reflects that '"[t]hey want to get rid of me cheaply"'; he remonstrates, '"[w]hy did they send just you!"' (Kafka 2000: 174). And yet, underlining K.'s utter abjection and impotence, I would argue that he does not provide an exhibition for his ghostly spectators to enjoy: his ignominious lack of resistance towards his executors parallels Block's earlier humiliating subjugation, which K. himself, as a spectator, found repugnant.[29]

By bringing Nietzsche's insights to my reading of Kafka's *The Trial*, I have emphasised K.'s persistent need to accord his suffering some form of significance. Doing so, I offer a new reading of the novel and also reconsider the relevance of Nietzsche's thought to this text. I have thus pointed to the role of interpretative activity in the novel and argued that the court primarily thwarts the defendants' exegetical capacity: the accused are reduced to a state of paralysis and dependence as they fail to comprehend the charges brought against them. Given that K. is besieged by the court's insidious and overpowering forces, I have read K.'s self-culpabilisation as signalling his active attempt to reclaim some form of meaning, and hence agency, as well as his surrender. Finally, as the novel's action remains radically indeterminate until the very last moment, I have suggested that even the self-incrimination that precipitates his complicity in his own execution remains inadequate: his preoccupation with his need to justify his useless, unredeemable suffering therefore constitutes the novel's theatrical denouement. This consideration of the role of the spectator that is central to the final chapter's hyperbolic theatricality is prevalent in Samuel Beckett's *Endgame* (1957). Furthermore, the inflated attention drawn to the artifice of the execution scene, pointing to the co-existence of art and the brutal ugliness of life, recalls Nietzsche's thought on the role of tragic art. As I now turn to examine Beckett's play in relation to suffering and nihilism, I shall illustrate that not only is the senseless and the unpalatable theatrically represented, but the play also echoes Nietzsche's views on ancient tragedy by calling attention to the role of art to justify life's horror.

NOTES

1. Quoted in Benno Wagner, 'Insuring Nietzsche: Kafka's Files', *New German Critique*, 99 (2006): 84.
2. See Walter H. Sokel, 'Nietzsche and Kafka: The Dionysian Connection', in *Kafka for the Twenty-First Century*, ed. by Stanley Corngold and Ruth V. Gross (Rochester, NY: Camden House, 2011), pp. 64–74; Stanley Corngold, 'Kafka's "Zarathustra"', *Journal of the Kafka Society of America*, 19 (1995): 9–15; Stanley Corngold, 'Nietzsche, Kafka and Literary Paternity', in *Nietzsche and Jewish Culture*, ed. by Jacob Golomb (London: Routledge, 1997), pp. 137–57; Linda C. Hsu, 'Klamotten: Reading Nietzsche Reading Kafka', *German Quarterly*, 67 (1994): 211–21.
3. Grimm claims: '[Bridgwater's] investigations and insights are constantly hampered by his lust for sweeping, all-too sweeping generalization, philosophical flights of fancy'. Reinhold Grimm, 'Comparing Kafka and Nietzsche', *German Quarterly*, 52 (1979): 41.
4. See also *OGM* III 7: 81.

5. See also Chapter 1, pp. 11–12; Chapter 2, p. 45, p. 55.
6. See, for example, Cyrena N. Pondrom, 'Kafka and Phenomenology: Josef K.'s Search for Information', in *Twentieth Century Interpretations of The Trial*, ed. by James Rolleston (Indiana University; Prentice-Hall, 1976), p. 50. Pondrom contends that K. is 'a reasonable man who assumes that cause and effect are inviolable and that everything has an explanation'. See also Rolf J. Goebel, 'The Exploration of the Modern City in *The Trial*', in *The Cambridge Companion to Kafka*, ed. by Julian Preece (Cambridge: Cambridge University Press, 2002), pp. 42–60 (p. 50). Goebel reads Josef K. as 'the detective who, persistently if in vain, seeks to impose rationality, logic, and legal analysis'.
7. See Chapter 2, pp. 39–40; Chapter 3, pp. 78–9.
8. See Chapter 2, footnote 34.
9. For other views see, for example: Elizabeth Boa, *Kafka: Gender, Class, and Race in the Letters and Fictions* (Oxford: Clarendon Press, 1996), p. 185; Anna Katharina Schaffner, 'Kafka and the Hermeneutics of Sadomasochism', *Forum for Modern Language Studies*, 46 (2010): 334–50 (335); David Tenenbaum, *Issues of Shame and Guilt in the Modern Novel* (New York: Edwin Mellen Press, 2009), p. 135. For further evidence of K.'s inability to bear others' suffering, see Kafka (2000: 51). This scene is also suggestive of others' hypersensitivity.
10. See, for example, Kafka (2000: 164).
11. I will illustrate this in more detail below. For further examples of K.'s thinking in these terms, see Kafka (2000: 72): K. feels 'indebted' to his uncle; Kafka (2000: 75): he feels that he 'owes' the family an explanation.
12. Bridgwater claims: 'However much K.'s rational self of Conscience may try to assert itself, he continually lacks moral concentration, and in every case eventually follows the Will, that is, his desires. In Biblical terms K. is, like Karl Rossman, the victim of original sin, for his very will is guilty'. *Kafka and Nietzsche* (Bonn: Bouvier, 1974), p. 61.
13. Robertson follows Ingeborg Henel here. See Ingeborg Henel, 'The Legend of the Doorkeeper and Its Significance for Kafka's *Trial*', in *Twentieth Century Interpretations of The Trial*, ed. by James Rolleston (Indiana University; Prentice-Hall, 1976), pp. 40–55 (42). Henel argues: 'At his arrest he ignored the inspector's admonition that he occupy himself less with his innocence and the authorities and reflect more about himself'.
14. The court thus diverges from Nietzsche's valorisation of the primitive justice system which, he claimed, acted to curb explosive, reactive feelings through the notion of 'equivalence'. See *OGM* II 4: 43; see Chapter 2, pp. 48–9.
15. See also *OGM* I 10: 23; Chapter 2, pp. 52–3; Chapter 3, pp. 86–7, 108–10.

16. See especially K.'s discussion with Titorelli. Kafka (2000: 118, 121). I shall discuss the priest's authoritative omniscience below.
17. See Chapter 2, pp. 51–2.
18. See Chapter 1, p. 10.
19. This story was originally published in the almanac, *Vom Jüngsten Tag* (Leipzig: Kurt Wolff Verlag, 1916).
20. Henel also invokes Zarathustra's maxim to pronounce judgement on K.: 'Can you be judge of yourself and avenger of your own law? It is terrible to be alone with the judge and avenger of one's own law' (*TSZ* I 17: 89).
21. See Chapter 1, p. 11.
22. For an example of K.'s objection to pity, see Kafka (2000: 53–4).
23. Chapter 2, p. 41.
24. See, for example, Kafka (2000: 41, 44, 112).
25. See Chapter 2, pp. 44–5.
26. See Chapter 2, p. 53.
27. For example, K. considers offering himself to the whipper for punishment in place of the guards because he feels powerless to prevent their whipping. See Kafka (2000: 69–70).
28. See, for example, Kafka (2000: 10, 53).
29. See Kafka (2000: 149–50). This point recalls Nietzsche's view on the savage who 'does not want to see a contemptible creature suffer, there is no enjoyment in that' (*D* 135: 86).

References

Alberts, Paul, 'Knowing Life Before the Law: Kafka, Kelsen, Derrida', in *Philosophy and Kafka*, ed. by Brendan Moran and Carlo Salzani (Plymouth: Lexington Books, 2013).

Allen, Neil, *Franz Kafka and the Genealogy of Modern European Philosophy: From Phenomenology to Post-Structuralism* (Lewiston, N.Y. : Edwin Mellen Press, 2005).

Anderson, Mark M., *Kafka's Clothes: Ornament and Aestheticism in the Habsburg Fin De Siècle* (Oxford: Clarendon Press, 1994).

Bridgwater, Patrick, *Kafka and Nietzsche* (Bonn: Bouvier, 1974).

Deleuze, Gilles, and Félix Guattari, *Kafka: Toward a Minor Literature*, trans. Dana Polan (Minneapolis: University of Minnesota Press, 1986).

Derrida, Jacques, 'Before the Law', in *Acts of Literature*, ed. by Derek Attridge (London: Routledge, 1992).

Foucault, Michel, *Discipline and Punish*, trans. Alan Sheridan (London: Penguin, repr., 1991).

Friedländer, Saul, *Franz Kafka: The Poet of Shame and Guilt* (New Haven: Yale University Press, 2013).

Grimm, Reinhold, 'Comparing Kafka and Nietzsche', *German Quarterly*, 52 (1979): 339–50.

Hawes, James, 'Faust and Nietzsche in Kafka's *Der Prozess*', *New German Studies*, 15 (1988): 127–51.

Heller, Peter, 'Kafka and Nietzsche', in *Proceedings of the Comparative Literature Symposium. Vol. iv: Franz Kafka: His Place in World Literature*, ed. by Wolodymyr T. Zyla, Wendell M. Aycock, and Pat Ingle Gillis (Lubbock: Texas Technology University, 1971), 71–95.

Henel, Ingeborg, 'The Legend of the Doorkeeper and Its Significance for Kafka's *Trial*', in *Twentieth Century Interpretations of The Trial*, ed. by James Rolleston (Englewood Cliffs, N.J. : Prentice-Hall, 1976), 40–55.

Janaway, Christopher, *Beyond Selflessness* (Oxford: Oxford University Press, 2007).

Kafka, Franz, *The Trial*, trans. Idris Parry (London: Penguin, repr., 2000).

Kavanagh, Thomas M., 'Kafka's *The Trial*: The Semiotics of the Absurd', in *Twentieth Century Interpretations of The Trial*, ed. by James Rolleston (Englewood Cliffs, N.J. : Prentice-Hall, 1976), 86–93.

Kuepper, Karl J., 'Gesture and Posture as Elemental Symbolism in Kafka's *The Trial*', in *Twentieth Century Interpretations of The Trial*, ed. by James Rolleston (Englewood Cliffs, N.J. : Prentice-Hall, 1976), 60–9.

Kundera, Milan, *Testaments Betrayed*, trans. Linda Asher (Chatham: Faber and Faber, 1995).

Lampert, Laurence, *Nietzsche's Task: An Interpretation of Beyond Good and Evil* (New Haven, CT: Yale University Press, 2004).

Leiter, Brian, *Routledge Philosophy Guidebook to Nietzsche on Morality* (London: Routledge, 2002).

May, Simon, *Nietzsche's Ethics and His War on 'Morality'* (Oxford: Oxford University Press, 1999).

Miller, James, 'Carnivals of Atrocity: Foucault, Nietzsche, Cruelty', *Political Theory*, 18 (1990): 470–91.

Muller-Lauter, Wolfgang, *Nietzsche: His Philosophy of Contradictions and the Contradictions of His Philosophy*, trans. David J. Parent (New York: University of Illinois Press, 1999).

Nietzsche, Friedrich Wilhelm, *The Will to Power*. trans. Walter Kaufmann and R. J. Hollingdale (New York: Vintage Books, 1968).

———, *Beyond Good and Evil: Prelude to a Philosophy of the Future*. trans. R. J. Hollingdale (Harmondsworth: Penguin, repr. 1990).

———, *The Birth of Tragedy*. trans. Shaun Whiteside (London: Penguin, 1993).

———, *On the Genealogy of Morality*. trans. Carol Diethe (Cambridge: Cambridge University Press, 1994).

———, *Thus Spoke Zarathustra*. trans. R. J. Hollingdale (London: Penguin, repr. 2003).

————, *The Anti-Christ* in *Twilight of the Idols* and *The Anti-Christ*. trans. R. J. Hollingdale (London: Penguin, repr. 2003).

————, *The Gay Science: With a Prelude in German Rhymes and an Appendix of Songs*. trans. Josefine Nauckhoff and Adrian Del Caro (Cambridge: Cambridge University Press, repr. 2003).

————, *Twilight of the Idols* in *Twilight of the Idols* and *The Anti-Christ*. trans. R. J. Hollingdale (London: Penguin, repr. 2003).

————, *Human, All Too Human*. trans. Marion Faber and Stephen Lehmann (London: Penguin, repr. 2004).

————, *Daybreak: Thoughts on the Prejudices of Morality*. trans. R. J. Hollingdale (Cambridge: Cambridge University Press, repr. 2007).

Norris, Margot, 'Sadism and Masochism in Two Kafka Stories: "In Der Strafkolonie" and "Ein Hungerkünstler"', *MLN*, 93 (3) (1978): 430–47.

Owen, David, *Nietzsche, Politics and Modernity: Critique of Liberal Reason* (London: Sage, 1995).

Pascal, Roy, *From Naturalism to Expressionism: German Literature and Society 1880–1918* (London: Basic Books, 1973).

Pondrom, Cyrena N., 'Kafka and Phenomenology: Josef K.'s Search for Information', in *Twentieth Century Interpretations of The Trial*, ed. by James Rolleston (Englewood Cliffs, N.J. : Prentice-Hall, 1976), 70–85.

Ridley, Aaron, *Nietzsche's Conscience: Six Character Studies from the Genealogy* (Ithaca: Cornell University Press, 1998).

Ring, Annie, 'In the Law's Hands: S/M Pleasure in *Der Proceß*, A Queer Reading', *Forum for Modern Language Studies*, 48 (2012): 306–22.

Robertson, Ritchie, *Kafka: Judaism, Politics and Literature* (Oxford: Clarendon, 1985).

Schaffner, Anna Katharina, *Modernism and Perversion; Sexual Deviance in Sexology and Literature, 1850–1930* (Basingstoke: Palgrave Macmillan, 2011).

Schaffner, Anna Katharina, and Shane Weller, *Modernist Eroticisms: European Literature After Sexology* (New York, NY: Palgrave Macmillan, 2012).

Schrift, Alan D., *Nietzsche and the Question of Interpretation: Between Hermeneutics and Deconstruction* (London: Routledge, 1990).

Staten, Henry, *Nietzsche's Voice* (Ithaca, NY: Cornell University Press, 1990).

Straus, Nina Pelikan, 'Grand Theory on Trial: Kafka, Derrida, and the Will to Power', *Philosophy and Literature*, 31 (2) (2007): 378–93.

Tusken, Lewis W., 'Once More with Chutzpah: A Brave Comparison of New Worlds in Nietzsche's *The Genealogy of Morals* and Kafka's *In the Penal Colony*', *Journal of Evolutionary Psychology*, 10 (1989): 342–51.

Wagner, Benno, 'Insuring Nietzsche: Kafka's Files', *New German Critique*, 99 (2006): 83–119.

Williams, Bernard, *Shame and Necessity* (Berkeley: University of California Press, 1993).

Ziolkowski, Theodore, *The Mirror of Justice: Literary Reflections of Legal Crises* (Princeton, NJ: Princeton University Press, 1997).

CHAPTER 5

Samuel Beckett's *Endgame* and the Economy of *Ressentiment*

Introduction: Theatre of Suffering

Hamm's opening soliloquy gestures towards the play's principal themes and points to one of the central predicaments that govern the drama:

> HAMM: Enough, it's time it ended, in the refuge too. [*Pause.*] And yet I hesitate, I hesitate to ... to end. Yes, there it is, it's time it ended and yet I hesitate to—[he yawns]—to end. God, I'm tired, I'd be better off in bed. (Beckett 1990: 93)

Exemplified by a suicidal desire that will remain unfulfilled, Hamm's fatigue recalls the state of paralysis that characterises K.'s ignominious death in Kafka's *The Trial* (1925). This desire to end coupled with the incapacity to actualise this wish recurs throughout Beckett's *Endgame* (1957), performing a central tension in a play characterised by constant strains and ambiguities. This predicament suggests one of the possible significances of the play's title. Hamm's meta-theatrical opening words, '[m]e—[*he yawns*]—to play', resonate with K.'s theatrical execution: both Hamm and K. corroborate Nietzsche's apprehension of the 'human-all-too-human' need for a witness to human suffering (93). That is, as I shall explore in greater depth below, this self-conscious performativity is directly related to the characters' experience as chronic sufferers: Beckett, like Kafka, dramatises the characters' various strategies to appropriate their useless

© The Author(s) 2018
S. Smith, *Nietzsche and Modernism*,
Palgrave Studies in Modern European Literature,
https://doi.org/10.1007/978-3-319-75535-9_5

suffering, including that of invoking and implicating the audience in the characters' exegetical impasse.

Discussing *Endgame*, the philosopher Stanley Cavell notes the link between suffering and performativity: '[i]t is a play performed not by actors, but by sufferers' (Cavell 1976: 158). Hamm's opening, self-re-flexive soliloquy may possess a hyperbolic quality, yet it also serves to point to the centrality of suffering in the drama:

> HAMM: Can there be misery—[*he yawns*]—loftier than mine? No doubt. Formerly. But now? [*Pause.*] My father? [*Pause.*] My mother? [*Pause.*] My ... dog? [*Pause.*] Oh I am willing to believe they suffer as much as such creatures can suffer. But does that mean their sufferings equal mine? No doubt. [*Pause.*] No, all is a—[*he yawns*] —bsolute, [*proudly*] the big-ger a man is the fuller he is. [*Pause. Gloomily.*] And the emptier. (Beckett 1990: 93)

As the play continually complicates the question of sympathetic identi-fication between characters and between characters and the audience, this speech adumbrates the import of the theme of the sufferer's radical ontological isolation in *Endgame*. This has significant ethical implications that I shall examine by appealing to Nietzsche's thoughts on suffering, sympathy, and cruelty.

Endgame is preoccupied with pain and cruelty, entropy and impo-tence. Beckett's characters are ageing, fragmented subjects who, as Clov puts it, are 'dying of their wounds' (132). To briefly illustrate this it may be noted that the drama both begins and ends with Hamm apostrophis-ing his handkerchief, 'old Stancher'. In his examination of the etymol-ogy of the verb stanch, Beckett scholar Russell Smith reveals its relation to mourning as well as its contemporary meaning, 'to stop the flow of blood' (Smith 2007: 100). I shall show that, as in D. H. Lawrence's *Lady Chatterley's Lover* (1928), these wounded characters deploy defen-sive and recuperative strategies in a struggle for mastery, to attain some form of self-coherence, to prevent further spillage of selfhood.

The refuge itself, as a space, epitomises such defensive withdrawal and self-enclosure. Furthermore, the claustrophobic setting of the shel-ter, combined with the characters' physical confinement, resonates with Elaine Scarry's observation on the phenomenology of pain as the shrinking of the self's universe: Clov is the play's only mobile charac-ter; Hamm is blind, paralysed and wheelchair bound; Hamm's parents,

Nagg and Nell, are legless and living in dustbins (see Scarry 1985: 32). Human existence in this play, then, as throughout the Beckettian world, is constituted through suffering and loss. As I attend to the sense of suffering and loss that permeates *Endgame*, I shall signal the relevance of Nietzsche given that his philosophy was particularly preoccupied with analysing the psychology of the crushed, the impotent and the sick.[1]

In the first part of my discussion I shall focus on sketching the characters' experience of passive, chronic suffering. Here I shall observe the characters' recourse to defensive, restricted economies and discuss this with reference to Nietzsche's analysis of *ressentiment*. I shall then turn to consider the characters' recuperative strategies, particularly focusing on the role of narrative in the play. However, as I note the characters' failed attempts to constitute an efficacious, willing selfhood through narrative, I shall then approach the pervasive appearance of cruelty in the play. Invoking Nietzsche's thought on this phenomenon to suggest ways in which the play's seemingly gratuitous aggression works to sustain the fatigued characters on the one hand, I will contend that this largely compensatory drive precipitates their mutual demise on the other. As I move from considering the self-destructive quality of the characters' interrelations, I shall conclude the chapter by examining the characters' performativity and concomitant invocation of an audience. This strategy, I contend, signals the characters' ultimate recourse to render their suffering significant and bearable.

DYING FROM THEIR WOUNDS

The world outside of the shelter is, according to Hamm, 'corpsed'. This vision of the world depicted in *Endgame* may be taken to be representative of a post-apocalyptic scenario. Theodor Adorno, for instance, relates the play's barrenness to the devastation wrought by World War Two (see Adorno 1982: 122).[2] Pursuing this reading would allow one to situate *Endgame* along with *Lady Chatterley's Lover* in terms of their respective depictions of post-war nihilism. I wish to add to this interpretation by focusing on Nietzsche's contention that our interpretative perspectives are embodied, that they are symptomatic of the particular physio-psychological constitution of the beholder: it is possible to argue that the characters' bleak outlooks can be related to their overriding physical deterioration and exhaustion. After all, as the critic Mary F. Catanzaro puts it, Hamm is 'the consummate picture of tired ennui'

(Catanzaro 2007: 185). By invoking Nietzsche's notion of perspectivism and yoking it to the characters' exhaustion and illness, I will then go on to observe the economy of *ressentiment* permeating the play. Perhaps the best place to begin to explore this notion of perspectival outlook in *Endgame* is by turning to Hamm's reminiscing of his visit to the madman who, in perceiving the world as 'ashen', seems to echo or presage the characters' habitation of a 'corpsed' world.

Thomas Dilworth and Christopher Langlois note that Hamm's remembered visit to the madman occurs at the centre of *Endgame*. They thus contend that as 'middleness is thematically emphasised' throughout the play, Beckett is gesturing towards its significance to the play as a whole (Dilworth and Langlois 2007: 168). Furthermore, Dilworth and Langlois identify the appearance of the madman in *Endgame* to signal the relevance of Nietzsche to this particular work. These critics stress Beckett's antagonism towards Nietzsche, noting 'Beckett establishes his play as thoroughgoing contradiction of the Nietzschean optimism about the putative nonexistence of God' (168). Accordingly, Hamm's depressing, apocalyptic mediation of the madman's vision is to be primarily read as a rebuttal of Nietzsche's supposed celebration of God's death as it is pronounced by the fictional madman in the marketplace. However, I hold that this view not only fails to attend to the profound ambivalence conveyed towards God's death by Nietzsche, but it also sells short the relevance of his thought as a whole to *Endgame*.

Pointing towards Nietzsche's ambivalent assessment of God's death, it is important to observe that Nietzsche's madman warns of a devastating disorientation attending this 'event'. The madman quizzes his indifferent marketplace audience: '[w]here are we moving to? [...] Aren't we straying through an infinite nothing?' (*GS* 125: 120). Nietzsche's writing consistently registers a tension regarding the demise of the ascetic ideal. For example, as I claimed in Chapter 2, Nietzsche argues in *On the Genealogy of Morality* (1887) that the ascetic ideal has persisted as it presents a direction or goal to motivate human willing while also offering the cognitive means to render human suffering bearable.[3] Thus, while Nietzsche may celebrate the potential exhilarating liberation that God's death may signify for those sufficiently strong and courageous 'free spirits', he is also cognisant that the loss of transcendent orientation points may signal a collapse into what he calls 'passive nihilism'. As discussed in Chapter 1, this term relates to a twinned condition of cognitive disorientation and affective exhaustion.[4] What is more, it is clear that Nietzsche's madman questions humanity's capacity to supplant God, to confer new direction or a new meaning to life: '[i]s the magnitude of this event not too great for us? Do we not ourselves have to become gods merely to appear worthy of it?' (*GS* 125: 119–20).

Furthermore, before returning to consider the ways in which the play captures the characters' responses to God's 'decomposition' and their struggle to replace 'Him' and 'become like gods', I will briefly register an alternative apprehension of nihilism regarding Nietzsche's famous passage, expounded by the critic J. Hillis Miller, to consider a connection between Nietzsche's and Hamm's respective madmen. According to Miller's reading of Nietzsche's pronouncement of God's death, modernity sees man becoming the centre of meaning, supplanting God (see Miller 1966: 3). However, rather than celebrate this development, Miller bemoans the unrestrained growth of man's imperialistic ego, relativising all. For Miller argues that as '[t]he will wants to assimilate everything to itself, to make everything a reflection within its mirror', there is a resultant loss of the objective world (4). Miller consequently claims: '[w]hen everything exists only as reflected in the ego, then man has drunk up the sea' (3). In other words, '[n]ihilism is the nothingness of consciousness when consciousness becomes the foundation of everything' (3). The nihilistic, narcissistic-relativism that Miller identifies as characterising modernity, manifests in Beckett's drama; this can be associated with Nietzsche's insights into the psychology of the chronic sufferer.

In *Endgame*, the contrasting perspectives held by Hamm and the madman whom he visited suggest that one's relationship to the outside world is constituted by one's own particular consciousness:

> HAMM: I once knew a madman who thought the end of the world had come. He was a painter—and engraver. I had a great fondness for him. I used to go and see him, in the asylum. I'd take him by the hand and drag him to the window. Look! There! All that rising corn! And there! Look! The sails of the herring fleet! All that loveliness! [*Pause.*] He'd snatch away his hand and go back into his corner. Appalled. All he had seen was ashes. [*Pause.*] He alone had been spared. [*Pause.*] Forgotten. [*Pause.*] It appears the case is ... was not so ... so unusual. (Beckett 1990: 113)

Hamm's perceptions of abundant life, of 'that rising corn' and the 'sails of the herring fleet', diverge dramatically from the madman's barren vision. These antithetical views, held respectively by Hamm and the madman, reverberate with Nietzsche's claim that '[t]here is *only* a perspective seeing, *only* a perspective "knowing"' (*OGM* III 12: 92). For Nietzsche, 'knowing' is an active interpreting and evaluating; it is a means to secure one's place in the world and attain mastery over the basic conditions of life. One's interpretation is symptomatic, then, of one's will to power, of one's strength to confer oneself and the world with meaning. Furthermore, as I shall argue in the central part of my discussion of *Endgame*, for Nietzsche this exegetical orientation is apprehended as an aesthetic activity. It is thus telling that the madman who considers the world as 'ashen' is no longer a painter or engraver: he has lost his creative or active, heuristic capacity. In other words, he is nihilistic: as Nietzsche puts it, '[t]his same species of man, grown one stage poorer, no longer possessing the strength to interpret, create fictions, produces nihilists' (*WP* 585 (A): 317). Attending this loss of interpretative or creative capacity, the correlative loss of effectual selfhood is apparent in the withdrawn, reclusive state of Hamm's madman.

Tellingly, as Francis Doherty points out, insofar as Hamm observes that the madman's 'case is ... was not so unusual', he 'disallows the possibility of treating him as mad, but allows the possibility for this unusual view to be shared by many' (Doherty 1971: 100). That the characters come to share the madman's perspective of an 'ashen' world is reinforced by their similar adoption of defensive, withdrawn postures. The characters' self-protective strategies and postures can be related to their experience of chronic suffering.

While the shelter has been variously interpreted by commentators, it may also simply figure as an extension of the self. As Scarry argues when discussing rooms generally:

> In normal contexts, the room, the simplest form of shelter [...] keeps warm and safe the individual it houses in the same way the body encloses and protects the individual within; like the body, its walls put boundaries around the self preventing undifferentiated contact with the world. (Scarry 1985: 38)

Hamm's desperate insistence upon a return to the centre when taken on his spin round the room points to an excessive vulnerability to the other and the outside world:

> HAMM: Do you hear? [*He strikes the wall with his knuckles.*] Do you hear? Hollow bricks! [*He strikes again.*] All that's hollow! [*Pause. He straightens up. Violently.*] That's enough. Back! (Beckett 1990: 104)

With Scarry's view of the room in mind, Hamm's distress at finding the walls 'hollow' suggests a fear of permeability. Here resembling Lawrence's portrayal of the paralysed Clifford Chatterley, Hamm's urgent injunction to return to the centre similarly suggests a fragility that requires a defensive foreclosure of contact with otherness.[5] What is more, despite being apparently sealed from the 'corpsed' world outside, the characters are aware that they remain part of natural processes. The refuge, and hence the self, remains porous, subject to natural ageing and decay, as this exchange illustrates:

> HAMM: No more nature! You exaggerate.
> CLOV: In the vicinity
> HAMM: But we breathe, we change! We lose our hair, our teeth!
> Our bloom! Our ideals! (97)

This notion of the fragile boundaries of selfhood subject to natural dissolution can be explored by invoking Nietzsche's binary of Apollo and Dionysus as he describes them in *The Birth of Tragedy* (1872): Apollo, on the one hand, symbolises the illusory boundaries of individual identity that allow us to conceive of a stable self and to function in an ordered world; Dionysus, on the other, represents nature's abundant, excessive forces that overwhelm and ultimately collapse this *principium individuationis* (principle of individuation) (*BT* 2: 20). While I discussed the Dionysian and the rupture of individual boundaries in the Lawrence chapter in terms of the erotic encounter, here I shift my emphasis to apprehend the Dionysian in terms of pain and decay, similarly operating to fragment the ego and dissolve the self's pursuit of self-contained identity.[6] In other words, the god that Nietzsche holds to symbolise life's abundance and regenerative potency also brings cognisance of time's inexorable movement and a painful awareness of our own finitude. Michael Worton comments on *Endgame*, in line with Nietzsche's view of the Dionysian, that '[i]f our one certain reality is that "we breath, we change! We lose our hair, our teeth! Our bloom! Our ideals!", this truth is very difficult to accept emotionally' (Worton 1996: 72).

A number of critics have focused on the characters' struggle to digest what I have referred to as the knowledge of the Dionysian. Calling *Endgame* a 'tragedy of perpetual loss', Judith Roof claims that '[t]he characters perceive their fragmentation in relation to a past wholeness' (Roof 1992: 145). That is, the characters' evince a particularly heightened sensitivity to depletion, suggesting an inability to absorb and recover from their decrepitude and pain. This observation echoes Freud's notion of melancholia which, as Jonathan Boulter discerns, signals an incapacity to appropriate one's losses in coherent narrative form (see Boulter 2008: 45). Returning to the crucial point of narrative below, here it is worth noting Boulter's assertion—that the melancholic is 'continually haunted by loss, by history'—to emphasise Roof's claim (45). The director Herbert Blau similarly observes that an awareness of inexorable loss and decay is apparent 'even at the start' of *Endgame*: Clov's opening speech upon the 'impossible heap' of grain signals 'nothing but loss, ineluctable and pitiless loss', according to Blau (Blau 2004: 97). For Hamm, change is perceived solely as deterioration. Sylvie Henning similarly contends that 'Hamm acquires a more simply negative, and even destructive, view of nature' (Henning 1992: 107). Hamm's perspective is thus partial, echoing his madman's limited, nihilistic vision: Hamm lacks a more inclusive vision of life's total economy, one that would encompass loss and gain, death and birth, and growth or enhancement as well as decay. In other words, he has lost sight of the vision of the 'herring fleet' that had earlier differentiated his perspective from the madman. In Nietzsche's idiom, Hamm evinces a 'low valuation of all that becomes': he derides life as flux, as change, as this, Nietzsche notes, is a fundamental source of suffering and loss (*WP* 585 (A): 317). Significantly, Nietzsche argues such an evaluative position, one that conceives of life in these negative terms, derives from physio-psychological suffering and impotence: '[w]hat kind of man reflects in this way? An unproductive, suffering kind, a kind weary of life' (317).

Hamm's hostility to the natural world can be illustrated in a related exchange that also implies an excessive vulnerability to the other:

HAMM: You stink already. The whole place stinks of corpses.
 CLOV: The whole universe.
HAMM: [*Angrily.*] To hell with the universe! (Beckett 1990: 114)

This outburst recalls Hamm's opening soliloquy and the first, harsh words addressed to Clov: '[y]ou pollute the air!' (92–3). Hamm cannot voluntarily deny his sense of smell; the other and the world at large are considered perfidious contaminants. Indeed, his frustrated condemnation of the world and his servant reverberates with Nietzsche's analysis of reactive *ressentiment*, the feelings of poisonous hatred that derive from a sense of powerlessness.[7] Recalling Zarathustra's teachings on vindictiveness and impotence in Chapter 2, the following passage from *Daybreak* (1881) captures a similar hatred towards the world as that articulated by Hamm, linking it to failure:

> *The World Destroyers*—This man fails in something; finally he exclaims in a rage: 'Then let the whole world perish!' This revolting feeling is the summit of envy, which argues: because there is *something* I cannot have, the whole world shall have *nothing*! The whole world shall *be* nothing! (*D* 304: 155–6)

Focussing upon the physio-psychological perspective of the powerless slaves in antiquity in the *Genealogy*, Nietzsche similarly holds that *ressentiment* manifests in a hostility to 'everything that is "outside", "other", "non-self"' (*OGM* I 10: 21). This attitude of negation inflects Christian values according to Nietzsche. Moreover, it cannot be overstated for the purposes of my reading of Beckett's play that Nietzsche argues that this principle of negation results from a particularly heightened sensitivity to suffering: the '*instinctive hatred of reality*: a consequence of an extreme capacity for suffering and excitement which no longer wants any contact at all because it feels every contact too deeply' (*AC* 30: 153–4). In a cognate passage from *Ecce Homo* (1888), Nietzsche elaborates upon this point and claims that such sensitivity is one of the effects of prolonged illness:

> If anything whatever has to be admitted against being sick, being weak, it is that in these conditions the actual curative instinct, that is to say the *defensive and offensive instinct* in man becomes soft. One does not know how to get free of anything, one does not know how to have done with anything, one does not know how to thrust back—everything hurts. Men and things come importunately close, events strike too deep, the memory is a festering wound. Being sick *is* itself a kind of *ressentiment*. (*EH* I 6: 15)

Endgame can be read as a dramatisation of Nietzsche's observations on the psychology of those afflicted by protracted pain. That is, Nietzsche's connection of an 'instinctive hatred of reality' to a heightened sensitivity deriving from physio-psychological weakness or illness illuminates readings of Beckett's play. This sensibility entails a consequent defensive withdrawal from such contact. With regards to Hamm these points can be readily evinced by focusing upon his relationship to his parents. Representing his past, his lineage, his embodiedness, it is significant that Hamm's parents, too, are perceived as corporeal invaders disturbing his desire for cerebral self-enclosure, or what Henning calls 'Hamm's solipsistic dreaming' (Henning 1992: 111). His parents are a painful intrusion, rupturing his attempt to attain a sealed, self-enclosed self-relation; they 'come importunately close' and largely signal further loss of selfhood. Cavell's comment on Hamm's subsequent order to Clov to violently eject Nagg and Nell is suggestive: '[t]he old father and mother with no useful functions any more are among the waste of society, dependent upon the generation they have bred, which in turn resents them for their uselessness and dependency' (Cavell 1976: 117). Implying that Hamm is governed by a calculative rationality that operates by seeking a return for any expenditure or loss, Cavell's point echoes Henning's aforementioned observations on Hamm's hostility towards natural decay and thus to life *per se*. Relatedly, Henning acutely discerns Hamm's view of the natural world: '[i]f there is neither absolute gain, nor anything free of change (and therefore of loss), better that the natural process should not exist at all' (Henning 1992: 107). Both Cavell's and Henning's contentions echo Nietzsche's analysis of the calculative reasoning that characterises the ascetic ideal, one that rationally economises all distress.[8] This interpretative strategy signals Hamm's position of weakness or hunger in Nietzsche's parlance. Hamm thus evinces the 'human-all-too-human' need to avert the unpalatable consideration of the self's complete expenditure. This prudential, calculative reasoning permeates *Endgame* even as, as I shall discuss below, it resists such rationalisations. It can also be said, as noted in previous chapters, that this outlook exemplifies the position of the Alexandrian or 'theoretical' man, outlined by Nietzsche in *The Birth of Tragedy*, who seeks to deny Dionysian, tragic knowledge.[9] Other characters assume this position: Clov, like his master, can be defined by his excessive desire for self-enclosure. His drive for withdrawal is similarly motivated by the need to assuage pain. As such, the theatre director Blau, in a retrospective of a production, explains the effort 'to seal him [Clov] off as much as possible from the air, the world, the presence of others, who are the source of pain' (Blau 2004: 75).

Not only do the characters suffer from physiological deterioration and various related ailments, but, as Blau observes, their interrelationships themselves are abusive, retaliatory and are clearly sources of wounding for all concerned. Speaking of Hamm and Clov, Laura Salisbury describes them as '[b]ound in what seems like a master-slave dialectic of violent hatred and mutual dependence' (Salisbury 2012: 113). The implicit masochistic dimension contained in his continued loyalty to Hamm confounds Clov. He petitions Hamm:

> CLOV: There's one thing I'll never understand. [*He gets down.*] Why I always obey you. Can you explain that to me? (Beckett 1990: 129)

This pivotal point in the play, in which Clov quizzes Hamm as to why he stays, signals not only Clov's continued dependence, but also the characters' need to account for their suffering. For, as Nietzsche notes, 'it is the experience of being powerless against men, not against nature, that generates the most desperate embitterment against existence' (*WP* 55: 35). One possible reason as to why the characters sustain their combative and cruel relationships is suggested in the final exchange between Hamm and Clov. This exchange features a logic of indebtedness or obligation that is also suggestive of the origin of Clov's subordinate position:

> HAMM: I'm obliged to you, Clov. For your services:
> CLOV: [Turning, sharply.] Ah pardon, it's I am obliged to you.
> HAMM: It's we are obliged to each other. (Beckett 1990: 132)

That this logic may underpin the characters' co-dependence seems consistent with their mutual desire to achieve a causal or logical closure such as that provided by a contractual structure. Clov, after all, 'love[s] order. It's [his] dream' (120). That is, echoing my discussion of the characters' preoccupation with the fear of loss regarding the natural processes of decay, this contractual logic of indebtedness is emblematic of a calculative rationality that promises the recuperation or augmentation of selfhood: all losses implicitly return within a closed, bound system. Furthermore, in linking Hamm's chronicle to his possible adoption of Clov, Paul Lawley observes that Hamm seeks to dominate and manipulate Clov by drawing attention to the latter's sense of indebtedness. As Lawley puts it, '[t]he adopted child is expected to feel that he owes a debt because he was *chosen*' (Lawley 1992: 120). Hamm thus invokes notions of indebtedness to configure himself as a parental creditor who should be recompensed: '[u]pon an adopted son he can bring to bear a pressure of obligation', as Lawley notes (120). Clov, then, may rationally apprehend his suffering, or his continued dependence upon Hamm, in these terms.

While Hamm and Clov's relationship can be seen to illustrate the pertinacity of contractual relations, of what Nietzsche discerns to be 'the oldest and most primitive personal relationship there is', *Endgame* operates through a series of tensions and ambiguities to repeatedly dissolve this logic (*OGM* II 8: 49). Not only do the characters appear to inexplicably reverse roles, but notions of obligation are themselves shown to be inherently unreliable. For instance, complaining of being denied a promised Turkish Delight 'in return for a kindness', most likely for attending to his son Hamm's stories, Nagg laments that '[o]ne must live with the times': he must resign himself to the fact that the 'times' are characterised by the failure to honour obligations or promises (Beckett 1990: 120). Rather, as Nagg implicitly discerns, the contractarian logic is manipulated by the dominant. This example, I would suggest, renders these notions of indebtedness as insufficient in themselves to bind the characters, or to be appealed to in order to account for their suffering.

NARRATIVE GESTURES

The breakdown of performative speech-acts such as promising is indicative of the general denudation of the significance of language in the refuge. Illustrating this point, and again exhibiting his dependence, Clov asks Hamm to 'teach' him 'new words' since the old ones no longer have any meaning. In contrast to Connie Chatterley's disillusion with those 'great words' in *Lady Chatterley's Lover*—exalted ideals such as hope, charity, and sacrifice—Clov despairs that even the most everyday words 'sleeping, waking, morning, evening [...] have nothing to say' (133).[10] As a consequence of inhabiting a world of empty signifiers, Boulter observes that there is an 'absence of true dialogical exchange' in the shelter (Boulter 1998: 42). Furthermore, Boulter contends that narrative operates to 'supplement' this absence: 'the narrative function is appropriated to mitigate the dialogical void at the heart of the drama' (42). Narrative, I shall show, not only 'mitigate[s]' the 'dialogical void', but it may be considered itself as the most necessary and sustaining palliative that the characters can call upon, given particularly that other forms, such as dialogue, Nagg's Turkish Delight, or Hamm's painkiller, consistently fail to materialise or satisfy.

Narrative gestures abound in *Endgame*. The content of these stories or fragments reveal a preoccupation with the need to narrate pain and painful experiences. Nagg and Nell, for example, share their reminiscences of their bicycle accident in which they lost their limbs. Subject to inexorable loss, paralysis and impotence, the characters in Beckett's drama deploy narrative in their attempts to augment and reconstitute their sense of selfhood. For, consonant with Nell's later remark that 'nothing is funnier than unhappiness', narrative here is offered as a palliative for her depression (Beckett 1990: 101–2). As Nagg puts it, the story is meant to 'cheer' Nell 'up' (101–2).

It is telling that Hamm's violent outburst against his parents occurs as they narrate this painful experience. While I have hinted above that this excessive reaction may arise from a particularly vulnerable sensibility stemming from prolonged illness, here it is worth focussing on Hamm's need to dominate the storytelling, to arrogate this privilege for himself. Hamm's imperialistic domination within the refuge is noted by John Sheedy who claims that Hamm is 'at once the writer, director and star actor-sufferer in the only show on earth' (Sheedy 1966: 317). Sheedy's keen observation, suggesting Hamm's self-aggrandising, narcissistic denial of the other, can be allied with my earlier invocation of Miller's discussion of the Nietzschean madman's proclamation of the death of God: nihilism signifies the loss of other and the world. Such a posture of solipsistic self-enclosure can be viewed as a defensive expression, an attempt to close oneself off from further loss and pain. Indeed, by referring to Hamm as an 'actor-sufferer', Sheedy implies that it Hamm's woundedness that that impels him to 'write', 'direct' and 'star' in his 'show'. Alluding again to Hamm's opening, self-reflexive soliloquy may corroborate this point: as Hamm asks if there can 'be misery loftier than' his, he announces his own urgent need to give his distress expression. For his pain, he surmises, is 'bigger': he can only 'believe' that other 'creatures' can suffer. While this exclamation implies a pathological incapacity to identify with others' suffering, it also follows that, since the other remains opaque or impenetrable, one's own experience of pain is the most palpable, the most demanding expression or relief. Returning below to explore the ethical ramifications concerning this notion of the self's fundamental isolation, I shall now adduce key arguments made by Scarry and Arthur W. Frank: both thinkers contend that the sufferer is forced to express the experience of pain or illness through narrative form.

Both Scarry and Frank have written persuasively on the correlation between pain and narrative. Registering pain's capacity to annihilate consciousness, Scarry contends that '[p]hysical pain has no voice, but when it at last finds a voice, it begins to tell a story' (Scarry 1985: 3). Frank echoes Scarry's view that pain, or illness, 'is a call for stories' (Frank 1997: 53). According to Frank, pain disrupts and possibly destroys the sufferer's sense of coherence. The sufferer becomes what he calls a 'narrative wreck' (54). Using the metaphor of wreckage to convey the devastating disorientation that besets the chronic sufferer, Frank claims that in 'conditions of fatigue, uncertainty, sometimes pain' it is stories that bring new orientation points to help render self-coherence. Frank argues: '[t]he way out of narrative wreckage is telling stories, specifically [...] "self-stories". [...] The self is being *formed* in what is told' (55). Significantly, Hamm insists that his story is a chronicle, suggesting a factual, biographical element. While the audience may perceive his story to be fictional, largely through Hamm's repeated intrusive and contradictory self-reflexive gestures, the performative aspect of the story is reinforced by Clov who retorts, on being compelled to listen to Hamm's story, that it is the one that he has 'been telling [himself] all of [his]... days' (Beckett 1990: 121). The story itself is bound to Hamm's self-constitution.

One of the most influential aspects of Nietzsche's work is that of the relation between aesthetic activity and the attainment of self-mastery or self-coherence. As discussed in Chapter 2, Nietzsche broadly conceives of the aesthetic to mean form-giving. Applied to his naturalistic conception of the self, this notion speaks of the need to hierarchically organise one's multiple, conflicting impulses.[11] As he puts it in *The Will to Power*, the coordination of these warring drives 'under a single predominant impulse results in a "strong will"' (*WP* 46: 28). The pathos of power is thus attained when the plurality of instincts is organised and harnessed by the command of one dominant drive, or several cooperating drives: directed by the telos of this dominant drive, one reflexively experiences oneself as a willing agent. Alexander Nehamas' seminal interpretation of Nietzsche's philosophy explores the emphatically aesthetic conception of this project. For Nehamas, not only are Nietzsche's key doctrines informed by aesthetic notions, but Nietzsche's espousal of self-fashioning takes literary narrative as its paradigm: by 'fashioning a literary character out of [oneself]', one organises 'everything into a coherent whole' (Nehamas 1985: 136–7). The literary project thus exemplifies the ordering, editing, and selecting of one's materials to attain an overall coherence.

In Hamm's case, his chronic illness significantly frustrates his capacity to constitute the self as a narrative achievement: Hamm's dominating fatigue is both symptomatic of, and further contributes towards, his inability to generate narrative self-coherence.[12] His suicidal desire therefore attends his complaint regarding the 'effort' to construct and sustain his narrative:

> HAMM: I don't know. [*Pause.*] I feel rather drained. [*Pause.*]
> The prolonged creative effort. [*Pause.*] If I could drag
> myself down to the sea! I'd make a pillow of sand for my
> head and the tide would come. (Beckett 1990: 120)

This passage suggests that Hamm's loss of creative strength manifests in, or leads to, a state of suicidal nihilism, a desire for self-destruction. His incapacity to creatively sustain a sense of self-coherence, in Nietzsche's idiom, is reflective of an inability to direct the self's plural impulses and engender a pathos of willing towards a goal. In the context of the play it is also suggestive of the power of chronic pain or illness to radically disturb the formation of self-coherence. As discussed in Chapter 2, pain consumes the self and impedes the subject's capacity to engender a pathos of self-integrity.[13] The consequent unravelling of selfhood, or the diffusion of the self's drives, results in a 'weak will', degenerating to an intolerable state of paralysis. With a diminishing creative capacity, Hamm comes to resemble the reclusive madman whom he had visited: nauseated, exhausted, life-negating.

Throughout Nietzsche's work the aesthetic is celebrated as a means to avert feelings of suicidal nihilism. In *The Gay Science* (1882–1887) he argues: '[*h*]*onesty* would lead to nausea and suicide. But now our honesty has a counterforce that helps us avoid such consequences: art, as the *good* will to appearance. [...] As an aesthetic phenomenon existence is still *bearable* for us' (*GS* 107: 104). In *The Will to Power* (1901) he similarly claims, '[w]e possess *art* lest we *perish of the truth*' (*WP* 822: 435). The philosopher Bernard Williams neatly grasps the significance of this assertion: 'Nietzsche does not mean that we possess art in place of the truth; he means that we possess art so that we can possess the truth and not perish of it' (Williams 2006: 322). To expand upon the role of art in Nietzsche's thought with this point in mind, and to signal its relevance to interpreting *Endgame*, it is useful to briefly return to his first published book, *The Birth of Tragedy*. Here Nietzsche hypothesises that the ancient Greeks, whom he claims were particularly sensitive to suffering, created the art form of ancient tragedy to overcome a view of existence captured in the ancient Greek folkloric wisdom of Silenus: '[t]he best of all things is something entirely outside your grasp: not to be born, not to *be*, to be *nothing*. But the second-best thing for you—is to die soon' (*BT* 3: 22). Prone to this pessimistic outlook, the Greeks, according to Nietzsche, created tragic art through a unique combination of the antithetical aesthetic impulses he attributes to the Greek deities Apollo and Dionysus. Having sketched these symbols with a different language above, it is worth clarifying that Apollo symbolises surface appearance and dream-like illusion, while Dionysus, the god who is dismembered in ancient myth, signals a pre-perceptual reality of senseless images and nature's unrestrained, excessive force. The fact that Dionysus is dismembered points to a radical dissolution of individuality that can be associated with both the tragic hero's death and with the audience's collective intoxicated state. Apollo, on the other hand, represents individual boundaries and so accounts for both the recognisable form of the heroic individual and the existence of an intelligible plot that propels the drama. As Nietzsche claims that it is the balance of these two impulses that enables Greeks to flourish and so repel the prevalent pessimism, it can be asserted that an imbalance, or over-reliance upon one of these impulses would fail to render tragedy's paradoxical energising impact: Apollonian illusion on its own, while remaining painfully aware of life's senselessness, leads to sterility without an energising glimpse of the Dionysian raw energy. 'Apollo could not live without Dionysus' as Nietzsche puts it (4: 26). Unmediated exposure to the Dionysian vision of existence, on the other hand, is nauseating and induces suicidal nihilism by bringing cognisance of the ephemeral nature of individual being. Nietzsche thus claims that, 'Apolline consciousness alone, like a veil, hid that Dionysiac world from his view' (2: 21). For Nietzsche, the death of tragedy in Greek culture is signalled by a subsequent excessive reliance upon a third principle, related to and yet distinct from the Apollonian impulse, namely Socratic rationality. The view heralded by this outlook, that the world is amenable to logical reflection, inherently precludes the possibility of registering the world's Dionysian senselessness. This rejection of the deeper Dionysian truth of the meaninglessness of existence also inflects Christian theodicy, given that the belief in a benign deity domesticises senseless suffering within a metaphysical rational economy.

In a 1936 entry from his 'Clare Street Notebook', Beckett seems to be deploying a similar psychological-metaphysical structure of appearance and reality to that found in Nietzsche's *The Birth of Tragedy*.

There are moments where the veil of hope is finally ripped away and the eyes, suddenly liberated, see their world as it is, as it must be. Alas, it does not last long, the perception quickly passes: the eyes can only bear such a merciless light for a short while, the thin skin of hope re-forms and one returns to the world of phenomena. [...] And even if the cataract can be pierced for a moment it almost always re-forms immediately; and thus it is with hope.[14]

Resembling Nietzsche's binary of truth and illusion in his early work, this passage suggests that Beckett's aesthetics can be read as being motivated by the wish to depict the world through 'liberated' eyes, to present it in a 'merciless light', denuded of 'hope'. Or, using Nietzsche's idiom, Beckett wishes to render the Dionysian truth, to offer a glimpse of the chaotic senselessness that is foreclosed by the veil generated by our perceptual and conceptual faculties.

Cavell's admiration for what he observes to be Hamm's attempts to 'defeat meaning, of word and deed', can be aligned with Beckett's view as it is expounded in this notebook entry (Cavell 1976: 148). That is, Cavell perceives Hamm to be something of a Nietzschean hero or overman engaged in 'the task of purposely undoing, re-evaluating all the purposes we have known' (150). Accordingly, Hamm is performing an active destruction of the Christian interpretation of existence to present the world innocent of this 'curse'. In its stead, according to Cavell, Hamm seeks '[o]nly a life without hope, meaning, justification, waiting, solution' (149).

Beckett's hostility to Christian soteriology and what Cavell calls 'its total, even totalitarian, success' (117), is also registered by Beckett biographer James Knowlson who invokes the poem 'Ooftish' (1938) to support his reading (Knowlson 1996: 67). In this poem Beckett expresses his contempt towards the totalising nature of eschatology:

> offer it up plank it down
> Golgotha was only the potegg
> cancer angina it is all one to us
> cough up your T.B. don't be stingy
>
> .....
>
> the whole misery diagnosed undiagnosed diagnosed
> get your friends to do the same we'll make use of it

> we'll make sense of it we'll put it in the pot with the rest
> it all boils down to blood of lamb. (Beckett 2012: 59)

In 'Ooftish' the rational optimism that structures theodicy, or the 'we'll make sense of it' notion in the poem, degrades others' particular, and perhaps useless, suffering: by appropriating others' distress within a universal narrative, theodicy thus performs a violence against the reality of the individual's experience of pain. Beckett's antipathy towards Christian theodicy may therefore be aligned with Nietzsche's repudiation of the Christian interpretation of suffering.

To reiterate, however: while Nietzsche's thought actively participates in the overcoming of the ascetic ideal on the one hand, he also points ambivalently to the nihilistic consequences of the dissolution of the Christian exegesis of existence on the other. Thus, echoing the ambivalence contained in his madman's pronouncement alluded to above, he argues: '[a]s we thus reject Christian interpretation and condemn its "meaning" as counterfeit, *Schopenhauer's* question immediately comes at us in a terrifying way: *Does existence have any meaning at all?*' (*GS* 357: 219–20). What is more, for Nietzsche the pursuit of the naked truth, such as that implied in Beckett's notebook entry, entails the onset of an awful predicament: on the one hand, the naturalistic sciences, which Nietzsche holds to embody the modern form of the ascetic ideal's relentless pursuit of the truth, comes to the 'realization that the way of the world is not at all divine—even by human standards it is not rational, merciful, or just' (346: 203–4); on the other hand, while 'we moderns' may accept that we have interpreted life 'falsely and mendaciously', doing so involves cognisance that we did so 'according to a *need*': interpreting the world as 'rational, merciful, or just' 'may have made it possible for us to *endure* life' (204). And this argument of a psychological 'need' for such an interpretation is reinforced in the climactic moments of the *Genealogy*: here Nietzsche accounts for the origins and persistence of the ascetic ideal by claiming that it primarily functioned to combat 'epidemics' of suicidal nihilism by offering an interpretation of 'senseless suffering' (*OGM* III 28: 127). Nietzsche thus claims that the dilemma to 'confront coming generations' is 'the terrible Either/Or: "Either abolish your venerations or—*yourselves!*"' (*GS* 346: 204). Taking our 'venerations' to refer to the interpretation of the world as 'rational, merciful, or just', Nietzsche concludes: '[t]he latter would be nihilism; but would not the former also be—nihilism? That is *our* question mark' (203–4).

This tension grips *Endgame*. This can be best illustrated when Hamm invokes the presence of a 'rational being' to confer significance on their existence at the very moment when he appears to corroborate Cavell's identification of an active evacuation of meaning. Hence Hamm first exclaims '[w]e're not beginning to ... to ... mean something?', before surmising (Beckett 1990: 108):

> HAMM: I wonder. [*Pause.*] Imagine if a rational being came back to earth, wouldn't he be liable to get ideas into his head if he observed us long enough. [*Voice of rational being.*] Ah, good, now I see what it is, yes, now I understand what they're at! [CLOV *starts, drops the telescope and begins to scratch his belly with both hands.* [*Normal voice.*] And without going so far as that, we ourselves ... [*with emotion*] ... we ourselves ... at certain moments ... [*Vehemently.*] To think perhaps it won't all have been for nothing! (108)

This strain, with regard to whether the characters can exist devoid of meaning or not, or without our 'venerations', is registered in the shifts in emotion gestured to in Beckett's stage directions. And while Hamm may express a desire to not 'mean something', giving currency to Cavell's view, it is clear that Hamm's radical oscillation from such a posture to one that invokes the possibility of new meaning in the form of the presence of a 'rational being' resonates with Nietzsche's analysis of the modern predicament. Otherwise put, 'senseless suffering', or the fear that it will 'all have been for nothing', impels one to seek a means to appropriate one's experiences of pointless distress: the self is propelled to reconstitute itself, attempting to generate coherence by conferring significance to the senselessness it encounters. That this attempt, I suggest, takes the form of an appeal to an imagined 'rational being' also implies the continued valence of God, or of the Christian narrative's interpretation of suffering, which I shall return to consider below. Additionally, while there are echoes here of the dialectical dynamic that Nietzsche describes in the Apollo-Dionysus relation as discussed particularly in Chapter 2, Hamm's vacillation, moreover, evokes Beckett's similar notebook entry: ineluctably the 'thin skin of hope re-forms' only moments after 'the veil of hope is finally ripped away'.

Regarding the importance of meaning constitution in *Endgame*, I think it is worthwhile to stress my divergence from critics such as Cavell and the Beckett scholar Eric Tonning. Tonning identifies Christianity as 'Beckett's fundamental antagonist' and supports Cavell's view of the characters' performance in terms of their resistance to those bequeathed, Christian meanings (Tonning 2014: 104). Contending that 'Hamm's *fear*' is to remain 'residually significant', Tonning also argues that in his opposition to 'the heroic-redemptive attitude', 'Beckett parodies the whole attempt to wrest meaning from the Void' (118–9). This deflationary reading of the import of meaning constitution in Beckett echoes Cavell's apprehension of a repudiation of significance in *Endgame*: as aforementioned, Cavell explicitly argues that, with regards to what he considers to be Hamm's heroic undoing of meaning, 'where existence is interpreted, sheltered, it is lost' (Cavell 1976: 151). Yet while these respective readings of *Endgame* may be aligned with a Nietzschean 'active nihilism' insofar as the characters seem to partake in a deconstruction of the persistent meaning of the ascetic ideal, I maintain that Beckett simultaneously dramatises the characters' incapacity to remain bereft of significance. Just as Nietzsche insists upon a necessary Apollonian reconstitution of meaning following an encounter with Dionysian senselessness in *The Birth of Tragedy*, so do the characters in *Endgame* evince an ineluctable desire to constitute and recuperate selfhood, to seek self-coherence, to give their suffering some significance and hence render it bearable.[15] While Cavell acknowledges this tension, my reading provides an alternative emphasis (see Cavell 1976: 132, 140, 145, 149): it is the characters' engagement with unredeemed 'senseless suffering' which I hold to constitute the central nihilistic problem of the play. Thus, where Cavell stresses 'that the play itself is about an effort to undo' the 'curse' of the Christian interpretation of existence, which entails the realisation that suffering 'has to *stop* meaning anything, and become the simple fact of life', I focus on the characters' ineluctable need to render their suffering bearable, and hence meaningful (Cavell 1976: 122, 151). As I have suggested above, this manifests particularly in the characters' narrative strategies. As Worton puts it, 'the very abundance of specifically narrative gestures in *Endgame* points to the desire for a degree of meaning formation' (Worton 1996: 63).

Clov's case most readily illustrates the characters' need to bestow their suffering existence with significance. His greater reliance upon traditional, external narrative means to apprehend his pain and avert the encounter with the what Nietzsche calls the '*horror vacui*', or the thought that it has all 'been for nothing', somewhat distinguishes his approach from Hamm's: for the persistence of the ascetic ideal in

Endgame is most apparent in Clov's interpretation of his suffering as punishment. Tellingly, Clov repeatedly gestures towards an inability to inhabit any alternative perspective, signalling a long-standing condition of physio-psychological paralysis: suggesting his appeal to traditional responses, Clov comments: '[a]ll life long the same questions, the same answers' (Beckett 1990: 94); similarly, he confirms his psychological stasis, stating at the end of the play: 'I feel too old, and too far, to form new habits' (Beckett 1990: 133). Recalling that Nietzsche argues in the *Genealogy* that the ascetic ideal provides a narrative that encourages the sufferer to 'understand his suffering itself as a *condition of punishment*', it is significant that both Clov's opening words and his final speech echo each other, suggesting both this state of stasis and that he apprehends his existence solely in these terms *(OGM* III 20: 111). Here in the latter speech he articulates his desire for his pain to end:

> CLOV: [*As before.*] I say to myself—sometimes, Clov, you must learn to suffer better than that if you want them to weary of punishing you—one day. (Beckett 1990: 133)

It is evident that Clov's thinking is dominated by the conception of the end of his unbearable suffering. Robert Kugelmann's discussion on the phenomenology of pain is pertinent to an appreciation of Clov's interpretative strategy: '[n]o greater deformation of the human condition can be imagined than endless pain which is called Hell—because pain promises an end. All writers on pain find themselves addressing eschatology, because that is the dynamism of pain' (Kugelmann 1999: 189).

A further dimension to this eschatological hermeneutic is that it permits Clov to rationally appropriate his suffering by appealing to the contractual logic that grounds and legitimises notions of punishment. Thus, echoing Josef K. in *The Trial*, whom I argued in the previous chapter rationalised his experience of senseless suffering in terms of guilt, Clov, too, can attain cognitive mastery of his distress insofar as he conceives of himself as a debtor who is legitimately repaying for debts incurred. As noted, this logic permits him to understand his continued service to Hamm. That this repayment entails one's suffering shall be further illuminated by my discussion of the role of cruelty below. Furthermore, through a Nietzschean lens, this punitive logic entails a concomitant sense of agency insofar as Clov can hold himself accountable for his suffering: rather than looking to some external source of his pain, he can discern his fault within himself and amend his behaviour accordingly, namely by suffering 'better'.[16] This is underpinned, somewhat paradoxically, by the conception of his pain ending.

Clov's notion of punishment also implies the presence of a perpetrator or spectator of his punishment: Clov's desire to suffer 'better' assumes an unnamed 'they' inflicting or spectating upon his pain. As Stan Gontarski observes, punishment 'implies fixation, order, somebody or something inflicting this' (Gontarski 2009: 142). Anthropomorphising senseless suffering by invoking a personal 'they' as perpetrators of his distress, Clov thus domesticates his encounter with the *horror vacui*. Doherty's perceptive comment corroborates this reading: '[m]an needs the fiction of punishment for a crime uncommitted in order that he bear up under the burden of an emptiness and isolation which are unbearable but must be borne' (Doherty 1971: 43). What is evident in this analysis of the role of punishment as Clov conceives it is that the hermeneutic of suffering provided by the ascetic ideal provides a means of shielding man from what Nietzsche calls the 'basic character of existence', namely its Dionysian senselessness (*BGE* 39: 68).

Returning to an entry from Nietzsche's mature work, *Beyond Good and Evil* (1886), in which he speaks of differing abilities to confront, and hence affirm, as much of life as possible, may draw out the distinction between Hamm's and Clov's respective exegetical approaches:

It might be a basic characteristic of existence that those who would know it completely would perish, in which case the strength of a spirit should be measured according to how much of the 'truth' one could still barely endure—or to put it more clearly, to what degree one would *require* it to be thinned down, shrouded, sweetened, blunted, falsified. (*BGE* 39: 68)

Calibrating strength in a language that conjures his metaphor of digestion, Nietzsche valorises those who can assimilate existence in a form that is minimally 'thinned down, […] sweetened, […] falsified'. In other words, for Nietzsche, the strong individual can perceive and affirm existence without appeal to transcendent structures. By conceiving the truth as ugly, nauseating and potentially fatal, Nietzsche inverts traditional notions of its permanence and beauty to contend that we all, to some degree, require illusion or untruth. While the stronger confront life as honestly as possible, swallowing as much of life's ugliness and bitterness as they can endure, the ascetic ideal performs the maximum amount of thinning down, sweetening and falsifying of the nauseating reality of existence.

Hamm's narrative, I believe, is suggestive of his larger digestive capacity to confront and absorb more of life's horror without recourse to those transcendent sweeteners that Clov draws upon. Not only is the content of Hamm's narrative largely cruel and disturbing, but his self-reflexive remonstration to his fictive characters points to an acknowledgement of an absence of any redemptive palliative: '[u]se your head, can't you, use your head, you're on earth, there's no cure for that!' (Beckett 1990: 118). By apparently exhibiting or exhorting realisation of a 'de-deified' world, Hamm here appears to corroborate Cavell's reading of his heroism.

Hamm's position regarding the Christian interpretation of existence dramatically vacillates, however. It can be first noted that when Clov asks Hamm to explain his sense of dependence, Hamm assumes an idiom that evokes notions of a deified status. That is, Hamm pompously asserts a position of hermeneutical superiority that suggests that he has supplanted God as an omniscient authority, declaring: '[a]h the creatures, the creatures, everything has to be explained to them' (113). Yet Hamm's incapacity to displace God as a creator is once again highlighted by his anguish at his inability to generate new characters, and thus a new self-narrative. This is apparent in his subsequent recourse to prayer that attends the suggested dissolution or incompletion of his narrative:

> HAMM: I'll soon have finished with this story. [*Pause.*] Unless I bring in other characters. [*Pause.*] But where would I find them? [*Pause.*] Where would I look for them? [*Pause. He whistles. Enter Clov.*] Let us pray to God. (118)

Here Hamm echoes the beleaguered, superstitious defendants in *The Trial* whose creative or exegetical paralysis is marked by their recourse to an external authority to confer value.[17] Moreover, the stage directions register his subsequent 'anguished protest' as he then exclaims '[t]he bastard! He doesn't exist!' (119). Hamm, then, whose perspective of the 'corpsed' universe brings to mind the apocalyptic vision of the madman whom he had previously visited, now evokes the Nietzschean madman who pronounces God's death: Hamm's indignation justifies the market-place madman's caution regarding our worthiness or ability to supplant God, to be creators. Borrowing Nietzsche's words, we can say that the 'delicate, sensitive, and ailing' characters, subject to prolonged, chronic pain and failing to constitute coherent selfhood, are likely to 'bleed to death from the truth' of God's non-existence (*HAH* 109: 78). Hamm's bitter pronouncement recalls Robert P. Pippin's suggestive comment on the modern condition, alluded to in Chapter 2:

> [with] no ultimate justice in the after-life, [...] human beings will come to see a finite, temporally mutable, contingent life as a kind of burden, a curse, or purposeless play, and they will exact revenge for having been arbitrarily thrown into this condition. (Pippin 2006: xxiv)

I will turn shortly to explore the pervasive play of retribution in *Endgame*, relating this to the characters' feelings of powerlessness. What is also suggested by Hamm's call to prayer is the characters' need for an audience to witness the theatre of human suffering. This need is implied at a number of key moments: a witness is imagined in Clov's apprehension of a 'they' who inflict his 'punishment'; it is also apparent with the characters' insistence upon an audience to attend to one's stories. Moreover, Hamm's invocation of a 'rational being' brings to mind Nietzsche's claim, regarding the ancient Greeks, that '[i]n order to rid the world of concealed, undiscovered, unseen suffering and deny it in all honesty, people were then practically obliged to invent Gods and intermediate beings at every level' (*OGM* II 7: 48). Not only does this contention stress the human need to avert encounters of senseless suffering, but Nietzsche's perception contains the notion that the Gods are enriched by the undeniable pleasure attained through the witnessing of human pain. For as Nietzsche puts it:

> All evil is justified if a god takes pleasure in it: so ran the primitive logic of feeling—and was this logic really restricted to primitive times? The gods viewed as the friends of *cruel* spectacles—how deeply this primeval concept still penetrates into our European civilization! (48)

Hamm, as 'writer, director' of his narratives may be seen to be attaining the pathos of distance of the spectating gods, surveying his dependent creatures' distress. Kathryn White's analysis of the content of Hamm's narrative is pertinent:

Hamm is a storyteller, reiterating tales of pain and misery. These stories may be an attempt to pass the time, but they may also provide relief by dwelling on a fictitious person's despair, the suffering of oneself may be momentarily alleviated. (White 2008: 14)

Hamm 'appears to take satisfaction in the knowledge that others also endure suf-fering', according to White (14). While agreeing with White's assertion that Hamm palliates his own pain through his fictions, further exploration of cruelty is required to unpack how, both in act and in imagined form, it performs this compensatory role. I shall now turn to examine *Endgame* as a spectacle of cruelty and suffering.

HAMM AND CLOV'S WAR

Cruelty is a central feature of Nietzsche's philosophy. It lies at the heart of his ideas of self-cultivation and cultural enhancement. He famously argues: '[a]lmost everything we call "higher culture" is based on the spiritualization and intensification of *cruelty*' (*BGE* 229: 159). He insists that the sublimation of one's raw, aggressive instincts, rather than their extirpation, is crucial to human development. As Simon May notes, 'discipline, to the point of self-cruelty, is central to all "higher culture"—providing that this self-cruelty hones and refines the "instincts" rather than simply suppresses them, that it enhances the alertness and range of the senses rather than shrinks them' (May 1999: 28). The life-denying form of cruelty, as the suppression or annihilation of instinctive being, dominates Nietzsche's analyses of the ascetic ideal. Furthermore, Nietzsche identifies compensatory, retaliatory gestures or actions, which may range in degree of refinement regarding their expression, with the notion of *ressentiment*. Appealing to this particular aspect of Nietzsche's thought on cruelty will expand the critical understanding of its role in *Endgame*, which has hitherto focused upon its seeming gratuitousness.[18] Scrutinising the appearance of aggression in *Endgame* through this notion will demonstrate that there is a distinctive 'logic of cruelty' operating in the characters' struggle for supremacy (Sheehan 2008: 86).

   Cruelty pervades *Endgame* and dominates the play's central relationship. As Beckett stressed to Michael Haertdter, 'there must be maximum aggression between [Hamm and Clov] from the first exchange of words onward. Their war is the nucleus of the play'.[19] Significantly, Hamm's cruelty predominantly manifests as a desire to afflict Clov with a sense of meaninglessness. For instance, it is with *'prophetic relish'* that Hamm conveys his prescient vision of a fatigued Clov losing his will, 'sitting there, a speck in the void, in the dark, for ever' (Beckett 1990: 109). According to Hamm, Clov's profound, future isolation will be character-ised by dramatic deterioration. For again conceiving the shelter as a figu-ration of the self's boundaries, Hamm informs his servant that the walls will disappear, '[i]nfinite emptiness will be all around', and he'll be 'like a little bit of grit in the middle of the steppe' (109–10). To emphasise the abjectness of Clov's confrontation with the *'horror vacui'*, Hamm gestures towards the uselessness of religious consolation as he proclaims 'all the resurrected dead of all the ages wouldn't fill' this darkness (109). Hamm's vision emphasises Clov's concomitant loss of efficacious agency. In doing so it recalls Nietzsche's claim from *The Birth of Tragedy* that 'insight into the terrible truth', awareness of the Dionysian meaningless-ness of existence, initiates paralysis: it 'outweighs every motive for action' (*BT* 7: 39). Having sketched some of the characters' defensive-recuper-ative strategies above, it is evident that Hamm's 'aggression' seeks to explode Clov's protective measures and to subject him to a depressive loss of willing.

While I have briefly alluded to Nietzsche's stress on the sublimation of our aggressive drives, which he valorises in distinction to both crude, uncontrolled expressions of these instincts and to the ascetic denial of them, it is worth alluding to a series of passages in which he seeks to wrest externally directed cruelty from a traditional moral perspective for the purposes of reading *Endgame*. Turning to an entry in *The Gay Science*, Nietzsche here juxtaposes acts of kindness with the perpetra-tion of cruelty by considering them as equally motivated by the primary desire for power:

> Benefiting and hurting others are ways of exercising one's power over them—that is all one wants in such cases! We *hurt* those to whom we need to make our power perceptible, for pain is a much more sensitive means to that end than pleasure: pain always asks for the cause, while pleasure is inclined to stop with itself and not look back. (*GS* 13: 38)

Cruelty, for Nietzsche, is primarily understood as a means to impact the other. While both '[b]enefiting and hurting others' involve a flow of energy back to the self, it is cruelty that provides a greater return: the person in pain, Nietzsche claims, is more inclined to acknowledge its source. From this model, then, the infliction of suffering is, like 'ben-efiting' others through acts of generosity or kindness, fundamentally a means to augment or intensify one's sense of self.

In his earlier work *Human All Too Human* (1878), Nietzsche is more explicit about the 'innocence' or amoral status of cruelty. He claims, '[m]alice does not aim at the suffering of the other in and of itself, but rather at our own enjoyment' (*HAH* 103: 71). This enjoyment is anal-ogous to the pleasure we take 'in breaking up twigs, loosening stones, fighting with wild animals, in order to gain awareness of our own strength' (72): we inflict cruelty to 'release our power on the other per-son and experience an enjoyable feeling of superiority', Nietzsche con-tends (71–2). Reinforcing this notion of self-intensification, Nietzsche argues in *Daybreak* that 'to practice cruelty is to enjoy the highest gratifi-cation of the feeling of power'. In this passage Nietzsche claims that 'the constantly imperilled community [...] refreshes itself and for once throws off the gloom of constant fear and caution' in the act of cruelty (*D* 18: 16). Aligning Beckett's fatigued characters with Nietzsche's contention that cruelty acts as 'a veritable seductive lure *to* life' may help explain why they inflict suffering upon each other with such 'relish' (*OGM* II 7: 47).

Insight into the dynamics of cruelty can be gained by referring to Nietzsche's idea of the will to power. As noted in Chapter 2, Nietzsche considers the feeling of overcoming resistances as integral to this notion. In one succinct passage Nietzsche explains: '[w]hat is happiness?—The feeling that power *increases*—that a resistance is overcome' (*AC* 2: 127). It is possible to read the perpetration of cruelty as the overcoming of the other's resistance, as Ivan Soll does when he observes that, 'in mak-ing others suffer we are made aware that we are making them experience things *against their will*' (Soll 1994: 180). Soll goes on:

> What differentiates cruelty from other behaviour that involves overcoming difficulty is that cruelty involves overcoming the opposed and resisting will of another person. [...] The joys of cruelty become the joys of the triumph of the will over other wills, of interpersonal domination. (180–1)

Given the ubiquity of strategies deployed by the characters to dominate the other in *Endgame*, which concomitantly provoke defensive meas-ures to resist such attempts, it is possible to see the characters stimulated by the desire to attain the pathos of power deriving from overcoming the other's will. What is more, one may situate Nietzsche's insistence on the need for a state of creative tension, in which no party or force completely dominates or annihilates the other, with Beckett's comments on *Endgame*. Turning first to Beckett: Beckett wrote to Alan Schneider that 'death is merely incidental to the end of "this...this...thing." ...I do not say "death game"' (Beckett 1998: 22). Salisbury cites this letter to persuasively argue that 'this play is emphatically not an extermination struggle' (Salisbury 2012: 129). In other words, Hamm's domination cannot be total, for that would spell the death, or end, of the game. Nevertheless, as I shall argue below, the play's denouement suggests that the characters dangerously flirt with this possibility.

Nietzsche's work repeatedly stresses the need for the generation of a creative tension, for the continual play of dominance and resistance. While distinguishing his stance from the hedonically orientated ascetic ideal, insofar as he avows the suffering integral to this state, he importantly holds that a productive condition of discord prevents the collapse into sterile tyranny and decay. The following passage captures this view regarding one's relation both to the external other and to the conflicting impulses that constitute the self:

> A further triumph is our spiritualization of *enmity*. It consists in profoundly grasping the value of having enemies: in brief, in acting and thinking in the reverse of the way in which one formerly acted and thought. The Church has at all times desired the destruction of its enemies: we, we immoralists and anti-Christians, see that it is to our advantage that the Church exist.... In politics, too, enmity has become much more spiritual—much more prudent, much more thoughtful, much more *forbearing*. Almost every party grasps that it is in the interest of its own self-preservation that the opposing party should not decay in strength; the same is true of grand politics. A new creation in particular, the *Reich* for instance, has more need of enemies than friends: only in opposition does it *become* necessary.... We adopt the same attitude towards the 'enemy within': there too we have spiritualized enmity, there too we have grasped its *value*. One is *fruitful* only at the cost of being rich in contradictions; one remains *young* only on condition that the soul does not relax, does not long for peace.... (*TI* V 3: 53–4)

According to Nietzsche, it is when harnessing one's resources to combat or overcome an adversary that one realises and intensifies one's strengths and capacities. The external 'enemy' or the 'enemy within' provides an opportunity for growth, presenting an obstacle or a resistance to be surmounted. The absence of a powerful adversary against which one tests oneself results in a state of relaxation, precipitating the disintegration of the inner organisation of the self's various drives. There is an attendant loss of force, a diminishing pathos of power.

The continued dynamic of dominance and resistance is key to the play. As Salisbury remarks concerning Hamm and Clov's conflict: 'each requires the other to remain in the game' (Salisbury 2012: 128). Clov, then, continually defies Hamm's attempts to subjugate him. Regarding Hamm's prophetic vision of Clov's decline, which imagines Clov sitting depressively in the dark 'for ever', Clov ruptures the potency of his master's cruel vision by reminding Hamm that he 'can't sit down' (Beckett 1990: 110). This assertion not only suggests that he will not succumb to the nihilistic collapse that his master envisages, but also acts to frustrate Hamm's attempt at configuring cognitive coherence, of generating another narrative form.[20]

What is more, in defying Hamm's imperialistic denial of his individuality by highlighting his overlooked disability, Clov's retort is also suggestive of the other's incapacity to identify with one's suffering, again signaling the self's radical isolation. This theme is also evident in what Beckett called '[o]ne of the cruellest sections of the play': Clov's refusal to administer Hamm's painkiller (Beckett 1992: 65). Rather than evincing Clov's resistance against his bullying master, this episode illustrates that Clov, too, is an active perpetrator of cruelty.[21] Such scenes demonstrate the frequent interchangeability of the characters' roles, contributing to the play's resistance to standard ethical readings. Observing that the perpetrator also fails to imaginatively identify with the other's suffering, even if this is only to register the degree to which the agent of pain can claim to impact its recipient, further complicates such interpretations of *Endgame*. Clov's enquiry as to whether Hamm's throat hurts—so as to maliciously deny him a lozenge—resonates with an earlier exchange in which Hamm sought to ascertain the degree to which he had made Clov suffer:

HAMM: I've made you suffer too much. [*Pause.*] Haven't I?
CLOV: It's not that.
HAMM: [*Shocked*] I haven't made you suffer too much?
CLOV: Yes!
HAMM: [*Relieved.*] Ah you gave me a fright! (Beckett 1990: 95)

Reading this dialogical exchange in conjunction with a series of passages from *Human All Too Human*, where Nietzsche again ruminates upon the 'innocence' of cruelty, is illuminating. Here Nietzsche surmises that 'when we injure out of so-called malice, the *degree* of pain produced is in any case unknown to us' (*HAH* 104: 73). Underpinning this argument is a recurrent view found in Nietzsche, namely that we display a lack of imagination to identify with the other: 'the idea of one's "neighbour" [...] is very weak in us; [...] [t]hat the other suffers *must be learned;* and it can never be learned completely' (101: 71). Nietzsche here anticipates Beckett's understanding of the self's essential ontological solitude.[22]

What is of primary significance regarding these claims is Nietzsche's intention to interpret human nature, and hence human cruelty, 'beyond good and evil'. He asks: '[c]an there be an injury out of pure *malice*, in cruelty, for example? If one does not know how painful an action is it cannot be malicious' (104: 73). Applying this point to *Endgame* further undermines conventional ethical readings of the characters' behaviour. [88] Paul Sheehan makes a similar observation when he notes that 'cruelty often requires an *other* to be able to function properly' (Sheehan 2008: 99): as cruelty and ethics depend 'to some extent, on the existence of an *other*', this absence of the other, as conceived by Nietzsche and dramatised by Beckett, extricates cruelty from traditional ethics (88). As implied above, the characters' narcissistic self-enclosure, which I argue is particularly heightened due to their chronic suffering, signals an increasingly attenuated awareness of the other. These points corroborate Shane Weller's reading of Beckett's admiration for both Racine's and the Marquis de Sade's 'dispassionate statement of human desire': Weller's interpretation of Beckett's 'dispassionate', or non-moral, statement of human motivation similarly situates humanity 'beyond good and evil' (Weller 2008: 114).

A second point to note in relation to Nietzsche's series of claims regarding cruelty is that there is a characteristic self-preservative dimension to this incapacity to relate to the other. As Nietzsche contends: '[b]ut do we ever completely *know* how painful an action is to the other person? As far as our nervous system extends, we protect ourselves from pain' (*HAH* 104: 73). As discussed in Chapter 2, Nietzsche holds that one's responsiveness towards others' pain has a depressive, nihilistic effect that threatens to overwhelm the self.[23] He argues, for example, that the individual capable of a deep, Dionysian identification with others' distress 'would collapse with a curse against existence' (33:

36). Consequently, Nietzsche claims, the vast majority of people remain sealed-off within themselves: 'everyone wills himself alone and stands his ground alone' to protect him or herself from participating in the 'vicissitudes and suffering' of others (36).

Beckett's presentation of the characters' postures of self-enclosure repeatedly evinces the threat posed by others' distress. For instance, it may be argued that Hamm's excessive outrage at his parents' disturbance was provoked by Nagg and Nell's narration of loss. Additionally, Nagg vindictively recollects his own harsh rejection of Hamm who, as 'a tiny boy [...] frightened, in the dark', woke his parents only to be moved 'out of earshot' so that they 'might sleep in peace' (Beckett 1990: 119–20). Elsa Baroghel observes that Nagg seeks 'a pain free psychosis, not disturbed or intruded upon by the other' (Baroghel 2010: 126). Furthermore, Nagg's point that he 'was asleep, happy as a king' (Beckett 1990: 119) echoes Hamm's refrain—of a desire to sleep—and resonates with Nietzsche's contention that the fatigued sufferer covets 'something akin' to '*hibernation*' as a release from deep pain (*OGM* II 17: 102–3). It can be inferred that the characters' chronic suffering motivates this pathological withdrawal from the other.

A further illustration of this fear of exposure to others' vulnerability is evident in Hamm's narrative. Perceiving the arrival of a desperate beggar as an 'invasion', the narrator avoids the beggar's face, 'black with mingled dirt and tears', and exclaims, '[n]o, no, don't look at me, don't look at me' (Beckett 1990: 117). It is telling that this event occurs as Hamm's fictional narrator prepares for the Christmas festivities: the narrator oscillates from paternal, generous postures to hostile defensive gestures, wishing to restrict the gift of refuge to the other, and thus limit the loss to the self that this would entail. For Boulter, Hamm's repeated return to his story suggests 'a nostalgic return to potency' given that 'he had the means and power to render real aid to someone' (Boulter 1998: 46). In other words, 'the story takes place in a time where some ethical action could have taken place' (47). Boulter's situating of potency with ethical action, or generosity, in the play anticipates my correspondent alignment of impotence with cruelty, *vis à vis* Nietzsche.

In Nietzsche's thought the notion of gift-giving is tied to his ideal of squandering. It is suggestive of a position of strength, of abundance, and this may apply to the individual or to the state. This strength or richness can be understood to reflect an accomplished state of coherence, of self-mastery: from a state of plenitude one can expend one's riches and absorb one's losses. As discussed in Chapter 2, this squandering or self-loss may be exemplified by his ideal of self-overcoming whereby the self voluntarily relinquishes one's existent self-containment in the pursuit of an ever-expanding, richer multiplicity; one's sense of inner strength may also be expressed by a capacity to exercise forgiveness towards one's malefactors: the well-constituted sovereign individual or powerful state controls or overcomes its reactionary punitive drive to endure its 'parasites'.[24]

The damaged, fragmented characters in Beckett's play stand in contradistinction to Nietzsche's notion of abundance and to the cognate ideal of squandering. As discussed above, the wounded subjects in *Endgame* who, largely determined by their recuperative postures, consider the other primarily as a threat. Mirroring Lawrence's characterisation of Sir Clifford Chatterley, Beckett's characters adopt prudential, self-preservative strategies to limit and control their contact with the other.[25] And rather than grant forgiveness for any perceived injury, Beckett's characters resemble Kafka's in seeking to assuage their pain by identifying someone to blame for their respective losses.[26] Nietzsche's insight into the psychology of the sufferer, who 'instinctively looks for [...] a culprit', is equally pertinent to *Endgame* (*OGM* III 15: 99): identifying a legitimate offender, Nietzsche contends, acts as a palliative insofar as it produces 'some kind of *excess of feeling*,—which is used as the most effective anaesthetic of dull, crippling, long-drawn-out pain' (III 19: 107). That is, blame cognitively prefigures the perpetration of cruelty upon the other who, as the identified culprit, shall be punished.

Blame is a chief feature of the suffering characters' responses to the world and to the other. Hamm, as noted above, reproaches life *per se*. He also condemns his father, whom he calls an 'accursed progenitor' (Beckett 1990: 96). White contends that 'Hamm resents Nagg and Nell for bringing him into this world, and essentially blames them for his suffering' (White 2008: 14). Catanzaro also notes that 'Nagg and Nell clearly have not been forgiven' for the more specific grievance of their neglect during his childhood (Catanzaro 2007: 173). Blame, then, in *Endgame* illustrates Nietzsche's claim that it primarily signals the bearer's impoverished condition: it is a reactive sentiment, motivated by the desire to compensate for the self's losses. Invoking Nietzsche's thoughts on punishment, we can again identify this aggrieved mentality appealing to the closed economy of the contractual logic: the sufferer, Nietzsche holds, considers him or herself as a creditor who may gain recompense through the perpetration of cruelty upon the guilty culprit.[27] Yet rather than serving to augment the self, blame and the perpetration of punitive action ultimately perpetuates the pathos of loss for the characters in *Endgame*. For as Nietzsche clarifies in his rumination on cruelty:

> The state in which we hurt others is certainly seldom as agreeable, in an unadulterated way, as that in which we benefit others; it is a sign that we are still lacking power, or it betrays a frustration in the face of this poverty; it brings new dangers and uncertainties to the power we do possess and clouds our horizon with the prospect of revenge, scorn, punishment, failure. (*GS* 13: 39)

The perpetration of cruelty, as sketched above, may act as a 'seductive lure to life' for the wearied characters; it may produce 'the most effective anaesthetic' for chronic pain. However, Nietzsche contends that it nevertheless signals powerlessness, evincing a lack of self-mastery. Cruelty is associated with 'the feeling of vengefulness and vindictiveness' which belong 'to weakness', Nietzsche claims: it reveals a dominant reactionary disposition (*EH* I 7: 17). Furthermore, insofar as cruelty self-perpetuates by containing the 'prospect of revenge', it impedes one from focusing on and realising one's own goal. It therefore frustrates one from experiencing oneself as a powerful, willing agent fulfilling one's purpose. In contrast to Nietzsche's healthy squanderer or powerful state able to bear its 'parasites', the play's characters remain inextricably bound to the game of blame and revenge. Beckett's *Endgame* demonstrates that while blaming the other may be driven by the desire to augment one's own fragile sense of selfhood and to override an extant sense of injustice, the perpetuation of retributive expressions comes dangerously close to destroying the other, and hence the self: the vindictive drive that manifests in the play stands in opposition to Nietzsche's aforementioned claim that it is necessary to realise that 'in the interest of [one's] own self-preservation' 'the opposing party should not decay in strength'.

THE END GAME

The final act of vengeance, Clov's indeterminate departure, leaves Hamm bereft of an audience for his narrative. The play's denouement thus highlights Hamm's impotence and meaningless isolation. Reinforcing the pervasive sense of inexorable loss, Hamm seems to presage this moment of utter abandonment earlier in the play:

HAMM: There I'll be, in the old refuge, alone against the silence and...
[*he hesitates*]... the stillness. If I can hold my peace, and sit quiet, it will be
all over with sound, and motion, all over and done with. [*Pause.*] I'll have
called my father and I'll have called my... [*he hesitates*]... my son. [...] I'll
say to myself, He'll come back. [*Pause.*] And then? [*Pause.*] And then?
[*Pause.*] He couldn't, he has gone too far. [*Pause.*] And then? [*Pause. Very
agitated.*] All kinds of fantasies! That I'm being watched! A rat! Steps!
Breath held and then... [he breathes out.] Then babble, babble, words,
like the solitary child who turns himself into children, two, three, so as to
be together, and whisper together, in the dark. (Beckett 1990: 126)

According to Mary Bryden, Hamm triumphs in the battle for power as
he 'conclude[s] the show on his own terms' (Bryden 1990: 219). The
final move, Bryden asserts, sees Clov as 'the sacrificial lamb, or, alterna-
tively, the scapegoat sent into the "Desert" recommended to him by Nell
in her final breath' (224). However, the idea of Hamm's ultimate vic-
tory, coupled with this notion of finality which I shall soon turn to, is
questionable: for Bryden also notes, by pointing to the fact that the herb
clove is used 'as a calming agent and a palliative for internal bleeding',
that Clov's absence means that 'there will be no more painkiller of any
sort' for Hamm (224). And it is the loss of the most potent palliative
going, namely the presence of an audience attending to one's stories,
that terrifies Hamm. Frank's comment on the relation between illness
and narrative is insightful on the ill self's particularly heightened dependency upon an audience:

The self-story is told both to others and to one's self; each telling is
enfolded within the other. The act of telling is a dual reaffirmation.
Relationships with others are reaffirmed, and the self is reaffirmed. [...]
The ill person needs to reaffirm that his story is worth listening to by others. He must also reaffirm that *he is still there*, an audience for himself. [...]
Illness is a crisis of self in the specific sense of an uncertainty that one's self
is still there as an audience. (Frank 1997: 56)

Hamm's bullying insistence that Clov fake an enthusiastic demand for his
narrative is indicative of his 'crisis of self'. His alternative tactic of bribing
Nagg to attend to his stories similarly conveys Hamm's urgent need for
an audience. What is more, Nagg's repudiation of this role anticipates
Clov's similar vindictive manoeuvre. Nagg is aware that Hamm, as Ruby

Cohn notes, 'is centre stage, always in need of an audience', as he brutally concludes his speech (Cohn 1980: 77):

> NAGG: I hope the day will come when you'll really need to have me listen to you, and need to hear my voice, any voice. [*Pause.*] Yes, I hope I'll live till then, to hear you calling me like when you were a tiny boy, and were frightened, in the dark, and I was your only hope. (Beckett 1990: 120–1)

Revealing Hamm's dependency while imagining a future reversal of the actual power structure, Nagg's disclosure of his past neglect of Hamm again evokes Nietzsche's notion of *ressentiment*: the powerless Nagg, always seduced by the promise of a sugar-plum to attend to Hamm's stories, resorts to an imaginary revenge given his incapacity to exercise an actual retribution.[28] Tellingly, Nagg's vindictive wish plays on Hamm's fear of solitude by envisaging his son's fundamental isolation much as Hamm's prophecy envisioned Clov's future destitution: in both cases the victim is to imagine himself alone in the 'dark'; it is significant that Clov had earlier reported to Hamm that Nell had died '[o]f darkness' (Beckett 1990: 129), the encounter with the void that provokes the realisation that all is 'meaningless and in vain' (*WP* 36: 23). The devastation wrought by Nagg's manoeuvre is suggested by Hamm's summative comment: 'our revels now are ended' (Beckett 1990: 120). With Nagg rejecting to play the role of audience to his son's narratives, Hamm's pronouncement is indicative of the terminal state of this relationship.

Denuded of any self-affirming spectator with Clov's absence at the end of the play, Hamm's final strategy is suggested by the 'fantasies' that he is 'being watched' in his premonitory vision. His ultimate appeal to an audience is noted by Salisbury: '[f]or in his final "gag" Hamm throws his whistle towards the auditorium, offering it up to these others "[w]ith my compliments". It is precisely the audience, then, alongside Clov, who are invoked in the final line "[y]ou ... remain"' (Salisbury 2012: 131). Hamm's appeal to an unseen and uncertain spectator constitutes his final recourse to avert suicidal nihilism, the collapse of all willing. For, as I have argued throughout, it is useless suffering that threatens to overwhelm and paralyse the self, precipitating suicidal dissolution: the characters in *Endgame* exhibit a fear of the realisation that their long-standing pain will have 'been for nothing' (Beckett 1990: 108). Hamm's strategy thus echoes Josef K.'s desperate search for a witness to observe his ignominious ending in *The Trial*. Hamm's self-reflexivity also parallels Nietzsche's description of the ancient Greeks who, Nietzsche argues, were 'full of tender consideration for "the spectator"' (*OGM* II 7: 49). That is, Hamm similarly exhibits the fundamental need to recoup something from the experience of pointless suffering. By inventing an audience, as the Greeks created the intermediary, spectating gods, Hamm's suffering is offered as a gift for the pleasure of the spectator. 'My compliments' therefore means: my suffering, a gift to you, for your pleasure. Tellingly, Clov had earlier directed his telescope to the auditorium, informing Hamm: 'I see…a multitude…in transports…of joy' (Beckett 1990: 106). A modicum of comfort is attained in considering one's suffering to be of value to a spectating audience: it is no longer 'unseen', or senseless.

Invoking an audience also allows the possibility of identifying with the spectator's detached position. This move permits one to imaginatively achieve distance from one's suffering. I believe something of this is also going on when Hamm speaks of multiplying himself like the 'solitary child who turns himself into children' (126). Moreover, remaining cognisant of Hamm's aggressive proclivity throughout the play in conjunction with this rumination recalls Nietzsche's depiction of the ascetic who splits himself 'asunder into sufferer and a spectator': the ascetic, Nietzsche claims, does not direct aggression outwards onto an external other like the crude barbarian, but rather, as these impulses must be expressed, intensifies the inward drive of one's cruel instincts; Hamm, similarly denied an outlet for his aggression in his state of solitude, parallels the depiction of the ascetic who continues to attain 'an unspeakable happiness at the *sight of torment*' through inflicting or witnessing his own suffering (*D* 113: 68). Given that Hamm's final destitution can be apprehended in terms of the absence of his two main sources of pain relief—an audience for his stories and an outlet for his aggression—his self-division thus resonates with Nietzsche's claim that 'there is also an abundant, over-abundant enjoyment of one's own suffering' (*BGE* 229: 159).

Nevertheless, despite gesturing towards this masochistic recuperative strategy, the final image of the isolated Hamm fantasising multiple presences and appealing to the unseen audience strikes one of profound loss and failure. For Clov's ambiguous departure, the provocation of radical uncertainty as to whether he has actually departed or not, comprises the final act of vengeance on Clov's part: Clov presents the blind Hamm with a final exegetical predicament that prevents him from interpretatively mastering the game. Exemplifying the play's continual frustration of closure, Gontarski notes: 'Clov's silent, unresponsive presence' signals 'a persistence that suggests that there may be at least one more turn to the wheel' (Gontarski 2009: 139–40). Clov's absence serves, then, to highlight Hamm's dependence on the other and the powerlessness characterising his solitude. Thus, rather than situate Nietzsche's analyses of (externally orientated) cruelty with Weller's reading of Beckett's 'dispassionate statement' of human nature, despite the suggested parallels, I hold that Nietzsche's reflections on cruelty as a compensatory gesture points more towards a reading of the characters' individual and collective impotence and ultimate failure. The revenge play between the characters that dominates the drama thus clearly undermines any notion, such as that held by Cavell, of Hamm's heroism or triumph.

Indeed, these cruel and masochistic dimensions of *Endgame* may account for the audiences' mixed responses to the play. On the one hand, *Endgame* may repel its audience as it presents its characters struggling to constitute some form of self-coherence and inescapably bound to destructive, compensatory strategies. On the other hand, however, by briefly noting *Endgame*'s relation to Nietzsche's analysis of ancient tragedy, outlined in Chapter 2, it is possible to identify a source of the audience's pleasure, albeit a rather masochistic one. For Nietzsche, pre-Socratic tragedy involved the dissolution and reconstitution of meaning and identity: through the intoxicated audience's collective identification with the hero's demise, the tragic experience entailed the decomposition of stable meaning and the rupture of Apollonian closure and boundaries; mirroring nature's exuberant fertility, the fragmented self did not collapse in this quasi-religious experience, but had the power to reconstitute itself. The participant-spectator of ancient tragedy passed through a Dionysian, nihilistic state yet was reinvigorated just as Dionysus was reborn following painful dismemberment. I shall now outline the relevance of this painful-pleasurable dialectical dynamic regarding the audience's experience of *Endgame* by firstly registering the audience's resistance towards Beckett's favourite play.

Julie Campbell's discussion of audience responses to the play is insightful. Alluding to Beckett critic Vivian Mercier's aversion to *Endgame*, Campbell acknowledges that reactions to the play may depend upon one's personal disposition and contextual situation: Mercier's repulsion from the play stemmed from personal crisis, from his wife's illness and death; his reaction points to the fact that Beckett's drama, in its unconventional presentation of human suffering and decay, may negatively impact its audience (see Campbell 2007: 269). This negative affect may be talked about in terms of nihilism. For Nietzsche, as aforementioned, considers one potential effect of tragedy, given that it is premised on the recognition that everyone 'must be prepared to face a sorrowful end', to be that of inducing feelings of suicidal despair (*BT* 17: 80).

Nietzsche's writings on nihilism shed further light on the way in which Beckett's dramatisation of his characters' decline provokes revulsion and resignation. For *Endgame*'s audience is arguably exposed to what Nietzsche calls 'the disgusting spectacle of the failed, the stunted, the wasted away' (*OGM* I 11: 26). As Nietzsche argues that '[t]he *sickly* are the greatest danger to man', for they 'introduce the deadliest poison and scepticism into our trust in life, in man, in ourselves', it may be said that the audience's engagement with 'the unfortunate, the downtrodden, [and] the broken' characters presented before them may induce feelings of nihilistic despair (III 14: 95). For, as Nietzsche succinctly puts it, '[t]he sight of man now makes us tired—what is nihilism today if it is not *that*?... We are tired of *man*' (I 12: 27).

That Beckett may have been aware of this possible impact upon his audience is suggested in his earlier novel, *Molloy* (1951). Here the eponymous narrator, similarly beset by debilitating physical ailments, confesses of his own wearied condition:

> It is indeed a deplorable sight, a deplorable example, for the people, who so need to be encouraged, in their bitter toil, and to have before their eyes manifestations of strength only, of courage and of joy, without which they might collapse, at the end of the day, and roll on the ground. (Beckett 2009: 20)

Coupled with this negative affective dimension of the play, *Endgame* presents its audience with a cognitive impasse. Otherwise put, the play repeatedly resists attempts at interpretative closure and mastery. Significantly, Beckett told Schneider that he wanted to provide a 'full evening's agony' with the performance of *Endgame* (Beckett 1998: 16). That this 'agony' may take the form of a hermeneutical obstacle that both the characters and the audience share can be elucidated, for example, by recalling Clov's final ambiguous departure: Hamm shares this conundrum with the audience that he repeatedly invokes. The audience's drive for hermeneutical closure or coherence thus mimics the characters' various attempts to attain a self-preservative self-enclosure. The characters' thwarted attempts to assemble the 'grains' of their identity, to construct a coherent 'heap' or whole, or an Apollonian individuated self, are transmitted to the witnessing audience (Beckett 1990: 93). For the characters' attempts to render power or interpretative mastery are largely shifting, paradoxical, and unintelligible.

Nietzsche's analysis of the self's appropriative economy is germane here with reference to the hermeneutical difficulties that the audience are presented with. For Nietzsche observes that a common means of attaining 'the *feeling* of growth, the feeling of increased power' is through the tendency 'to assimilate the new to the old, to simplify the complex, to overlook or repel what is wholly contradictory' (*BGE* 230: 160–2). This drive for the superficial or for an Apollonian assimilation of the complex and paradoxical to categories of stable identity is, however, thwarted for the audience of *Endgame*. As Gabriele Schwab observes, the audience cannot rely upon notions of psychic continuity, 'of circumscribed wholes', given the characters' fragmentary and interchangeable natures (Schwab 1992: 89). She also makes the general observation that: '[T]he pervasive structure of negation and contradiction frustrates all partial investments of meaning and thereby fundamentally impedes every gesture of interpretation which strives for closure' (91). By disturbing the stable categories of meaning and identity that we rely upon, the audience is subject to an 'endgame' which plays with the limits of our subjectivity. Drawing on Schwab's thesis, Campbell notes that it is possible to see a dialectic of opening and closure characterise the audience's experience of the play: '*Endgame* encourages the spectator to make sense of what is happening on stage, but then challenges this very procedure' (Campbell 2007: 268). The audience's attempt to attain a state of interpretative coherence amounts to a gesture of closure towards the play's refractory otherness. Yet the play repeatedly resists this imperialistic endeavour, disturbing these ineluctable attempts at closure, at assimilation. The experience of this play thus involves an expenditure of the rationally closed, coherent, or Apollonian self. We are propelled, as Schwab discerns, to engage with new openings that then impel us to posit new interpretations. Of course, these new positions, gesturing towards closure, are themselves being continually ruptured by the constant strains, ambiguities and contradictions that characterise this play. Presented with this exegetical recalcitrance, the self must invest more of itself in this drive to assimilate or digest that which resists such attempts at assimilation. This dynamic, which mirrors the Apollonian-Dionysian dialectic of meaning evacuation and reconstitution as Nietzsche presents it, may account for both the joy and the hostility that *Endgame* generates.

For some, the absence of gestures or signals that point towards an interpretative consensus or closure may provoke hostility and depression. Recalling Nietzsche's minimal psychological principle that the self experiences the pathos of power as it overcomes resistances, it may be surmised that Beckett's play, rather, with its refractory nature, stimulates an antithetical pathos of impotence. This resistance or blockage, it must be stressed, that provokes such repugnance is not solely cognitive. For the cognitive and the affective are intertwined: the characters' embodied pain manifests in their cognitive failings which are purveyed to the audience. It is thus this presentation of the characters' physio-psychological breakdown, and not just psychic dissolution, that the audience seeks to appropriate and which it may stumble at. And yet the experience of dissolution that *Endgame* subjects us to is pleasurable. As Campbell wonderfully puts it: '[t]here is no message in *Endgame,* there is no consoling panacea, but there is something indefinable and also magical going on' (270).

In confronting the audience with the characters' senseless suffering, *Endgame* presents a truly Dionysian vision, one of a world devoid of hope. It resists attempts to reconstitute palliatives or restoratives that would engender some form of meaning. And yet we, as creatures with consciousness, are impelled to construct meaning. We are thus provoked to engage with the resistances the play presents us with. And this entails 'agony'. For, as Nietzsche maintains, suffering is integral to feelings of pleasure, or rather, to the pathos of power:

> Displeasure, as an obstacle to its will to power, is therefore a normal fact, the normal ingredient of every organic event; man does not avoid it, he is rather in continual need of it; every victory, every feeling of pleasure, every event, presupposes a resistance overcome. (*WP* 702: 373)

The dialectic of opening and closure I have just sketched suggests that *Endgame* presents resistances which we are 'in continual need of'. For the play continually invites and resists interpretative closure. And if we are to grow, according to the thinker, we require to engage with such resistances. Thus, just as Nietzsche saw the tragic Greeks embrace Silenus's wisdom, with the dissolution of ego-security this entailed, so *Endgame*'s masochistic dimension may spell a paradoxical feeling of life-enhancement in the midst of such nihilistic despair. For in this encounter with the text's unassimilable otherness, the self may just find itself temporarily assuming the position of Nietzsche's 'genius of the heart': 'broken open, [...] more uncertain perhaps, more delicate, more fragile, more broken, but full of hopes that as yet have no names' (*EH* III 6: 47).

NOTES

1. In terms of Beckett's philosophical influences much attention has been given to his admiration of Arthur Schopenhauer, Nietzsche's 'Great and Only Teacher'. Christopher Janaway, *Willing and Nothingness: Schopenhauer as Nietzsche's Educator* (Oxford: Oxford University Press, 2008), p. 8. In a well-known letter, Beckett wrote to Thomas MacGreevy in July 1930: 'I am not reading philosophy, not caring whether he is right or wrong or a god or worthless metaphysician. An intellectual justification of unhappiness—the greatest that has ever been attempted—is worth [...] an examination'. Cited in Elsa Baroghel, 'From Narcissistic Isolation to Sadistic Pseudocouples: Tracing the Genesis of Endgame', *Samuel Beckett Today/Aujourd'hui: An Annual Bilingual Review/Revue Annuelle Bilingue*, 22 (2010): 123–33 (123). There are many critical considerations of Schopenhauer's contribution to Beckett's pessimistic work. For an extended discussion, see Ulrich Pothast, *Metaphysical Vision: Arthur Schopenhauer's Philosophy of Art and Life and Samuel Beckett's Own Way to Make Use of It* (New York: Peter Lang Publishing, 2008)). As noted in Chapter 1, Nietzsche identified Schopenhauer with modern forms of nihilism. That is, having initially been 'overpowered' by Schopenhauer, Nietzsche came to distance himself from his 'master' and strove to articulate an opposing, life-affirming philosophy. Chistopher Janaway, *Willing and Nothingness: Schopenhauer as Nietzsche's Educator* (Oxford: Oxford University Press, 2008), p. 1. Yet while Nietzsche's repudiation of Schopenhauer was complex and never absolute—he continued to pay homage to Schopenhauer throughout his later work—it is fair to surmise that the apparent divergences characterising Nietzsche's and Beckett's respective views of Schopenhauer have inflected critical discussions of the Nietzsche-Beckett relation. Paul Sheehan, for instance, argues that: '[i]n depicting life as an existential realm detached from human being, Beckett might seem not so different from Nietzsche who excoriated the human

disposition to abjure life for "antilife"—slave morality, bad conscience, *ressentiment*. But for Nietzsche life, or its correlate, power, nevertheless possesses inherent value, which it clearly does not in the Beckettian estimate (where the correlate for life is not power but impotence). See Paul Sheehan, *Modernism, Narrative, Humanism* (Cambridge: Cambridge University Press, 2009), p. 163. Steven J. Rosen briefly discusses Nietzsche's influence on Beckett in terms of his critique of nihilism before noting Beckett's rejection of Nietzsche. According to Rosen it was 'the positive side of Nietzsche's thought' that Beckett repudiated: 'the trouble with' Nietzsche's philosophy, 'to Beckett's way of thinking, lies in the insufficient extremity of its nihilism'. Steven J. Rosen, *Samuel Beckett and the Pessimistic Tradition* (New Brunswick, NJ: Rutgers University Press, 1976), p. 132. Mary M. F. Massoud reads *Waiting for Godot* 'as written in defiance of Nietzsche's jubilant announcement that "God is dead!"'. Mary M. F. Massoud, 'Beckett's Godot: Nietzsche Defied', *Irish University Review: A Journal of Irish Studies*, 40 (2010): 42–53 (42). For an unorthodox juxtaposition of Nietzsche and Beckett, see Richard Lane's essay. Lane unusually 'examines the writing lives of Beckett and Nietzsche, and the interconnected positioning of the two writers *as* characters in one another's texts'. Richard Lane, 'Beckett and Nietzsche: The Eternal Headache', in *Beckett and Philosophy*, ed. by Richard Lane (Basingstoke: Palgrave Macmillan, 2002), pp. 166–76 (168). Of particular relevance for this chapter, Stanley Cavell repeatedly frames his discussion of *Endgame* with reference to Nietzsche's understanding of active nihilism and its relation to theodicy. Stanley Cavell, 'Ending the Waiting Game', in *Must We Mean What We Say?: A Book of Essays* (Cambridge: Cambridge University Press, 1976), pp. 115–62. I shall invoke this powerful essay throughout this chapter.

2. Theodor Adorno, '*Trying to Understand* Endgame', trans. Michal T. Jones, *New German Critique*, 26 (1982): 119–50 (122). Adorno states: 'French existentialism had tackled history. In Beckett, history devours existentialism. In *Endgame*, a historical moment is revealed, the experience which was cited in the title of the culture industry's rubbish book *Corpsed*. After the Second War, everything is destroyed, even resurrected culture, without knowing it; humanity vegetates along, crawling, after events which even the survivors cannot really survive, on a pile of ruins which even renders futile self-reflection of one's own battered state'.

3. See Chapter 2, pp. 50–1.

4. See Chapter 1, pp. 7–8.

5. See Chapter 3, pp. 82–3.

6. This point echoes my discussion of pain in Chapter 2. See pp. 36–7.

7. See Chapter 2, p. 50.

8. See Chapter 2, pp. 47–52.
9. See Chapter 2, p. 27, and my discussion of the ascetic ideal on p. 50.
10. See Chapter 3, pp. 74–5.
11. See Chapter 2, pp. 31–2.
12. In noting Hamm's inadequacy as a storyteller, I disagree with Doherty's comment that Hamm delights in 'his own skill at telling' given that his 'invention and memory are in satisfactory working order for sufficient doling out of words'. Francis Michael Doherty, *Samuel Beckett* (London: Hutchinson, 1971), p. 90. Countering this suggestion that Hamm is able to achieve a proficient sense of self-coherence, I concur, rather, with Stan Gontarski's observation that '[t]he dominant trope of these narratives is their sense of unending, which manifests itself formally in fragmentation and incompletion.' Stan E. Gontarski, 'A Sense of Unending: Samuel Beckett's Eschatological Turn', *Samuel Beckett Today/Aujourd'hui* (2009): 135–49 (141).
13. See Chapter 2, pp. 36–7.
14. Quoted in Erik Tonning, *Modernism and Christianity* (Basingstoke: Palgrave Macmillan, 2014), p. 117.
15. Stan Gontarski echoes my view, arguing that 'although Hamm fears the actual end, he fears insignificance more'. Stan E. Gontarski, 'A Sense of Unending: Samuel Beckett's Eschatological Turn', *Samuel Beckett Today/Aujourd'hui* (2009): 135–49 (141).
16. See Chapter 2, p. 50.
17. See Chapter 4, p. 126.
18. For example, Paul Sheehan claims that cruelty operates 'outside the framework of cause and effect' in Beckett. See Paul Sheehan, 'A World Without Monsters: Beckett and the Ethics of Cruelty', in *Beckett and Ethics*, ed. by Russell Smith (London: Continuum, 2008), pp. 86–101 (86). Francis Doherty sums up his analysis of *Endgame*: '[a]ll we can say is that, in the end, man's role is absurd and meaningless in a world designed for cruelty'. Francis Michael Doherty, *Samuel Beckett* (London: Hutchinson, 1971), pp. 99–100. Paul Lawley asserts: 'Hamm's *need*, both then and now (despite Nagg's claim), is the need to exert power wilfully, even arbitrarily'. Paul Lawley, 'Adoption in Endgame', in *Waiting for Godot and Endgame: Samuel Beckett*, ed. by Steven Connor (London: Macmillan, 1992), pp. 119–27 (121).
19. Quoted in Elsa Baroghel, 'From Narcissistic Isolation to Sadistic Pseudocouples: Tracing the Genesis of Endgame', *Samuel Beckett Today/Aujourd'hui: An Annual Bilingual Review/Revue Annuelle Bilingue*, 22 (2010): 123–33 (124).
20. Dina Sherzer similarly registers the use of paradox, tautology and mimicry among the subtle and manifold strategies deployed by Clov to undermine

and resist Hamm's dominance. Dina Sherzer, 'Beckett's Endgame, Or What Talk Can Do', *Modern Drama,* 22 (1979): 291–303 (295–6).

21. Smith similarly points out that Clov undertakes his master's orders to 'bottle' Nagg and Nell with brutal efficacy: 'he is a more-than-willing Executioner [...] whose zeal to exterminate all remaining forms of life exceeds even his master's'. See Russell Smith, 'Endgame's Remainders', in *Samuel Beckett's Endgame,* ed. by Mark S. Byron and Michael J. Meyer (New York: Rodopi, 2007), 99–120 (108).

22. See Chapter 2, p. 61.

23. See Chapter 2, pp. 61–2.

24. See Chapter 2, pp. 52–3.

25. See Chapter 3, pp. 82–3.

26. See Chapter 4, pp. 135–6.

27. See Chapter 2, pp. 48–9.

28. See Chapter 2, pp. 51–2.

REFERENCES

Adorno, Theodor, '*Trying to Understand* Endgame', trans. Michal T. Jones, *New German Critique,* 26 (1982): 119–50.

Baroghel, Elsa, 'From Narcissistic Isolation to Sadistic Pseudocouples: Tracing the Genesis of *Endgame*', *Samuel Beckett Today/Aujourd'hui: An Annual Bilingual Review/Revue Annuelle Bilingue,* 22 (2010): 123–33.

Beckett, Samuel, *Endgame,* in Samuel Beckett, *The Complete Dramatic Works* (London: Faber, 1990), 89–134.

——————, *The Theatrical Notebooks of Samuel Beckett. Volume II: Endgame,* ed. by S. E. Gontarski (London: Faber and Faber, 1992).

——————, *No Author Better Served: The Correspondence of Samuel Beckett and Alan Schneider,* ed. by Maurice Harmon (Cambridge, MA: Harvard University Press, 1998).

——————, *Three Novels: Molloy, Malone Dies, the Unnamable* (New York: Grove Press, 2009).

——————, *The Collected Poems of Samuel Beckett: A Critical Edition,* ed. by Seán Lawlor and John Pilling (London: Faber and Faber, 2012).

Blau, Herbert, *Sails of the Herring Fleet: Essays on Beckett* (Ann Arbor: University of Michigan Press, 2004).

Boulter, Jonathan, '"Speak No More": The Hermeneutical Function of Narrative in Samuel Beckett's *Endgame*', in *Samuel Beckett: A Casebook,* ed. by Jennifer M. Jeffers (New York: Garland, 1998), 39–62.

——————, *Beckett: A Guide for the Perplexed* (London: Continuum, 2008).

Bryden, Mary, 'The Sacrificial Victim of Beckett's *Endgame*', *Literature & Theology: An International Journal of Theory, Criticism and Culture,* 4 (1990): 219–25.

Campbell, Julie, '*Endgame* and Performance', in *Samuel Beckett's Endgame*, ed. by Mark S. Byron (New York: Rodopi, 2007), 253–74.

Catanzaro, Mary F., 'Masking and the Social Construct of the Body in Beckett's *Endgame*', in *Samuel Beckett's Endgame*, ed. by Mark S. Byron and Michael J. Meyer (Amsterdam: Rodopi, 2007), 165–88.

Cavell, Stanley, 'Ending the Waiting Game', in *Must We Mean What We Say?: A Book of Essays* (Cambridge: Cambridge University Press, 1976), 115–62.

Cohn, Ruby, *Just Play: Beckett's Theater* (Princeton, NJ: Princeton University Press, 1980).

Dilworth, Thomas, and Christopher Langlois, 'The Nietzschean Madman in Beckett's *Endgame*', *Explicator*, 65 (2007): 167–71.

Doherty, Francis Michael, *Samuel Beckett* (London: Hutchinson, 1971).

Frank, Arthur W., *The Wounded Storyteller: Body, Illness, and Ethics* (London: University of Chicago Press, 1997).

Gontarski, Stan E., 'A Sense of Unending: Samuel Beckett's Eschatological Turn', *Samuel Beckett Today / Aujourd'hui* (2009): 135–49.

Henning, Sylvie Debevic, 'Endgame: On the Play of Nature', in *Waiting for Godot and Endgame: Samuel Beckett*, ed. by Steven Connor (London: Macmillan, 1992), 100–18.

Knowlson, James, *Damned to Fame: The Life of Samuel Beckett* (London: Bloomsbury, 1996).

Kugelmann, Robert, 'Pain, Pathos, Place', in *Challenges to Theoretical Psychology*, ed. by Wolfgang Maiers (North York, ON: Captus University Publisher, 1999), 182–99.

Lawley, Paul, 'Adoption in *Endgame*', in *Waiting for Godot and Endgame: Samuel Beckett*, ed. by Steven Connor (London: Macmillan, 1992), 119–27.

May, Simon, *Nietzsche's Ethics and His War on 'Morality'* (Oxford: Oxford University Press, 1999).

Miller, J. Hillis, *Poets of Reality: Six Twentieth-Century Writers* (Oxford: Oxford University Press, 1966).

Nehamas, Alexander, *Nietzsche: Life as Literature* (Cambridge, MA: Harvard University Press, 1985).

Nietzsche, Friedrich Wilhelm, *The Will to Power*. trans. Walter Kaufmann and R. J. Hollingdale (New York: Vintage Books, 1968).

———, *Beyond Good and Evil: Prelude to a Philosophy of the Future*. trans. R. J. Hollingdale (Harmondsworth: Penguin, repr. 1990).

———, *Ecce Homo: How One Becomes What One Is*. trans. R. J. Hollingdale (London: Penguin, repr. 1992).

———, *The Birth of Tragedy*. trans. Shaun Whiteside (London: Penguin, 1993).

———, *On the Genealogy of Morality*. trans. Carol Diethe (Cambridge: Cambridge University Press, 1994).

———, *The Anti-Christ* in *Twilight of the Idols* and *The Anti-Christ*. trans. R. J. Hollingdale (London: Penguin, repr. 2003).

————, *The Gay Science: With a Prelude in German Rhymes and an Appendix of Songs*. trans. Josefine Nauckhoff and Adrian Del Caro (Cambridge: Cambridge University Press, repr. 2003).

————, *Twilight of the Idols* in *Twilight of the Idols and The Anti-Christ*. trans. R. J. Hollingdale (London: Penguin, repr. 2003).

————, *Human, All Too Human*. trans. Marion Faber and Stephen Lehmann (London: Penguin, repr. 2004).

————, *Daybreak: Thoughts on the Prejudices of Morality*. trans. R. J. Hollingdale (Cambridge: Cambridge University Press, repr. 2007).

Pippin, Robert B., 'Introduction', in Friedrich Wilhelm Nietzsche, *Thus Spoke Zarathustra*, trans. Adrian del Caro (Cambridge: Cambridge University Press, 2006), viii–xxxv.

Roof, Judith A., 'A Blink in the Mirror: Oedipus and Narcissus in *Waiting for Godot* and *Endgame*', in *Waiting for Godot and Endgame: Samuel Beckett*, ed. by Steven Connor (London: Macmillan, 1992), 141–9.

Salisbury, Laura, *Samuel Beckett: Laughing Matters, Comic Timing* (Edinburgh: Edinburgh University Press, 2012).

Scarry, Elaine, *The Body in Pain: The Making and Unmaking of the World* (Oxford: Oxford University Press, 1985).

Schwab, Gabriele, 'On the Dialectic of Closing and Opening in *Endgame*', in *Waiting for Godot and Endgame: Samuel Beckett*, ed. by Steven Connor (London: Macmillan, 1992), 87–99.

Sheedy, John J., 'The Comic Apocalypse of King Hamm', *Modern Drama*, 9 (3) (1966): 310–8.

Sheehan, Paul, 'A World Without Monsters: Beckett and the Ethics of Cruelty', in *Beckett and Ethics*, ed. by Russell Smith (London: Continuum, 2008), 86–101.

Smith, Russell, '*Endgame*'s Remainders', in *Samuel Beckett's Endgame*, ed. by Mark S. Byron and Michael J. Meyer (New York: Rodopi, 2007), 99–120.

Soll, Ivan, 'Nietzsche on Cruelty, Asceticism, and the Failure of Hedonism', in *Nietzsche, Genealogy, Morality: Essays on Nietzsche's Genealogy of Morals*, ed. by Richard Schacht (Berkeley: University of California Press, 1994), 168–92.

Tonning, Erik, *Modernism and Christianity* (Basingstoke: Palgrave Macmillan, 2014).

Weller, Shane, 'The Anethics of Desire: Beckett, Racine, Sade', in *Beckett and Ethics*, ed. by Russell Smith (London: Continuum, 2008), 102–17.

White, Kathryn, *Beckett and Decay* (London: Continuum, 2008).

Williams, Bernard, *The Sense of the Past: Essays in the History of Philosophy* (Princeton, NJ: Princeton University Press, 2006).

Worton, Michael, '*Waiting for Godot* and *Endgame*: Theatre as Text', in *The Cambridge Companion to Beckett*, ed. by John Pilling (Cambridge: Cambridge University Press, 1996), 67–87.

CHAPTER 6

Conclusion: Affective Modernism

ILLNESS: 'THE GREAT EXPERIENCE'?

In her well-known essay, 'On Being Ill' (1926), Virginia Woolf complains that 'illness has not taken its place with love and battle and jealousy among the prime themes of literature' (Woolf 2012: 3). Woolf's essay addresses literature's neglect of this most bodily of experiences by celebrating suffering's transformative potential and valorising the insights disclosed in illness. Broadly speaking, her conviction that one experiences 'tremendous [...] spiritual change' through illness, as it discloses 'undiscovered countries' and the 'wastes and deserts of the soul' (3), coincides with Nietzsche's exaltation of suffering as the occasion to 'see everything [...] in a new light', as an opportunity for self-examination and self-growth (*D* 114: 70). Suffering in illness, for Woolf as for Nietzsche, presents a 'great experience' for spiritual self-transformation (Woolf 2012: 8).

As observed in Chapter 2, Nietzsche's discourse on suffering is beset by a series of tensions, however: his affirmative rhetoric is especially undermined by focussing upon his views on others' distress. Similar strains operate in Woolf's essay: Woolf champions the receptivity to otherness fostered by illness on the one hand; her rejection of sympathy suggests an acute vulnerability to the fear of nihilistic collapse on the other. The issue of the self's affective being comes to the fore: while both figures endorse notions of an expansive, porous self, their visions seem to

© The Author(s) 2018
S. Smith, *Nietzsche and Modernism*,
Palgrave Studies in Modern European Literature,
https://doi.org/10.1007/978-3-319-75535-9_6

be at odds with their respective stress on protecting autarkic selfhood. By charting the strains in Woolf's essay, I aim to highlight some of the salient points of this study and bring it to a conclusion by suggesting its relevance to the field of modernist studies more generally.

THE NEED FOR ILLUSION

One consequence of being ill according to Woolf is that 'the whole landscape of life lies remote and fair' (Woolf 2012: 8). In contrast to the narrow and familiar outlook held by the healthy, industrious majority, this sense of perspectival detachment, or pathos of distance, defamiliarises the everyday world. Speaking from the vantage point of the invalid, Woolf thus attends to the overlooked, 'extraordinary spectacle' of the sky before her (12). Ruminating on how busy, productive life works in conjunction with our anthropomorphic projections to impede awareness of the celestial, aesthetic play of shapes and colours in constant flux, her initial joy gives way to ambivalence as she ponders nature's indifference: '[d]ivinely beautiful is also divinely heartless. Immeasurable resources are used for some purpose which has nothing to do with human pleasure or human profit' (13–14). Moral judgement displaces aesthetic appreciation, for such useless expenditure 'seems to call for comment and indeed for censure' (14). Despite finding her own illness and 'irresponsible' freedom valuable, Woolf seeks to economise this endless and unfathomable squandering: 'the waste of Heaven' must be made 'use of'; there is a need to extract some 'human profit' from this 'divinely heartless' performance (13–14). Otherwise put, Woolf follows Nietzsche in acknowledging not only that 'the way of the world is [...] not rational, merciful, or just', but also of the human need to confer value to the indifferent world shorn of transcendent significance (*GS* 346: 204). As Nietzsche argues:

> Think of a being such as nature is, prodigal beyond measure, without aims or intentions, without mercy or justice, at once fruitful and barren and uncertain; think of indifference itself as power—how *could* you live according to such indifference? To live—is that not precisely wanting to be other than this nature? Is living not valuating, preferring, being unjust, being limited, wanting to be different? (*BGE* 9: 39)

Woolf's essay is clearly grappling with the conundrum confronting modernity as Nietzsche articulates it. What is more, Woolf claims that the ill are particularly sensitive to these disclosures: 'only the recumbent', she contends, are aware of one's place within the natural order, of one's ephemerality; the productive majority defend themselves from cognisance of the self's ultimate insignificance, which 'Nature is at no pains to conceal—that she in the end will conquer; heat will leave the world; [...] the sun will go out' (Woolf 2012: 16). For Nietzsche, the revelation of man's 'smallness and accidental occurrence in the flux of becoming and passing away' is akin to tragic, Dionysian knowledge (*WP* 4: 9). As observed throughout this study, the ill, impotent and beleaguered characters who populate the fictional worlds of *Lady Chatterley's Lover* (1928), *The Trial* (1925), and *Endgame* (1957) are especially vulnerable to the thought of one's finitude; exposure to an unbearable fear of nothingness, the *horror vacui*, provoked by such Dionysian insights, the characters are beset by despair and paralysis, the pathos of nihilism. Following Nietzsche's contention that we are impelled to resist the Dionysian, I thus highlighted the characters' various strategies to recuperate significance against this unpalatable knowledge, to configure themselves as willing beings.

Woolf's essay resonates with Nietzsche's claim that it is only as 'an aesthetic phenomenon existence is still *bearable* for us' (*GS* 107: 104). Woolf points to the inevitability of the Apollonian artistic gesture, of the human need to shield oneself from a full knowledge of Dionysian flux and senselessness through the imposition of artificial boundaries: she claims that man's creative activity 'must have drawn some firm outline' to generate the illusion that 'there will be some green isle for the mind to rest on even if the foot cannot plant itself there' (Woolf 2012: 17). More specifically, Woolf contends that 'the co-operative imagination of mankind' has 'wished [...] into existence' the 'universal hope—Heaven, Immortality' to resist the threat of suicidal paralysis, to entice us to remain willing beings who do not 'stiffen peaceably into glassy mounds' (17).

Woolf treats Christian belief as one more fictional illusion, expressing human 'hopes and desires' that stand to counter nature's grand indifference (18). On such terms, as to whether it effectively engenders willing agents sustained by its illusory powers, she assesses its value: discerning that the 'little company of believers lags and drags and strays', and suggesting that their 'tired' and 'worn' appearance is symptomatic of their imaginative fatigue, Woolf points to the frailty of the Christian fiction to contend that 'Heaven-making must be left to the poets' (18). As Woolf then turns to literature to provide solace and the generation of new meaning, she argues that poetry in turn finds its inspiration in nature, exemplified by that which is 'very small and close and familiar', the 'self-sufficient' flowers she directs her attention towards (14). Curiously, Woolf's meditation, which advances as it responds to the unpalatable realisation of nature's grand indifference to human endeavour, valorises the rose in similar terms: '[W]onderful to relate, poets have found religion in nature; people live in the country to learn virtue from plants. It is in their indifference that they are comforting' (15). That the rose demonstrates 'a demeanour of perfect dignity and self-possession', the flowers can be read to exemplify a self-contained insouciance towards nature's grand squandering and carelessness (15–16). Or more exactly, they embody an indifference towards human sorrow. For Woolf claims that 'the great artists, the Miltons and the Popes', inspired by nature, 'console not by their thought of us but by their forgetfulness' (16). Further scrutiny of Woolf's ideology of self-sufficiency suggests that art must detach us from unbearable encounters with others' distress.

SYMPATHY AND THE PATHOS OF NIHILISM

A recurrent theme explored in the preceding chapters is the individual's fundamental isolation.[1] Woolf holds a similar view of human existence, claiming that illness reveals that '[w]e do not know our own souls, let alone the souls of others. Human beings do not go hand in hand the whole stretch of the way' (11). In illness, Woolf argues, the 'make-believe' of a collective identity 'ceases' (12). The singular nature of one's suffering is, for Woolf, an occasion to be celebrated: '[h]ere we go alone, and like it better so. Always to have sympathy, always to be accompanied, always to be understood would be intolerable' (11–12). Valorising one's suffering as an opportunity to explore one's 'inner virgin forest' or untouched 'snowfield' (11–12), Woolf's position strongly resembles Nietzsche's view that one's suffering is 'what is truly personal': '[w]hat we most deeply and most personally suffer from is incomprehensible and inaccessible to nearly everyone else' (*GS* 338: 191). Pity, for Nietzsche, thus denies the personal value of one's suffering: as a superficial, homogenising construal of distress, compassion intervenes to foreclose the sufferer's encounter with 'terrors, deprivations, impoverishments, midnights, adventures, risks, and blunders' that are 'necessary' for one's convalescence and self-transformation (*GS* 338: 191).

While both Nietzsche and Woolf reject the value of compassion within affirmative notions of self-sufficiency and self-growth, further examination of Woolf's treatment of sympathetic feelings reveals the presence of similar reactive postures as those observed in Nietzsche.[2] Departing from the rhetoric of dignified self-discovery regarding one's own suffering, Woolf denounces compassion by claiming that '[s]ympathy nowadays is dispensed chiefly by the laggards and the failures' (Woolf 2012: 10). It is useful to recall Nietzsche's view that compassion is exercised by 'those who have little pride and no prospect of great conquests' (*GS* 13: 39): the weak and impoverished espouse and practice compassion as a recourse to dominate the other, Nietzsche contends. As Woolf apprehends sympathy to be 'fantastic and unprofitable', exercised by those who have 'dropped out of the race', she evokes a key argument established in my reading of Nietzsche (Woolf 2012: 10): sympathising with others is 'unprofitable', it is a form of useless expenditure that promises no return to the self. As with nature's grand squandering, Woolf suggests that suffering is an excessive force, indifferent to the economy of the individual. Indeed, suffering's overwhelming nature is hinted at in Woolf's initial complaint that illness rarely features as a literary theme: 'there is the poverty of the language' to describe pain (6); 'the experience cannot be imparted' (8). Moreover, Woolf explicitly discusses suffering's power to shatter one's sense of self-sufficiency when one encounters others' distress. For others' suffering provokes the self to reflexively consider its own unredeemed grievances:

> As is always the way with these dumb things, his own suffering serves but to wake memories in his friends' minds of *their* influenzas, *their* aches and pains which went unwept last February, and now cry aloud, desperately, clamorously, for the Divine relief of sympathy. (18–19)

Despite valorising the transformative, life-enhancing potential of illness and pain at length, Woolf suggests here that one's own past wounds actually remain raw, unappropriated. The senseless, irredeemable nature of one's injuries induces the sufferer to 'desperately' seek others' sympathetic responses. Nevertheless, despite this drive to render one's grievances bearable and valuable by appealing to the other, and hence to a common meaning, Woolf warns against compassionate feelings:

But sympathy we cannot have. Wisest fate says no. If her children, weighted as they already are by sorrow, were to take on them that burden too, adding in imagination other pains to their own, buildings would cease to rise; roads would peter out into grassy tracks; there would be an end of painting and of music; one great sigh alone would rise to Heaven, and the only attitudes of men and women would be those of horror and despair. (9)

Such feelings, Woolf contends, precipitate the onset of suicidal nihilism: human agency is denuded as one's own suffering is amplified in pity, becoming intolerable. As 'there would be an end of painting and of music', artistic endeavour would similarly collapse in the contagion of grief. And yet Woolf again points to the necessity of art: art provides one means to 'prevent one from turning the old beggar's hieroglyphic of misery into volumes of sordid suffering' (9). Woolf's emphasis in this passage on pity as intensifying existent suffering to nihilistic ends does, of course, reverberate with Nietzsche's pronounced hostility to compassion. Nietzsche declares:

Pity stands in antithesis to the tonic emotions which enhance the energy of the feeling of life: it has a depressive effect. One loses force when one pities. The loss of force which life has already sustained through suffering is increased and multiplied even further by pity. Suffering itself becomes contagious through pity; sometimes it can bring about a collective loss of life and life-energy which stands in an absurd relation to the quantum of its cause. (AC 7: 130)

Attention to modernism's complex discourse on suffering reveals a repeated fear of nihilistic collapse: Woolf may valorise suffering as an occasion for self-insight in this essay, yet she simultaneously betrays a fear of losing her sense of self-possession as she is exposed to others' and hence her own unredeemed grievances. As discussed in Chapter 2, Nietzsche holds that it is experiences of meaningless distress that accelerate individual and collective feelings of suicidal nihilism. Indeed, I argued there that Nietzsche, as an 'exceptional man' sensitive to others' misery, was particularly vulnerable to this pathos. Given that one implication of God's death is that we moderns no longer have the traditional means to appropriate our suffering, to render it valuable by providing an overarching purpose for it, modernist literature, I contend, conveys our particularly heightened susceptibility to this nihilistic pathos.

Woolf's essay suggestively provokes a further comparison with Nietzsche and with the modernist works discussed in this study. Recalling, for instance, discussions of Lawrence's depictions of his characters' recourse to postures of protective self-enclosure in conjunction with observations upon the prevalence of compensatory expressions of cruelty in *The Trial* and *Endgame*, Woolf's discourse on suffering articulates its own reactive-defensive negation of the other. That is, as Woolf follows Nietzsche in denouncing those 'laggards and failures' who champion pity, Woolf's essay similarly indexes a restrictive digestive capacity regarding others' suffering. For, as noted throughout this study, others' distress, with its concomitant threat to autarkic selfhood, provokes a necessary, self-preservative drive for distance. As examination of the twinned issues of senseless suffering and nihilism has illuminated the presence of this impulse to closure and detachment, of a resistance to or rejection of the other, it may be suggested that attending to the complex ways in which sympathy and suffering are depicted in relation to such defensive-reactive feelings may offer a fresh approach to analysing modernist texts. By reading these restricted and reactive economies on such terms, this study can also be read in conjunction with other texts examining modernist writers and their relations to reactionary ideologies and politics.

MODERNISM AND THE DIONYSIAN AFFECT

Woolf's lament regarding the paucity of literature engaging with the body in illness can be extended to contemporary critical discourse. As Terry Eagleton notes, the fragile body in pain, illness or emotional disturbance features rarely within 'body-orientated academia' (Eagleton 2003: xiv). The reason for this, according to Eagleton, is that 'the suffering body is largely a passive one': 'hardly able to compete with the sexual, disciplined or carnivalesque body', the suffering, passive one stands at odds with postmodernism's 'ideology of self-fashioning' (xiv).

Sianne Ngai's *Ugly Feelings* departs from this critical tendency and focuses upon bodily emotions in a range of literary and cultural works. Seeking 'to expand and transform the category of "aesthetic emotions"' (Ngai 2005: 6), Ngai contends that negative feelings such as envy, anxiety and paranoia issue from 'the general situation of obstructed agency' (13–14). By largely focusing on two further affects bound to 'the situation of passivity itself', namely nihilism and *ressentiment*, my study may complement Ngai's work (12). Within the field of modernist studies more specifically, my approach to wounded subjectivities marks a shift from Jonathan Flatley's *Affective Mapping* (2008): while Flatley seeks to uncover the productive or useful qualities of negative affects such as melancholy in modernist literature, I have stressed the ubiquity of reactionary and impotent feelings attending the pathos of frustrated agency.[3]

Woolf's essay calls for a new language for the body, 'more primitive, more sensual, more obscene', and for 'a new hierarchy of the passions' to correspond to the body's predominant experiences (Woolf 2012: 7). Woolf challenges the tendency within literary discourse to privilege the experiences of the mind. As Woolf acknowledges, this proclivity is rooted in fear of the body; it will take courage to confront the afflictions and affects of the corporeal, for it brings awareness of one's ultimate passivity, of the 'inevitable catastrophe' (5):

> To look these things squarely in the face would need the courage of a lion tamer; a robust philosophy; a reason rooted in the bowels of the earth. Short of these, this monster, the body, this miracle, its pain, will soon make us taper into mysticism, or rise, with rapid beats of the wings, into the raptures of transcendentalism. (5–6)

Registering the proclivity to shield oneself, to varying degrees, from the Dionysian truth of existence, Woolf considers illness to not only promise new self-insight but also to disturb the cerebral barriers that foreclose contact with otherness. Woolf insists that illness fractures the self's boundaries, usurping the mind's rigid hegemony that serves to restrict the body's immediate, sensual awareness of otherness: in health, 'intelligence domineers over our senses' (21). Woolf celebrates this affective receptivity as 'the barriers go down' (23): the self's 'overweening arrogance' (23), its 'cautious respectability' in health, is breached in illness (11). One fruitful consequence of this heightened sensual sensibility is that one's reception of great literature, and especially of poetry, is enhanced: grasping 'what is beyond' the words' 'surface meaning' (21), the poem 'is all the richer for having come to us sensually first' (22). Similarly, one benefits from a more immediate relation with high literature, unimpeded by the power of authoritative criticism and predisposed ideas: '[i]llness, in its kingly sublimity, sweeps all that aside and leaves nothing but Shakespeare and oneself' (23).

While the term 'affect' is commonly held to be synonymous with the emotions, it may connote the self's relation to both one's inner plurality of feelings and to one's surrounding world. Lisa Blackman's definition is helpful: '[r]ather than considering bodies as closed physiological and biological systems, bodies are open, participating in the flow or passage of affect, characterised more by reciprocity and co-participation than boundary and constraint' (Blackman 2012: 2). As Flatley puts it, '*affect* indicates something relational and transformative' (Flatley 2008: 12–13). Observing that '[p]eople write always of the doings of the mind', Woolf's essay is suggestive of how literature, for Woolf, enacts its own restrictive economy, limiting one's affective sensibility (Woolf 2012: 5): literature neglects '[t]hose great wars which the body wages with the mind a slave to it' to foreclose terrifying encounters with the other within and without (5). Literature is marked by 'boundary and constraint'. Woolf conceives of literature as a cultural form that distances us from our very passivity to our bodies: in its neglect of illness, literature averts awareness of our ultimate finitude, the realisation that when sick we 'go down into the pit of death and feel the waters of annihilation close above our heads' (Woolf 2012: 3). It is possible to say then that, in Nietzschean terms, 'On Being Ill' challenges the prevalent modern, Alexandrian tendency to deny knowledge of the Dionysian.

As suggested above, Woolf's essay is characterised by a series of tensions. On the one hand, her essay explores the transformative experience of illness, evincing the affective nature of one's suffering: illness provides an exploratory platform for investigating the self, expanding the relations between known and unknown aspects of the self, while also permitting a more immediate, sensual contact with otherness. This heightened state of relationality in illness, which discloses new insights into the nature of self and world, Woolf celebrates. On the other hand, however, illness's revelation of our affective permeability entails a concomitant vulnerability. Corresponding to the strains operating in Nietzsche and the modernist works discussed in this study, Woolf's essay simultaneously champions notions of self-possession. This posture of closure finds expression in her condemnation of sympathetic feelings: the boundaries of the self must be fixed or shored up to prevent one drowning in the flood of despair and bitterness provoked by others' unassuaged grievances. This affective porosity, and the heightened sense of fragility, is especially exposed by others' suffering which produces life-nauseating feelings of suicidal nihilism. Woolf's essay thus demonstrates a courage and willingness to explore and valorise profound suffering and yet suggests, as seen throughout this study, the necessity to erect life-preserving barriers to stem one's flow of feeling towards others in distress. As noted in previous chapters, this self-defensive posture, marking the self's affective-digestive limits, is both inevitable and yet signals a reactive closure towards others and otherness.

Another way to account for these strains in Woolf's essay is to align these with her implicit claim that great art engenders a fruitful tension between the Apollonian and the Dionysian, or between postures of openness and closure. Discussing the 'masters', Woolf celebrates their capacity to disturb readers' attempts to attain exegetical mastery, thwarting the 'arrogant' boundary of self-contained identity imposing itself. Great literature, she contends, frustrates or suspends one's pathos of agency: 'the masters themselves often keep us waiting intolerably while they prepare our minds for whatever it may be—the surprise, or the lack of surprise' (24). Similarly, Woolf valorises illness for its capacity to shatter our illusion of cerebral self-control. For modern culture, as Woolf conceives it, leaves us locked up in the fortresses of our mental egos, secure, and yet vitally and affectively sealed off. In response to our proclivity to assume excessive self-protective postures, to restrict 'participating in the flow or passage of affect' and the vulnerability this entails, Woolf's essay is suggestive of Nietzsche's view that the Dionysian nature of existence must be glimpsed. Calling for literature to address the body in illness, to explore one's affective receptivity and fragility, entails fracturing an 'arrogant' self-containment that is identifiable with Nietzsche's notion of 'theoretical' Alexandrian culture. Woolf's exhortation for the literary to turn to the multiple, porous, fragile and yet expansive corporeality is suggestive of the necessity of transcribing and exploring the Dionysian affect.

This study has examined works that produce this Dionysian affect, rupturing the self's comfortable self-containment. In different ways the writings of Lawrence, Beckett and Kafka expose the reader, or the audience, to human vulnerability, to experiences of useless suffering, to senseless or compensatory cruelty, to the problem of nihilism. Frustrating our drive for hermeneutic mastery and emotional self-possession, these works present the Dionysian, unpalatable and excessive character of existence. And herein lies their value, opening us up to our own and to the world's otherness. As Kafka wonderfully puts it:

We need books that affect us like a disaster, that grieve us deeply, like the death of someone we loved more than ourselves, like being banished into forests far from everyone, like a suicide. A book must be the axe for the frozen sea inside us. (Kafka 1977: 16)

Notes

1. See Chapter 2, p. 34, 61; Chapter 3, pp. 106–7; Chapter 5, pp. 189–90.
2. See Chapter 2, p. 63.
3. See, for instance, Flatley 2008: 2. Flatley claims that 'melancholizing is something that one *does*. [...] It is a practice that might, in fact, produce its own kind of knowledge'.

References

Blackman, Lisa, *Immaterial Bodies: Affect, Embodiment, Mediation* (London: Sage, 2012).

Eagleton, Terry, *Sweet Violence: The Idea of the Tragic* (Oxford: Blackwell, 2003).

Flatley, Jonathan, *Affective Mapping: Melancholia and the Politics of Modernism* (Cambridge, MA: Harvard University Press, 2008).

Kafka, Franz, *Letters to Friends, Family and Editors* (New York: Schocken, 1977).

Ngai, Sianne, *Ugly Feelings* (Cambridge, MA: Harvard University Press, 2005).

Nietzsche, Friedrich Wilhelm, *The Will to Power*. trans. Walter Kaufmann and R. J. Hollingdale (New York: Vintage Books, 1968).

———, *Beyond Good and Evil: Prelude to a Philosophy of the Future*. trans. R. J. Hollingdale (Harmondsworth: Penguin, repr. 1990).

———, *The Birth of Tragedy*. trans. Shaun Whiteside (London: Penguin, 1993).

———, *The Anti-Christ* in *Twilight of the Idols* and *The Anti-Christ*. trans. R. J. Hollingdale (London: Penguin, repr. 2003).

———, *The Gay Science: With a Prelude in German Rhymes and an Appendix of Songs*. trans. Josefine Nauckhoff and Adrian Del Caro (Cambridge: Cambridge University Press, repr. 2003).

———, *Daybreak: Thoughts on the Prejudices of Morality*. trans. R. J. Hollingdale (Cambridge: Cambridge University Press, repr. 2007).

Woolf, Virginia, *On Being Ill: With Notes from Sick Rooms by Julia Stephens* (Ashfield, MA: Paris Press, 2012).

BIBLIOGRAPHY

Adamowski, T. H., 'The Natural Flowering of Life: The Ego, Sex, and Existentialism', in *D. H. Lawrence's 'Lady': A New Look at Lady Chatterley's Lover*, ed. by Michael Squires and Dennis Jackson (Athens: University of Georgia Press, 1985), 36–57.

Adorno, Theodor, '*Trying to Understand* Endgame', trans. Michal T. Jones, *New German Critique*, 26 (1982): 119–50.

Alberts, Paul, 'Knowing Life Before the Law: Kafka, Kelsen, Derrida', in *Philosophy and Kafka*, ed. by Brendan Moran and Carlo Salzani (Plymouth: Lexington Books, 2013).

Allen, Neil, *Franz Kafka and the Genealogy of Modern European Philosophy: From Phenomenology to Post-Structuralism* (Lewiston, N.Y.: Edwin Mellen Press, 2005).

Anderson, Mark M., *Kafka's Clothes: Ornament and Aestheticism in the Habsburg Fin De Siècle* (Oxford: Clarendon Press, 1994).

Ansell-Pearson, Keith and Duncan Large (eds.), *The Nietzsche Reader* (Oxford: Blackwell, 2009).

Aschheim, Steven E., *The Nietzsche Legacy in Germany, 1890–1990* (London: University of California Press, 1994).

Baroghel, Elsa, 'From Narcissistic Isolation to Sadistic Pseudocouples: Tracing the Genesis of *Endgame*', *Samuel Beckett Today/Aujourd'hui: An Annual Bilingual Review/Revue Annuelle Bilingue*, 22 (2010): 123–33.

Beardsworth, Richard, 'Nietzsche, Nihilism and Spirit', in *Nihilism Now!: Monsters of Energy*, ed. by K. J. Ansell-Pearson and Diane Morgan (Basingstoke: MacMillan, 2000), 37–69.

© The Editor(s) (if applicable) and The Author(s) 2018
S. Smith, *Nietzsche and Modernism*,
Palgrave Studies in Modern European Literature,
https://doi.org/10.1007/978-3-319-75535-9

Beckett, Samuel, *Endgame*, in Samuel Beckett, *The Complete Dramatic Works* (London: Faber, 1990), 89–134.

——, *The Theatrical Notebooks of Samuel Beckett. Volume II: Endgame*, ed. by S. E. Gontarski (London: Faber and Faber, 1992).

——, *No Author Better Served: The Correspondence of Samuel Beckett and Alan Schneider*, ed. by Maurice Harmon (Cambridge, MA: Harvard University Press, 1998).

——, *Three Novels: Molloy, Malone Dies, the Unnamable* (New York: Grove Press, 2009).

——, *The Collected Poems of Samuel Beckett: A Critical Edition*, ed. by Seán Lawlor and John Pilling (London: Faber and Faber, 2012).

Bell, Michael, *D. H. Lawrence: Language and Being* (Cambridge: Cambridge University Press, 1992).

——, 'Nietzscheanism: "The Superman and the All-Too-Human"', in *A Concise Companion to Modernism*, ed. by David Bradshaw (Oxford: Blackwell, 2003), 56–74.

——, 'Reflections on Violence: Writing and/as Violence in Lawrence', *Etudes Lawrenciennes*, 31 (2004): 49–64.

Bending, Lucy, *The Representation of Bodily Pain in Late Nineteenth-Century English Culture* (Oxford: Oxford University Press, 2000).

Bentley, Eric, *The Cult of the Superman: A Study of the Idea of Heroism in Carlyle and Nietzsche with Notes on Other Hero-Worshippers of Modern Times* (Gloucester, MA: Peter Smith, 1969).

Blackman, Lisa, *Immaterial Bodies: Affect, Embodiment, Mediation* (London: Sage, 2012).

Blau, Herbert, *Sails of the Herring Fleet: Essays on Beckett* (Ann Arbor: University of Michigan Press, 2004).

Boa, Elizabeth, *Kafka: Gender, Class, and Race in the Letters and Fictions* (Oxford: Clarendon Press, 1996).

Boothroyd, David, 'Beyond Suffering I Have No Alibi', in *Nietzsche and Levinas: "After the Death of a Certain God"*, ed. by Jill Stauffer and Bettina Bergo (New York: Columbia University Press, 2009), 150–64.

Boulter, Jonathan, '"Speak No More": The Hermeneutical Function of Narrative in Samuel Beckett's *Endgame*', in *Samuel Beckett: A Casebook*, ed. by Jennifer M. Jeffers (New York: Garland, 1998), 39–62.

Boulter, Jonathan, *Beckett: A Guide for the Perplexed* (London: Continuum, 2008).

Bradbury, Malcolm, and James Walter McFarlane, *Modernism: 1890–1930* (Harmondsworth: Penguin, 1976).

Bridgwater, Patrick, *Nietzsche in Anglo-Saxony: A Study of Nietzsche's Influence on English and American Literature* (Bristol: Leicester University Press, 1972).

——, *Kafka and Nietzsche* (Bonn: Bouvier, 1974).

Bryden, Mary, 'The Sacrificial Victim of Beckett's *Endgame*', *Literature & Theology: An International Journal of Theory, Criticism and Culture*, 4 (1990): 219–25.

Burns, Wayne, '*Lady Chatterley's Lover:* A *Pilgrim's Progress* for Our Time', in *D. H. Lawrence: Critical Assessments Vol. 3, the Fiction (2)*, ed. by David Ellis and Ornella De Zordo (Mountfield: Helm Information, 1993), 84–102.

Campbell, Julie, '*Endgame* and Performance', in *Samuel Beckett's Endgame*, ed. by Mark S. Byron (New York: Rodopi, 2007), 253–74.

Carey, John, *The Intellectuals and the Masses: Pride and Prejudice Among the Literary Intelligentsia, 1880–1939* (London: Faber and Faber, 1992).

Carr, Karen Leslie, *The Banalization of Nihilism: Twentieth-Century Responses to Meaninglessness* (Albany: State University of New York Press, 1992).

Catanzaro, Mary F., 'Masking and the Social Construct of the Body in Beckett's *Endgame*', in *Samuel Beckett's Endgame*, ed. by Mark S. Byron and Michael J. Meyer (Amsterdam: Rodopi, 2007), 165–88.

Cavell, Stanley, 'Ending the Waiting Game', in *Must We Mean What We Say?: A Book of Essays* (Cambridge: Cambridge University Press, 1976), 115–62.

Childs, Peter, *Modernism* (London: Routledge, 2000).

Cohn, Ruby, *Just Play: Beckett's Theater* (Princeton, NJ: Princeton University Press, 1980).

Conway, Daniel W., 'Heidegger, Nietzsche, and the Origins of Nihilism', *Journal of Nietzsche Studies* 3 (1992): 11–43.

————, 'Beasts of Prey: How We Became What We Are: Tracking the "Beasts of Prey"', in *A Nietzschean Bestiary: Becoming Animal Beyond Docile and Brutal*, ed. by Christa Davis Acampora and Ralph R. Acampora (Lanham, MD: Rowman & Littlefield, 2004), 156–79.

Corngold, Stanley, 'Kafka's "Zarathustra"', *Journal of the Kafka Society of America*, 19 (1995): 9–15.

————, 'Nietzsche, Kafka and Literary Paternity', in *Nietzsche and Jewish Culture*, ed. by Jacob Golomb (London: Routledge, 1997), 137–57.

Daleski, H. M., *The Forked Flame* (London: Faber and Faber, 1965).

de Beauvoir, Simone, *The Second Sex* (London: Jonathan Cape, 1953).

Deleuze, Gilles, and Félix Guattari, *Kafka: Toward a Minor Literature*, trans. Dana Polan (Minneapolis: University of Minnesota Press, 1986).

Derrida, Jacques, *The Ear of the Other*, trans. Peggy Kamuf (London: University of Nebraska Press, 1988).

————, 'Before the Law', in *Acts of Literature*, ed. by Derek Attridge (London: Routledge, 1992).

————, 'Structure, Sign and Play in the Discourse of the Human Sciences', in *Modern Criticism and Theory*, ed. by David Lodge (New York: Longman, repr., 1993), 108–23.

Dews, Peter, *The Idea of Evil* (Oxford: Blackwell, 2008).

Dilworth, Thomas, and Christopher Langlois, 'The Nietzschean Madman in Beckett's *Endgame*', *Explicator*, 65 (2007): 167–71.

Doherty, Francis Michael, *Samuel Beckett* (London: Hutchinson, 1971).

Dollimore, Jonathan, *Death, Desire and Loss in Western Culture* (London: Penguin, 1998).

Dyer, Geoff, *Out of Sheer Rage: In the Shadow of D. H. Lawrence* (London: Little, Brown and Company, repr., 2009).

Eagleton, Terry, *Sweet Violence: The Idea of the Tragic* (Oxford: Blackwell, 2003).

Ellis, David, *Death and the Author: How D. H. Lawrence Died, and Was Remembered* (Oxford: Oxford University Press, 2008).

Fernihough, Anne, *D. H. Lawrence: Aesthetics and Ideology* (Oxford: Oxford University Press, 1993).

Flatley, Jonathan, *Affective Mapping: Melancholia and the Politics of Modernism* (Cambridge, MA: Harvard University Press, 2008).

Forth, Christopher E., *Zarathustra in Paris: The Nietzsche Vogue in France, 1891–1918* (DeKalb: North Illinois University Press, 2001).

Foster, John Burt, *Heirs to Dionysus: A Nietzschean Current in Literary Modernism* (Princeton, NJ: Princeton University Press, 1981).

Foucault, Michel, *Discipline and Punish*, trans. Alan Sheridan (London: Penguin, repr., 1991).

Frank, Arthur W., *The Wounded Storyteller: Body, Illness, and Ethics* (London: University of Chicago Press, 1997).

Fraser, Giles, *Redeeming Nietzsche: On the Piety of Unbelief* (London: Routledge, 2002).

Friedländer, Saul, *Franz Kafka: The Poet of Shame and Guilt* (New Haven: Yale University Press, 2013).

Garrard, Greg, 'Nietzsche Contra Lawrence: How to Be True to the Earth', *Colloquy: Text Theory Critique*, 12 (2006): 11–27.

Gillespie, Michael Allen, *Nihilism Before Nietzsche* (Chicago: University of Chicago Press, 1995).

Glicksberg, Charles I., *The Literature of Nihilism* (London: Bucknell University Press, 1975).

Goebel, Rolf J., 'The Exploration of the Modern City in *The Trial*', in *The Cambridge Companion to Kafka*, ed. by Julian Preece (Cambridge: Cambridge University Press, 2002), 42–60.

Gontarski, Stan E., 'A Sense of Unending: Samuel Beckett's Eschatological Turn', *Samuel Beckett Today/Aujourd'hui* (2009): 135–49.

Gooding-Williams, Robert, *Zarathustra's Dionysian Modernism* (Stanford: Stanford University Press, 2001).

Green, Eleanor H., 'Blueprints for Utopia: The Political Ideas of Nietzsche and D. H. Lawrence', *Renaissance & Modern Studies*, 18 (1974): 141–61.

Griffin, Roger, *Modernism and Fascism: The Sense of a Beginning Under Mussolini and Hitler* (Basingstoke: Palgrave Macmillan, 2007).

Grimm, Reinhold, 'Comparing Kafka and Nietzsche', *German Quarterly*, 52 (1979): 339–50.

Haar, Michel, *Nietzsche and Metaphysics*, trans. Michael Gendre (Albany: State University of New York Press, 1996).

——, 'Nietzsche and the Metamorphosis of the Divine', in *Post-Secular Philosophy*, ed. by Philip Blond (London: Routledge, 1998), 157–76.

Hawes, James, 'Faust and Nietzsche in Kafka's *Der Prozess*', *New German Studies*, 15 (1988): 127–51.

Heidegger, Martin, 'Who Is Nietzsche's Zarathustra?', in *The New Nietzsche: Contemporary Styles of Interpretation*, ed. by David B. Allison (Cambridge, MA: MIT Press, 1985), 64–79.

Heller, Peter, 'Kafka and Nietzsche', in *Proceedings of the Comparative Literature Symposium. Vol. iv: Franz Kafka: His Place in World Literature*, ed. by Wolodymyr T. Zyla, Wendell M. Aycock, and Pat Ingle Gillis (Lubbock: Texas Technology University, 1971), 71–95.

Henel, Ingeborg, 'The Legend of the Doorkeeper and Its Significance for Kafka's *Trial*', in *Twentieth Century Interpretations of The Trial*, ed. by James Rolleston (Englewood Cliffs, N.J.: Prentice-Hall, 1976), 40–55.

Henning, Sylvie Debevic, '*Endgame*: On the Play of Nature', in *Waiting for Godot and Endgame: Samuel Beckett*, ed. by Steven Connor (London: Macmillan, 1992), 100–18.

Higgins, Kathleen Marie, 'Suffering in Nietzsche's Philosophy', in *Reading Nietzsche at the Margins*, ed. by Steven V. Hicks and Alan Rosenberg (West Lafayette, IN: Purdue University Press, 2008), 59–72.

Hough, Graham, *The Dark Sun* (Aylesbury: Duckworth, repr., 1975).

Hsu, Linda C., 'Klamotten: Reading Nietzsche Reading Kafka', *German Quarterly*, 67 (1994): 211–21.

Huenemann, Charlie, 'Nietzsche's Illness', in *The Oxford Handbook of Nietzsche*, ed. by Ken Gemes and John Richardson (Oxford: Oxford University Press, 2013), 63–80.

Humma, John B., 'D. H. Lawrence as Friedrich Nietzsche', *Philological Quarterly*, 53 (1) (1974): 110–20.

Janaway, Christopher, *Beyond Selflessness* (Oxford: Oxford University Press, 2007).

Janaway, Christopher (ed.), *Willing and Nothingness: Schopenhauer as Nietzsche's Educator* (Oxford: Oxford University Press, 2008).

Kafka, Franz, *Letters to Friends, Family and Editors* (New York: Schocken, 1977).

——, *The Trial*, trans. Idris Parry (London: Penguin, repr., 2000).

Kavanagh, Thomas M., 'Kafka's *The Trial*: The Semiotics of the Absurd', in *Twentieth Century Interpretations of The Trial*, ed. by James Rolleston (Englewood Cliffs, N.J.: Prentice-Hall, 1976), 86–93.

Kinkead-Weekes, Mark, 'Eros and Metaphor: Sexual Relationship in the Fiction of Lawrence', in *Lawrence and Women*, ed. by Anne Smith (London: Vision Press, 1978), 122–35.

Knowlson, James, *Damned to Fame: The Life of Samuel Beckett* (London: Bloomsbury, 1996).

Koh, Jae-kyung, *D. H. Lawrence and the Great War: The Quest for Cultural Regeneration* (Oxford: Peter Lang, 2007).

Kuepper, Karl J., 'Gesture and Posture as Elemental Symbolism in Kafka's *The Trial*', in *Twentieth Century Interpretations of The Trial*, ed. by James Rolleston (Englewood Cliffs, N.J.: Prentice-Hall, 1976), 60–9.

Kugelmann, Robert, 'Pain, Pathos, Place', in *Challenges to Theoretical Psychology*, ed. by Wolfgang Maiers (North York, ON: Captus University Publisher, 1999), 182–99.

Kundera, Milan, *Testaments Betrayed*, trans. Linda Asher (Chatham: Faber and Faber, 1995).

Lampert, Laurence, *Nietzsche's Task: An Interpretation of Beyond Good and Evil* (New Haven, CT: Yale University Press, 2004).

Lane, Richard, 'Beckett and Nietzsche: The Eternal Headache', in *Beckett and Philosophy*, ed. by Richard Lane (Basingstoke: Palgrave Macmillan, 2002), 166–76.

Lawley, Paul, 'Adoption in *Endgame*', in *Waiting for Godot and Endgame: Samuel Beckett*, ed. by Steven Connor (London: Macmillan, 1992), 119–27.

Lawrence, D. H., 'We Need One Another', in *Phoenix: The Posthumous Papers of D. H. Lawrence*, ed. by Edward D. McDonald (London: Heinemann, repr., 1961b), 188–95.

——, *Fantasia of the Unconscious and Psychoanalysis and the Unconscious* (London: Penguin, repr., 1971).

——, 'Blessed Are the Powerful', in *D. H. Lawrence: A Selection from Phoenix*, ed. by A. A. H. Inglis (Harmondsworth: Penguin, 1979), 505–13.

——, *Study of Thomas Hardy and Other Essays*, ed. by Bruce Steele (Cambridge: Cambridge University Press, 1985).

——, 'A Propos of "Lady Chatterley's Lover"', in D. H. Lawrence, *Lady Chatterley's Lover* (London: Penguin, repr., 2006), 305–35.

——, *Lady Chatterley's Lover* (London: Penguin, repr., 2006).

Leiter, Brian, *Routledge Philosophy Guidebook to Nietzsche on Morality* (London: Routledge, 2002).

Lévinas, Emmanuel, *On Thinking of the Other: Entre Nous* (London: Athlone, 1998).

Lewis, Pericles, *Religious Experience and the Modernist Novel* (Cambridge: Cambridge University Press, 2010).

Luckhurst, Roger, 'Religion, Psychical Research, Spiritualism, and the Occult', in *The Oxford Handbook of Modernisms* (Oxford: Oxford University Press, 2016), 429–44.

Ludwigs, Marina, '"A Democracy of Touch": Masochism and Tenderness in D. H. Lawrence's *Lady Chatterley's Lover*', *Anthropoetics: The Journal of Generative Anthropology*, 16 (2011): 1–22.

Macleod, Sheila, *Lawrence's Men and Women* (London: Paladin Books, 1987).

Martin, Kirsty, *Modernism and the Rhythms of Sympathy* (Oxford: Oxford University Press, 2013).

Massoud, Mary M. F., 'Beckett's Godot: Nietzsche Defied', *Irish University Review: A Journal of Irish Studies*, 40 (2010): 42–53.

May, Keith M., *Nietzsche and Modern Literature: Themes in Yeats, Rilke, Mann and Lawrence* (Basingstoke: Macmillan, 1988).

May, Simon, *Nietzsche's Ethics and His War on 'Morality'* (Oxford: Oxford University Press, 1999).

Miller, James, 'Carnivals of Atrocity: Foucault, Nietzsche, Cruelty', *Political Theory*, 18 (1990): 470–91.

Miller, J. Hillis, *Poets of Reality: Six Twentieth-Century Writers* (Oxford: Oxford University Press, 1966).

Millett, Kate, 'D. H. Lawrence (*Lady Chatterley's Lover, The Plumed Serpent*, 'The Woman Who Rode Away')', in *D. H. Lawrence*, ed. by Peter Widdowson (Burnt Mill: Longman, 1992), 69–89.

Milton, Colin, *Lawrence and Nietzsche: A Study in Influence* (Aberdeen: Aberdeen University Press, 1987).

Mulhall, Stephen, *Philosophical Myths of the Fall* (Princeton, NJ: Princeton University Press, 2007).

Muller-Lauter, Wolfgang, *Nietzsche: His Philosophy of Contradictions and the Contradictions of His Philosophy*, trans. David J. Parent (New York: University of Illinois Press, 1999).

———, 'Experiences with Nietzsche', in *Nietzsche, Godfather of Fascism, On the Uses and Abuses of a Philosophy*, ed. by Jacob Golomb and Robert S. Wistrich (Princeton, NJ and Oxford: Princeton University Press, 2002), 66–89.

Murdoch, Iris, *Metaphysics as a Guide to Morals* (London: Penguin, 1993).

Nehamas, Alexander, *Nietzsche: Life as Literature* (Cambridge, MA: Harvard University Press, 1985).

Ngai, Sianne, *Ugly Feelings* (Cambridge, MA: Harvard University Press, 2005).

Nietzsche, Friedrich Wilhelm, *The Will to Power*, trans. Walter Kaufmann and R. J. Hollingdale (New York: Vintage Books, 1968).

———, *Beyond Good and Evil: Prelude to a Philosophy of the Future*, trans. R. J. Hollingdale (Harmondsworth: Penguin, repr., 1990).

———, *Ecce Homo: How One Becomes What One Is*, trans. R. J. Hollingdale (London: Penguin, repr., 1992).

———, *The Birth of Tragedy*, trans. Shaun Whiteside (London: Penguin, 1993).

———, *On the Genealogy of Morality*, trans. Carol Diethe (Cambridge: Cambridge University Press, 1994).

———, *The Gay Science: With a Prelude in German Rhymes and an Appendix of Songs*, trans. Josefine Nauckhoff and Adrian Del Caro (Cambridge: Cambridge University Press, repr., 2003).

————, *Thus Spoke Zarathustra*, trans. R. J. Hollingdale (London: Penguin, repr., 2003).

————, *Twilight of the Idols* and *The Anti-Christ*, trans. R. J. Hollingdale (London: Penguin, repr., 2003).

————, *Human, All Too Human*, trans. Marion Faber and Stephen Lehmann (London: Penguin, repr., 2004).

————, *Daybreak: Thoughts on the Prejudices of Morality*, trans. R. J. Hollingdale (Cambridge: Cambridge University Press, repr., 2007).

Norris, Margot, 'Sadism and Masochism in Two Kafka Stories: "In Der Strafkolonie" and "Ein Hungerkünstler"', *MLN*, 93 (3) (1978): 430–47.

————, *Beasts of the Modern Imagination: Darwin, Nietzsche, Kafka, Ernst, & Lawrence* (Baltimore: Johns Hopkins University Press, 1985).

Nussbaum, Martha C., 'Pity and Mercy: Nietzsche's Stoicism', in *Nietzsche, Genealogy, Morality: Essays on Nietzsche's Genealogy of Morals*, ed. by Richard Schacht (Berkeley: University of California Press, 1994), 139–67.

Owen, David, *Nietzsche, Politics and Modernity: Critique of Liberal Reason* (London: Sage, 1995).

Owen, David, and Aaron Ridley, 'Dramatis Personae: Nietzsche, Culture, and Human Types' in *Why Nietzsche Still?*, ed. by Alan D. Schrift (London: University of California Press, 2000), 136–53.

Parry, Idris, 'Introduction', in *The Trial*, ed. by Franz Kafka (London: Penguin, repr., 2000), ix–xv.

Pascal, Roy, *From Naturalism to Expressionism: German Literature and Society 1880–1918* (London: Basic Books, 1973).

Phillips, Adam, and Barbara Taylor, *On Kindness* (London: Penguin, 2010).

Pippin, Robert B., 'Nietzsche and the Origin of the Idea of Modernism', *Inquiry*, 26 (1983): 151–80.

————, 'Introduction', in Friedrich Wilhelm Nietzsche, *Thus Spoke Zarathustra*, trans. Adrian del Caro (Cambridge: Cambridge University Press, 2006), viii–xxxv.

Pondrom, Cyrena N., 'Kafka and Phenomenology: Josef K.'s Search for Information', in *Twentieth Century Interpretations of The Trial*, ed. by James Rolleston (Englewood Cliffs, N.J.: Prentice-Hall, 1976), 70–85.

Pothast, Ulrich, *Metaphysical Vision: Arthur Schopenhauer's Philosophy of Art and Life and Samuel Beckett's Own Way to Make Use of It* (New York: Peter Lang Publishing, 2008).

Reginster, Bernard, *The Affirmation of Life: Nietzsche on Overcoming Nihilism* (London: Harvard University Press, 2006).

Ridley, Aaron, *Nietzsche's Conscience: Six Character Studies from the Genealogy* (Ithaca: Cornell University Press, 1998).

Ring, Annie, 'In the Law's Hands: S/M Pleasure in *Der Proceß*, A Queer Reading', *Forum for Modern Language Studies*, 48 (2012): 306–22.

Roberts, Tyler T., *Contesting Spirit: Nietzsche, Affirmation, Religion* (Princeton: Princeton University Press, 1998).

Robertson, Ritchie, *Kafka: Judaism, Politics and Literature* (Oxford: Clarendon, 1985).

Roof, Judith A., 'A Blink in the Mirror: Oedipus and Narcissus in *Waiting for Godot* and *Endgame*', in *Waiting for Godot and Engame: Samuel Beckett*, ed. by Steven Connor (London: MacMillan, 1992), 141–9.

Rosen, Steven J., *Samuel Beckett and the Pessimistic Tradition* (New Brunswick, NJ: Rutgers University Press, 1976).

Ruderman, Judith, 'The Symbolic Father and the Idea of Leadership', in *D. H. Lawrence*, ed. by Peter Widdowson (Burnt Mill: Longman, 1992), 103–18.

Salisbury, Laura, *Samuel Beckett: Laughing Matters, Comic Timing* (Edinburgh: Edinburgh University Press, 2012).

Sallis, John, 'Dionysus—In Excess of Metaphysics', in *Exceedingly Nietzsche: Aspects of Contemporary Nietzsche Interpretation*, ed. by David Farrell Krell and David Wood (London: Routledge, 1988), 2–7.

Sanders, Scott R., 'Lady Chatterley's Loving and the Annihilation Impulse', in *D. H. Lawrence's 'Lady': A New Look at Lady Chatterley's Lover*, ed. by Michael Squires and Dennis Jackson (Athens: University of Georgia Press, 1985), 1–16.

Scarry, Elaine, *The Body in Pain: The Making and Unmaking of the World* (Oxford: Oxford University Press, 1985).

Schaffner, Anna Katharina, 'Kafka and the Hermeneutics of Sadomasochism', *Forum for Modern Language Studies*, 46 (2010): 334–50.

———, *Modernism and Perversion; Sexual Deviance in Sexology and Literature, 1850–1930* (Basingstoke: Palgrave Macmillan, 2011).

Schaffner, Anna Katharina, and Shane Weller, *Modernist Eroticisms: European Literature After Sexology* (New York, NY: Palgrave Macmillan, 2012).

Schneider, Daniel J., *D. H. Lawrence: The Artist as Psychologist* (Lawrence, KS: University Press of Kansas, 1984).

Schrift, Alan D., *Nietzsche and the Question of Interpretation: Between Hermeneutics and Deconstruction* (London: Routledge, 1990).

Schwab, Gabriele, 'On the Dialectic of Closing and Opening in *Endgame*', in *Waiting for Godot and Endgame: Samuel Beckett*, ed. by Steven Connor (London: Macmillan, 1992), 87–99.

Seaford, Richard, 'Tragedy and Dionysus', in *A Companion to Tragedy*, ed. by Rebecca Bushnell (Malden, MA: Blackwell, 2005), 25–38.

Sheedy, John J., 'The Comic Apocalypse of King Hamm', *Modern Drama*, 9 (3) (1966): 310–8.

Sheehan, Paul, 'A World Without Monsters: Beckett and the Ethics of Cruelty', in *Beckett and Ethics*, ed. by Russell Smith (London: Continuum, 2008), 86–101.

————, *Modernism, Narrative, Humanism* (Cambridge: Cambridge University Press, 2009).

Sherzer, Dina, 'Beckett's *Endgame*, or What Talk Can Do', *Modern Drama*, 22 (1979): 291–303.

Shiach, Morag, 'Work and Selfhood in *Lady Chatterley's Lover*', in *The Cambridge Companion to D. H. Lawrence*, ed. by Anne Fernihough (London: Cambridge University Press, 2001), 87–102.

Simpson, Hilary, *D. H. Lawrence and Feminism* (London: Croom Helm, 1982).

Smith, Russell, '*Endgame*'s Remainders', in *Samuel Beckett's Endgame*, ed. by Mark S. Byron and Michael J. Meyer (New York: Rodopi, 2007), 99–120.

Sokel, Walter H., 'Nietzsche and Kafka: The Dionysian Connection', in *Kafka for the Twenty-First Century*, ed. by Stanley Corngold and Ruth V. Gross (Rochester, NY: Camden House, 2011), 64–74.

Soll, Ivan, 'Nietzsche on Cruelty, Asceticism, and the Failure of Hedonism', in *Nietzsche, Genealogy, Morality: Essays on Nietzsche's Genealogy of Morals*, ed. by Richard Schacht (Berkeley: University of California Press, 1994), 168–92.

Solomon, Robert C., '"A More Severe Morality": Nietzsche's Affirmative Ethics', in *Nietzsche as Affirmative Thinker*, ed. by Yirmiyahu Yovel (Dordrecht: Martinus Nijhoff Publishers, 1986), 69–89.

————, *Continental Philosophy Since 1750: The Rise and Fall of the Self, a History of Western Philosophy* (Oxford: Oxford University Press, 1988).

Spilka, Mark, 'Lawrence's Quarrel with Tenderness', *Critical Quarterly*, 9 (4) (1967): 363–77.

————, 'On Lawrence's Hostility to Wilful Women: The Chatterley Solution', in *Lawrence and Women*, ed. by Anne Smith (London: Vision Press, 1978), 189–211.

Squires, Michael, *The Pastoral Novel: Studies in George Eliot, Thomas Hardy and D. H. Lawrence* (Charlottesville: University Press of Virginia, 1975).

Staten, Henry, *Nietzsche's Voice* (Ithaca, NY: Cornell University Press, 1990).

Steinhauer, H., 'Eros and Psyche: A Nietzschean Motif in Anglo-American Literature', *Modern Language Notes*, 64 (1949): 217–28.

Straus, Nina Pelikan, 'Grand Theory on Trial: Kafka, Derrida, and the Will to Power', *Philosophy and Literature*, 31 (2) (2007): 378–93.

Surin, Kenneth, *The Turnings of Darkness and Light* (Cambridge: Cambridge University Press, 1989).

Tenenbaum, David, *Issues of Shame and Guilt in the Modern Novel* (New York: Edwin Mellen Press, 2009).

Thatcher, David S., *Nietzsche in England, 1890–1914: The Growth of a Reputation* (Toronto: University of Toronto Press, 1970).

Tonning, Erik, *Modernism and Christianity* (Basingstoke: Palgrave Macmillan, 2014).

Tusken, Lewis W., 'Once More with Chutzpah: A Brave Comparison of New Worlds in Nietzsche's *The Genealogy of Morals* and Kafka's *In the Penal Colony*', *Journal of Evolutionary Psychology*, 10 (1989): 342–51.

Wagner, Benno, 'Insuring Nietzsche: Kafka's Files', *New German Critique*, 99 (2006): 83–119.

Wallace, Jeff, *D. H. Lawrence, Science and the Posthuman* (Basingstoke: Palgrave Macmillan, 2005).

Warren, Mark, *Nietzsche and Political Thought* (Cambridge, MA: MIT Press, 1988).

Weller, Shane, 'The Anethics of Desire: Beckett, Racine, Sade', in *Beckett and Ethics*, ed. by Russell Smith (London: Continuum, 2008), 102–17.

———, *Modernism and Nihilism* (Basingstoke: Palgrave Macmillan, 2011).

White, Kathryn, *Beckett and Decay* (London: Continuum, 2008).

Widmer, Kingsley, 'Lawrence and the Nietzschean Matrix', in *D. H. Lawrence and Tradition*, ed. by Jeffrey Meyers (Amherst: University of Massachusetts Press, 1985), 115–31.

Williams, Bernard, *Shame and Necessity* (Berkeley: University of California Press, 1993).

———, *The Sense of the Past: Essays in the History of Philosophy* (Princeton, NJ: Princeton University Press, 2006).

Woolf, Virginia, *On Being Ill: With Notes from Sick Rooms by Julia Stephens* (Ashfield, MA: Paris Press, 2012).

Worthen, John, *D. H. Lawrence and the Idea of the Novel* (London: MacMillan, 1979).

Worton, Michael, '*Waiting for Godot* and *Endgame*: Theatre as Text', in *The Cambridge Companion to Beckett*, ed. by John Pilling (Cambridge: Cambridge University Press, 1996), 67–87.

Young, Julian, *The Death of God and the Meaning of Life* (Abingdon: Routledge, 2003).

Ziolkowski, Theodore, *The Mirror of Justice: Literary Reflections of Legal Crises* (Princeton, NJ: Princeton University Press, 1997).

INDEX

© The Editor(s) (if applicable) and The Author(s) 2018
S. Smith, *Nietzsche and Modernism*,
Palgrave Studies in Modern European Literature,
https://doi.org/10.1007/978-3-319-75535-9

231